# A YEAR OF SPACE

# A YEAR OF
# SPACE

*A Chapter in Autobiography*

BY

## ERIC LINKLATER

THE REPRINT SOCIETY
LONDON

FIRST PUBLISHED 1953
THIS EDITION PUBLISHED BY THE REPRINT SOCIETY LTD.
BY ARRANGEMENT WITH MACMILLAN & CO. LTD.
1954

PRINTED IN GREAT BRITAIN BY RICHARD CLAY AND COMPANY, LTD.,
BUNGAY, SUFFOLK

WITH ENCOMPASSING AFFECTION TO
SIR COMPTON MACKENZIE
ON HIS SEVENTIETH BIRTHDAY

# CONTENTS

# I

## PRELUDE IN THE WRONG KEY

I HAD been caught—indeed, caught out—in a scene that looked as if it had been contrived, that framed me in apparent affectation. I was dining alone, rather late, in the Opera Cellars in Stockholm, when a pleasant and shy young man from the newspaper *Svenska Dagbladet* arrived at my table and gently interrupted my reading. I was reading the new English translation of Stendhal's *The Green Huntsman*, and the book was propped against a wicker basket that held a half-bottle of Pontet Canet of 1934. Such company —the author and the claret together—was a little too ostentatiously good.

The young man from *Svenska Dagbladet* wanted to know why and how I had become an author, and what was my justification for continuing the practice of authorship; but I was unwilling, at so short notice, to discuss a subject that was of large importance to me, but to the general public could be of no interest unless my answer, in careful phrases, presented an effective case—or so I felt—for the defence. Instead, being a little anxious to guard myself against a charge of snobbery, I began to talk about Stendhal, and said that one of the interesting things about him was that while he was held in high esteem by our contemporary intellectuals, his style and habit of writing were strikingly dissimilar from contemporary fashions. Stendhal, I said, though relatively new-esteemed, is old-fashioned. He has

9

the courtesy to make his story and his purpose as clear to every reader as labour and talent can achieve; but clarity and courtesy are not typically our present mode. He has, too, the traditional belief in the necessity of a managed story, and in the value of characters whom the reader can accept as credible and whose activities will hold the reader's interest; but this is not a faith that gets much respect from the intellectual writers of to-day. Stendhal, who adored the ruthless young Buonaparte, was not obsessed by the grimness of politics, but saw in politics merely another field where man could release his romantic nature.

As for the Pontet Canet of the good year 1934, I said that I had always been fond of claret, and of whisky too—especially a malt whisky such as Highland Park, or Talisker, or Lagavulin—and many other sorts of drink, from vodka to the little white wines of Switzerland and Alsace. Having no appetite for power, I explained, I was free to enjoy the pleasures, so much more rewarding, that are called simple. We drank some cognac, and perhaps I talked too much; but I kept the conversation from myself—from my inner self. I was on holiday, I had earned my holiday, and I had no wish to spoil it by introspection and self-analysis.

In the long, cold winter that drenched with rain the latter part of 1950 and bound in ice the dark beginning of 1951, I had been working hard, in my house in Easter Ross, on a novel that had previously defeated my endeavour to give it the shape I wanted; and I had translated a play by Jean Anouilh called *La Répétition*. I cannot speak French, or any other language but my own. Many years ago, as a fairly clever schoolboy, I had some knowledge of Greek and Latin, but that has melted in the heat and fret of time, and

neither the practice of a Scotch grammar school before the
first German war, nor my course of life thereafter, gave me
any good opportunity to acquire the useful modern tongues.
I undertook the translation of *La Répétition* because, at first
sight, it seemed beyond my strength, and I thought it ridiculous that it should be; and after wearisome days with
grammar-book and a large dictionary I found some keys to a
forgotten syntax, I caught the tail of an idiom as it vanished
like a lizard into the crevice of a wall, and worked with
increasing pleasure; as much, sometimes, by the nose as by
the eye. The translation I finished before Christmas, and
the novel, that I called *Laxdale Hall*, on Easter Sunday, 1951.
Four days later I flew to Sweden, intent upon a holiday, but
with the opportune excuse for my journey that the State
Theatre of Gothenburg was to produce, in a Swedish translation, a small comedy I had written a year or two before, and
the theatre at Malmö would play it a fortnight later.

To say this, is not to boast of a continental triumph. In
the State Theatres of Sweden there are two stages, two
auditoriums; a large arena for classical plays and those that
promise commercial reward, a little stage for experimental
and imported pieces. *Love in Albania* was presented to
audiences that numbered about two hundred and twenty,
and so pleased was I by the genial and accomplished production at Gothenburg that I almost concluded, during the
supper which followed the first night, that an audience of
two or three hundred, in a theatre made to measure, was the
ideal and proper attendance at any play.

The camaraderie of a good repertory company prolonged
the supper to far past midnight, and it was in a sentimental
mood that I left the last-wakeful of the players when dawn

was breaking over cold grey streets that hummocks and
dirty ridges of belated snow encumbered.  But the wind of
dawn was immensely exhilarating, it came with an almost
effervescent assertion of its northern freshness, and after a
few hours in bed I got up to enjoy a breakfast of uncommon
robustitude : a few pieces of herring well soused in vinegar
and flavoured with dill, three or four slices of underdone,
cold roast beef, a glass of schnapps, and a bottle of beer.  I
was on holiday, I told myself, and presently drove north out
of Gothenburg to the great ruined castle of Bohus to
meditate on history.

How violent, how explosively improbable, was Sweden's
history from the burly assertion of nationality by Gustavus
Vasa to the reckless brilliance of Charles XII—from the
patriotic rising of the peasants and miners of Dalecarlia under
their stern, shrewd, aristocratic leader in the early years of
the XVIth century, to the disastrous wild heroism of Pol-
tava, and defeat by the Russians, in 1709—and in Stockholm
I found a new inducement to think of Swedish history.
Since my last visit, so far as I could judge, there had been a
change in the temper of the people.  Two or three years
before, there had been a hushed and nervous apprehension of
Russia, but now, in what talk I heard, there seemed a crescent
assurance of power, a resurgence of confidence; and in the
capital the flashing waters of its dividing streams shone
bright as burnished armour.  The busy streets were full of
men, darkly and expensively clad : Stockholm in the winter
appears to be a masculine city.  The men are tall, well built,
rather stern and solemn of aspect; they are so carefully and
conservatively dressed that their civilian clothes look like a
uniform, and if to their severe demeanour, their stalwart

bearing, were added buff jerkins and steel helmets, instead of broadcloth and black Homburgs, they might look very like the well cared-for, gravely disciplined, Protestant musketeers and pikemen of Gustavus Adolphus.

My friend Karl Ragnar Gierow—poet, dramatist, and gourmet, a man with a passionate distaste for sleep—had lately been appointed Director of the Royal Dramatic Theatre of Stockholm, and to show me the scope of his new domain he took me, one Sunday afternoon, to see the second act of Eliot's *Cocktail Party*, played in a cone of deliberately theatrical light against Rembrandtesque darkness; after dinner, to the middle act of Anouilh's *Ring Round the Moon*, a sumptuous exhibition of stage-craft dominated by the deep voice and delighted malice of Tora Teje, a remarkable actress; and then to the last act of *The Lady's not for Burning*, in which bright colour and a lusty release of animal spirits did not quite compensate for lost poetry.

Supper followed. 'Has every cook and waiter here, as well as the *maître d'hôtel*,' I asked, 'a sense of vocation?'

'If a cook is not serious,' said Gierow, 'he has no right to be a cook. And when the food is good, it must be served with respect.' I saw another dawn before I went to bed, and smelt again the first breath of day blowing from new-lit snow.

Before the end of the week, however, I felt the need of exercise, and taking train to Åre on the Norwegian border of Jämtland—a night's journey—I walked idly for a day on the packed snow of hillside paths, and then accepted a casual invitation to climb the mountain. I knew neither the name of the mountain nor its height; but someone lent me a pair of heavy, sharp-cornered boots, someone else a wind-proof jacket, dark glasses, and a ski-stick. Most of the party were skiers, but three or four were only taking a walk. Not until we were half-way up, slowly lifting heavy feet from soft snow on a slope like the roof of a house, did I learn the height of Åreskutan and feel, as I panted for breath, that I should have asked before. 1420 metres is not a major eminence, but after a close winter's work and the luxury of Stockholm it was enough to make muscle complain and lungs protest— and then, irrationally, to wake a puritanical, anti-luxurious pleasure in the slavish labour of calf and thigh, and the merited pain of tobacco-drugged lungs that open at last, with a despairing crack, their dusty pockets and neglected crannies and cry for air. The view, moreover, was superb : range after range of white hills fading into Norway, a lake that we almost overhung, and pine-woods, green when we climbed through them, that now, from the bare and windy upper heights, were a thunderous dark blue.

On the crest of Åreskutan the alpine hut where we ate sandwiches and drank our coffee was crowded with immensely tall, broad-shouldered young Swedes—great fair-haired girls and long, lean men—and with them were two elderly persons of inferior stature who had endured, not only labour in the snow, but all the years of our troubled century. I was one of them, and the other, who was taking his spring holiday in Åre, carried a British passport too. We were older by twenty years than the rest of the company, and for a moment I was tempted to philosophise. Did our presence on the mountain-top indicate a certain perdurable quality in the holders of British passports, a stubborn indifference to time and the climate of our age—or only a habit of mind persistently infantile? But when we went out again the question was blown away by a wind that whistled through icicle-teeth, and with long, sliding, slithering steps I scurried and slipped down the dropping slopes to find warmth in movement.

I woke in the morning, in a south-bound train, to see a land lying dark and miserable under the last of winter. Over drab snowfields, crusty and shrunken, and lakes held prisoner in ice discoloured and patched by rain that had fallen only to freeze, a sullen sky depended. Winter, like a shrivelled, mean old man with black veins and bloodless fingers, ruled all the land until, in the early afternoon, we approached the southernmost province of Scania, where the sun broke through the clouds—and quite suddenly the lakes were free. The little lakes and meres were no longer dark and still and prisoned by the ice, but wide-awake, running to reedy shores, rippling as if with laughter, and bluer than the sky above. The snow had gone, and spring had brought the world to life again. Spring was on the march, and winter, grumbling still, retreated to the north. The very time, I thought, for holiday.

I was going to stay with friends whose house had been built in that period of grace and elegance that Gustavus III inspired : its gate-posts carried, not griffons, lions, or bears, but, as a promise of geniality, great stone loving-cups— and the library, as I remembered it, was sunlit from within by light reflected from long rows of books bound in pale golden calf, as many English books as Swedish, almost as many French, but only a shelf or two of German. I was looking forward to my visit, and the pleasure of arrival suddenly expanded when I saw, in a corner of the library, the

broad and ponderous figure, the rough grey head, of Frans
Bengtsson : the most popular of living Swedish authors
and a writer as much esteemed by scholars as the laity.

He began at once to upbraid me for my affection to
Stendhal, of which he had read in *Svenska Dagbladet*. This
favouring of French authors, he said, was one of the worst
of British affectations. If a man writes in French, or paints
in French, or philosophises in French, he is always sure of an
audience—in England. But why, above all, read Stendhal?
In *La Chartreuse de Parme* Stendhal, like a proper Frenchman,
had deliberately set himself the task of belittling the Duke of
Wellington's great victory by looking at Waterloo through
the bewildered eyes of Fabrizio del Dongo, and seeing only
chaos on the field, run-away dragoons, a dog's-breakfast of a
battle that anybody might have won by the sheer incom-
petence of the other side—whereas, of course, the Duke,
after initial error, had fought a firmly controlled action and
brilliantly earned his brilliant victory.

Not for several years, Bengtsson told me, had he spoken
English, but under the spur of emotion—the Duke sits very
high in his esteem—his fluency was remarkable; and having
dealt with Stendhal, he asked me, still indignant, 'Why
don't you read a good author, as I do? A good English
author?'

'What are you reading?'

'*Peter Simple*. You don't think much of Captain Marryat,
I suppose? No, of course not! But you would if he had
written in French. All your intellectuals would read him
then, and talk seriously about his style, which is very good,
and the psychology of his heroes, which is not without
interest. I am so sorry for poor Captain Marryat. He

would have a great reputation in England—if only he had written in French!'

A day or two later my wife arrived. She had flown without mishap from Prestwick to Copenhagen, but by an oversight had left all her luggage in the train from Malmö. It was an unfortunate lapse, for we had been invited to dine in considerable grandeur that night. A dinner-party of thirty or more in a moated castle. . . . There was a lot of feminine bustle and excitement, the borrowing and trying-on of frocks and shoes, and tactful adjustment here and there with needle and thread; and then, when a little calmness supervened, she said: 'I didn't bring your letters, I didn't think you'd want to see them—except one, and that's in my suitcase unfortunately, and where my suitcase is I don't know. It's from someone called Sir Robert Fraser, at the—I think I've got it right—at the Central Office of Information. He wants you to go to Korea.'

'*Korea?* I'm damned if I do!'

'It's for the War Office, he says. To write a short history of the campaign.'

'Nothing will induce me to go to Korea! I've seen two wars, or bits of them, and that's more than enough. I don't like wars, I'm frightened of them. Especially in Korea; it's full of disease. And anyway, I'm on holiday.'

'I thought you'd be more interested. The Admiralty want you to write about naval operations as well as the war on land.'

'Look here! I've been working all winter, I haven't had a holiday for a long time——'

'It's not very long.'

'For a long, long time! But now I *am* on holiday, I'm

enjoying myself, and I mean to enjoy myself all summer. I'm going to New Zealand in August, and between now and then I don't intend to give a serious thought to anything except fishing.   So you needn't talk about Korea.'

'I don't want you to go!   That's the last thing I want. But I thought you'd be excited——'

'Well, you're wrong.   Quite wrong.—Korea, my God!'

# II

# THE DOUBTFUL DECISION

A WEEK later I was walking across St. James's Park on one of those days when spring, as it seems, sets out to win all London with gaiety and the bright hues of innocence; and in the park, meeting its fifth column of budding trees and rising grass and sparkling water, establishes its bridge-head. The air was flushed with conquest, and in the distant noise of traffic one could almost hear the obdurate forces of winter pulling out, at last, from untenable positions. The sun promised heat, and the ducks in the lake, clapping their wings, scattered bright water-drops and announced the rising tide of their affections. A pen-swan, graciously submerging her pointed body, accepted the regal caress of her mate and permitted him to tread her.

On the benches sat pale citizens, tired men and listless women, to breathe new air and be revived. They were not beautiful, but gratitude gave them a look of kindliness. They spread their knees and lifted their faces to the sky. An idiot, a gentle sun-worshipper, stood stock-still, head lifted back—then quickly walked a few paces and looked up to be surprised again. He opened his mouth, and with a shudder drew his breath in ecstasy.

I crossed the bridge, admired a little fleet of tufted duck, and at the west end of the lake, between the lesser island and the shore, discovered a more vivacious scene. As though in a conflict of emotions, in a mood both bridal and

Bank Holiday—and playful, too, with the excitement of girls picnicking—the ducks, mallard and tufted for the most part, were paddling to and fro, quickly feeding, flirting, rushing here and there with half-lifted wings. But in the midst of them, solitary and beautiful, a lonely foreigner swam.

He was a mandarin drake, and among the others he looked unnaturally handsome. He was a work of art, rather than of nature. His colours were so diverse, so precisely patterned, and he sat upon the water with the elegance of one accustomed to the mirror-calm of ornamental pools. His wing-tips rose above his tail in a little delicate pavilion, and all his movements were sedate. By the vulgarians about him he was quite ignored. His beauty made him lonely, and for his air of painted aristocracy he was ostracised.

I felt—not pity, indeed, for I am no sentimentalist—but indignation, a strong resentment against such manifest injustice. The mandarin, who deserved a harem to pick and choose from, was alone unmated. The proletarians splashed and scampered, and took their easy pleasure, while he, the strange and elegant, had none to keep him company and let him realise the spring. It was an intolerable situation.

I was living at my club, and there, that night, I told my story of the lonely drake. It roused immediate sympathy, and the aggregate of opinion was that *something must be done*. There was, we discovered, a senior official of the Zoo playing cards upstairs, and to him we sent our compliments and an invitation to have a drink when he had finished the rubber. He came, in a little while, but was less helpful than we had expected. The Zoo, he said, had no surplus of she-mandarins for St. James's Park, and he could suggest no other source of supply. He was, perhaps, in a hurry to get back to the bridge-table.

We stood about the bar in a defeated silence. The plight of the mandarin—that I had told as a passing tale—now seemed a matter of grave importance. We shared responsibility for his unhappiness; and the solitude of the little painted drake, on a night so warm for his companions, seemed quite intolerable. But what could be done?

Frowning and perplexed, manifestly suffering, one of our company suddenly turned and left us. His stride was long and purposeful. He had, we knew, a vested interest in such affairs, for his father had been one of the leading—indeed, dominating—ornithologists of the century. With a renewal of hope, and ordering another round of drinks, we awaited his return.

A little flushed by the heat of action, with a smile of pleasure half-breaking the muscular tension of resolve, he presently came back. 'If all goes well,' he said, 'he'll have his duck to-morrow afternoon.'

'How did you manage it?' we asked.

'I sent an imperative telegram to the Duke of Bedford.'

Loudly we applauded him. 'You have brought in the old world to redress the balance of the new,' said someone who remembered schoolroom history and the name of George Canning. It was pleasant indeed to think that there still existed a Duke—a Duke with a private zoo—who could be relied on to come to the assistance of a visiting mandarin. And we had, of course, shelved our responsibility.

A little while later—pacified by the thought of ducal sympathy and a bride for the stranger—I went upstairs to bed; but, to put off the tiresome business of undressing, smoked another cigarette—and remembering how I had spent the day, fell at once out of complacency into doubt and fear.

I had gone to the War Office in the morning, and then to the Air Ministry and the Admiralty; and I had promised to go, by and by, to Korea. It was impossible to fit Korea into the holiday pattern I had been arranging, and the horrid peninsula threw a shadow across the warmth of spring weather. I disliked intensely the prospect of long days in an aeroplane, and I was frightened, above all, of the gloom I should feel when I saw new ruins and more refugees. Too much of our world has been broken down, too much up-rooted, and I did not want to breathe again the sour smell of shattered houses, the stink of humanity on the run, and see its tear-stained children. What, I wondered, was the Korean for *Niente mangiare*?

I could not quite understand why I had agreed to go. My first reply, when Marjorie in Sweden brought me the invitation, had been a flat refusal, and I was still unwilling to give up my summer idleness for a strenuous, uncomfort-able journey to a country that hung from farthest Asia like a gangrened appendix of the world.—I was, of course, a little moved by vanity. It had been flattering to be told that my nomination for the task had been approved by all three Services; and none of us is immune to flattery. But there was more to it than that, and rather unwillingly —with some degree of surprise, as well as reluctance—I discovered in myself a persisting strain of puritanism: I should not enjoy my long holiday, fishing loch and river, if I refused what was—what would immediately have been recognised in the older world in which I grew up—a call to duty. My sense of duty is nothing like so large or robust as once it was, but a vestige remains; and no one had a better claim to it than the soldiers who twice had saved our century. If they wanted a clerk to record their latest bravery, it would indeed be shabby to refuse them. And having admitted that—having, as it were, confirmed to myself what I had already promised to my new masters—I felt, I confess, a little pleasant quiver of excitement. As Marjorie, in Sweden, had foreseen I would.

I had, moreover, succeeded in fitting my new task into the pattern of a farther journey to which I was committed. Some months before I had accepted an invitation by the British Council to lecture in New Zealand, in September, and in Ceylon on my way home.

I do not take easily to lecturing, for I have no expert knowledge of anything, no special subjects such as stamp-collecting, Cretan antiquities, or modern sanitation on which, being expected to lecture, I keep my knowledge up-to-date and my notes in readiness. Nor, though I am stiff in belief and stubborn in opinion, do I feel much desire to convert other people to my own creed and habit of thought. The novelist, as André Gide has said, 'does not long to see the lion eat grass'. To the novelist the lion is valuable in his proper character; it would be wasteful to make a lamb of him.—Without the knowledge, then, to set up an exhibition of it, or the zeal to seek converts, I have to compose my lectures as if composing a short story or a one-act play; but I was willing to do some work for the reward of seeing New Zealand and Ceylon. My masters in the War Office and the Admiralty did not want me to go to Korea before the end of

June, and when my task was done there, I could turn southward to the Antipodes. My longer journey was not to be
spoiled, but dramatically enlarged—and my sense of duty,
as I pondered this, began to look like a threshold to self-
indulgence.

I decided that too much scrutiny of one's motives led
nowhere; and started to undress. Action is more significant than the psychological springs of action, I told myself;
and usually more interesting. I slept soundly.

I could not wait to see whether the mandarin received
his bride, but took train to the north and in Highland
Scotland found winter, like a surly bailiff, still in possession.
The trees, at the beginning of May, were only a tracery of
leafless branches, the east wind blew, and the high hills to
which my windows look across a sandy bay wore a new
cape of snow. We had had too much of winter, and I fell
ill with my recurrent distemper : which is something worse
than indolence and rather less than accidie. It is a lethargy,
a moral impotence, a physical inertia; my appetite is un-
impaired, I sleep well, but my will dissolves and mind
hibernates in a trance that is only faintly disturbed by
promise of reparation to-morrow. The promise is not kept,
and a complication appears. 'What', asks the newest germ,
'is the moral argument for reparation? There is none.
Regular and persistent work is a perversion brought in by
the Protestant Reformation and the Industrial Revolution.
Your world is over-capitalised—both morally and materially
—and you sweat to pay the interest on it. But why not
show your independence, your right to idleness, and deny
the debt?'

A letter came which said that before I could go to Korea

I must be inoculated or vaccinated against typhoid, typhus, tetanus, cholera, yellow fever, and smallpox. Lethargy was not mentioned.

'It's a nuisance,' said the doctor, 'that you're so hairy.'

'In the early months of the last war,' I said, 'when I was manning—but very inefficiently—the defences of Scapa Flow, I fell and broke a rib. I had walked across a shingle beach that was all brown and greasy with oil from the *Royal Oak*, which had been sunk a few days before, to visit a destroyer whose captain I knew. I lost my footing on a steel ladder—my shoes were still slippery—and fell across a ledge or flange in the deck, and cracked a bone. I was strapped up in a vest of sticking-plaster, and when the time came to remove it a surgeon made a cut up the front, and with one merciless wrench tore the whole thing off. It took every hair with it. It looked as warm as a fleece when he held it up for admiration. It would, he said, make a fine fur-coat for a midget.'

'It would have done, I'm sure,' said the doctor; and slipped a needle into my arm.

There are many advantages in growing old, and one's re-actions to inoculation, love, and a late night are all mollified; but though they did not seriously upset me, the cholera and typhoid germs induced a queasiness that postponed my mind's recovery. The days were now bright and warm. Larches were putting out their spring tufts and dark-red nipples, crumpled beech-leaves silkily unfolded, and as the snow melted on its great flanks Ben Wyvis, against a sky of Wedgwood blue, lay striped like a tiger. I was so far convalescent that I was able to catch a few brown trout in a hill-loch, a sea-trout in a river-pool; but my spirit failed at the thought of writing lectures for New Zealand or starting to analyse the causes of war in Korea. Since writing, however, is both my habit and my trade—my pleasure and my pain, my only craft, and therefore, perhaps, my vocation—I decided to keep—oh, not a strict journal—but some record of the year's events, and their impact on me.

When I write a novel I see, from the beginning, the rough shape of all that should happen; for the story of my own travel, to the Antipodes by way of Korea, I could rely only on fortune to draw the design. But snobbery or no snobbery, I would, I thought, start it in good company: in the Opera Cellars in Stockholm, with Stendhal and a bottle of claret.

# III

## IN PARENTHESIS

Is a house, I asked myself, as desirable a possession as one used to suppose? It is costly to maintain, it is full of apparatus and furnishings that constantly require the attention of plumbers, electricians, painters, and the like. It is a running sore in one's bank account, it is a kind of sickroom for leaking taps, and smoking chimneys, and desquamating walls. A shelter against the weather—grant it so much—but also a veil upon the spirit, a resistance to bird-song and the Pleiades.

I had bought, in 1946, a larger house than I needed. 'I bought a big house,' I said, 'because I couldn't afford a little one.' That was taken as a joke, but it was true enough. The house was much cheaper than some trim, tidily designed, well-engineered, neater constructions that I had considered—and it stood most beautifully in a little wood on the westward slope of a hill, looking over a broad and shallow bay to mountains nobly shaped. The view was what I had first decided to buy, and the view was cheap at any price. The place, moreover, had been neglected, and I felt the temptation to improve it. The oldest part of the house dated from the latter years of the XVIIIth century, but a couple of generations ago, in the fashion of the time, its roofs and windows had been decorated with stony points and pinnacles: these would have to come down, and a jungle-growth of saplings, suckers, snowberry, laurels, and sprawling poplars must be removed. There was a big walled

27

garden overcrowded with old fruit-trees, and a long her-
baceous border that looked like a bank of the Amazon.    I
thought greedily of the profits of market-gardening, I swung
a heavy bill-hook with lively pleasure, and remembered that
I had once learnt to use an axe.

Tall trees came down, shrubberies were thinned, and the
view enlarged.   We looked across the water to the coro-
neted height of Fyrish, dark against the snow on Ben Wyvis,
and a pair of cruisers anchored in the bright firth off Inver-
gordon;  to the south, through a little wood carefully
cleared, we saw the lights of Cromarty, the native place of
the fantastical Sir Thomas Urquhart, who had been born
in that quiet corner to write so noisily : to translate Rabelais,
and die of laughter, if the story be true, when the end of the
Puritan revolution was the restoration of Charles II.   I had
the Maitland Club edition of his *Works*, a roughened copy
that had belonged to Sir Walter Scott's son-in-law, Lock-
hart; there was a propriety, I thought, in bringing it so near
its home.

I felled another tree or two, and in a cheerful demolition
the Victorian points and pinnacles and a great, tottering,
ornamental chimney came crashing down.   We began to
regard the house, as well as the view, with some complacency;  and on my fiftieth birthday I planted twelve
hundred young beeches to make a frontal hedge.

My predecessor in the house was a son of George
Romanes, the biologist and friend of Darwin, whose studies
had proceeded on a troubled course from the nervous
system of starfish to the nature of God.   An earlier tenant
had been Dr. Brydon, once famous as the only survivor of
the British army of four thousand fighting men and twelve

thousand camp-followers that, retreating from Kabul to Jalalabad in the winter of 1842, was massacred by the Afghans. Some prisoners were recovered later, but only Dr. Brydon, wounded and riding a grey pony, reached Jalalabad. He brought his pony home, and when it died it was buried in the grounds of the house that had become mine. Its fame lived in local memory, and when I had an iron boundary fence repaired I found that a part of it which was bent and twisted had carefully been left untouched. 'Because,' I was told, 'that's what Dr. Brydon's pony did one day when he jumped it.' There are more conspicuous monuments to military fame, in these Highland parts that have nourished so much of it, but my bent railing is an autograph, the very signature of hardiness.

Until a few years ago these domestic interests would have been regarded as a natural, even a laudable activity. I had four children, and it is the proper nature of a parent to make a comforting home for his young. The care and improvement of one's property, moreover, are traditionally a duty, not only to oneself, but to the community. Good fences make good neighbours, and the general well-being, the aggregate comeliness, of any part of the country are dependent on the respect that each man has for his own. All I had been doing was in the sound tradition that descends from Coke of Norfolk to the careful gardener of a window-box—but now the tradition was out of favour, and our egalitarian governors regarded private property and its improvement with a disliking frown.

I had not calculated with sufficient care the taxes that would be demanded from me. I can turn a sentence with tolerable fidelity to my intended meaning, but I cannot always expect the right answer when I do sums; and I am usually too busy—with ideas that may eventually be framed in sentences—to spend much time on sums. I was, in consequence, surprised by the fearful bills that presently the Board of Inland Revenue sent in; then worried, and perturbed; and finally dismayed. The attack on tradition —the Coke-of-Norfolk to window-box tradition—was more savage than I had realised; and the house which I had so benevolently improved, the garden I had so virtuously ploughed, became a burden to me, a penal load.

I am, perhaps, not an ideal specimen of the householder. There are times when I grow tired of possessions. I enjoy buying books, but I am not sure that I really enjoy having books. To acquire a bright new volume, or a set of old volumes in smooth, tobacco-brown calf, is indeed delightful, and promptly I sit down with them, intent on knowing what they have to say and how they say it; resentful of interruption till I have satisfied my curiosity. But a year or two later, sitting upright on their shelves, they often wear a sullen, heavy look. They deserve, I know, more careful consideration than I have given them, but if I gave them what they deserve I should have no time to write books of my own; for others to neglect.—And all property is the same: it demands attention. Slates on the roof after a February gale, linoleum for the bathroom, paint for the kitchen door, and dung for the garden. Property cannot look after itself, and is therefore a nuisance.

For a good many years of my life I could put almost all my possessions into a couple of suitcases, and I lived—no, never contentedly, but without envy of those who owned more. In the years that followed the Kaiser's war, when I

had very little money, I was extremely careful with it and spent all I had on pleasure. In pubs and bookshops, that is. My clothes cost almost nothing, for Orkney tweed, made on a cottage loom, never wore out, and my dead father's shirts, when I had grown to fit them, were sufficient for many years. The games I played were of the rougher sort, that required no expensive equipment. I had a shot-gun, a fishing-rod, and a ten-foot dinghy; and when I was thirty I bought a good but rather cumbersome hand-made gramophone. That was the total of my possessions until I married; and after marriage, for two or three years, my wife and I still avoided the burdens of house-owning. And now—well, walls are useful for hanging pictures, and books are necessary, and one can hardly enjoy domestic life without a kitchen and a bed; but when such things and their surroundings (a few trees, let us say, and a potato-field) cannot be given the care they should have until one has helped pay for the medical, educational, housing, and belly needs of one's fellow-citizens, the old-fashioned joy of ownership is somewhat curtailed—and one may look back, rather wistfully, to the suitcase days.

Indeed, as the time of departure came nearer, I was, I found, looking forward with a growing eagerness to the recurrence of suitcase days. I could not, of course, slough my domestic responsibilities, but I could lose sight of them for a little while. By means of an excellent device called a power of attorney I could let my wife pay my bills; and this, though it would not save money, would save me the pain of writing cheques. I abandoned my original pretence that I was going to Korea at the call of duty, and admitted that I was running away from householding. It saved a

little of my self-respect to know that I was running in the direction of evil-smelling ruins and Chinese Communists; and I should have to travel in aeroplanes, of which I am still somewhat afraid.

I went to London to do some shopping and get more instruction in my duties, and my arrival was saddened by the first news I heard.

Philip Jordan was dead. He had died in his sleep, early that morning, after a recurrent nightmare which had tormented him since, in Yugoslavia, he had marvellously escaped death in a burning aeroplane.—He was a good man, moved intensely by a sense of duty; but I would not, I think, have cared to say so in his hearing, for his tongue could be harsh and he detested anything that sounded of sentimentality as does a pious Moslem the idolater. Delicately built, ivory-pale and coldly handsome, he concealed his goodness and a great kindness behind a chilling wit and sometimes a front of arrogance. He wore himself out in service to all he believed in, and in the romantic fashion he found belief in Britain when Britain had to stand in the old folk-tale posture, like Horatius on the bridge, between civilisation and the barbarians.

With the fervour of an early Radical he detested Conservative policy and principles—or lack of principles, he would have said—and in the early months of the war he showed no great liking for the Army. Time and experience changed that, however. He saw the Army in many parts of the world, and acquired the warmest affection for the British soldier, the liveliest admiration of his qualities. But he continued to look sourly at the world good soldiers must live in. In his *Tunis Diary*, a book both typically

opinionative and sharply picturesque, he described with a schoolboy's zeal the heroical bayonet-charges of the Hampshires at Tebourba, and a page or two later quoted with approval a sentence from Bernanos' *Les Grands Cimetières sous la lune*: 'J'endure même humblement le ridicule de n'avoir encore que barbouillé de l'encre cette face de l'injustice dont l'incessant outrage est le sel de ma vie'.— And throughout the war, with salty imagination and ceaseless energy, he followed its rough course from Kuibyshev to Rangoon, from North Africa to Italy and the Rhine.

I shared some memorable days with him in Italy, in 1944, but when I heard of his death I remembered, first of all, a ridiculous and exuberant occasion that preceded the war by several years; when I dined with him in a newly opened restaurant in London. They made there, we had been told, a Spanish omelette of superlative quality: redolent of onions, furious with chillies, rich with mushrooms and strongly cured ham.—But with such an omelette, we said, we must drink a crude young wine, something harsh and burly, a stark vintage for the peasantry. 'What', said Philip to the *sommelier*, 'is the worst red wine you have?'

The restaurant was smartly furnished. It was attended by the most desirable sort of customers. The waiter was surprised and hurt. 'We have no bad wine,' he said.

'What nonsense!' said Philip. 'All restaurants have bad wine, and we want the worst you can find.'

The *sommelier* called the *maître d'hôtel*, to whom Philip repeated his request. The *maître d'hôtel*, though surprised, was sympathetic; and a claret that had been bottled for some suburban railway was brought. We tasted it, and shook our heads. 'Not nearly bad enough.'

B

More bottles were carried in.   The produce of a derelict vineyard blasted by a torrid sun, the sour survivor of a cold rain-swept year, a bitter wine from Pesaro or thereabout, a revolting juice from the Landes, I think, and a bottle of singular unpleasantness out of the Peloponnese.   'They are all very bad,' said Philip, 'but not of the sort of badness we want.   What else can you offer?'

The table was by now a little crowded, and more waiters grew interested in our quest.—We tasted a thick red wine from Blida or Sidi bel Abbès, and a gross Danubian brew. We were still dissatisfied, and after frowning colloquy a waiter was sent down to the kitchens.   Presently he returned with a bottle that looked as if it held horse-liniment, and was, we learnt, the private property of some under-cook or dish-washer.   And now at last we were pleased.   The wine tasted of copper and goatskins, it smelt of hot flint, it was rough as a file, and sour and strong.

'It will suit us admirably,' said Philip.   'Where does he belong to, this wise and sympathetic under-cook who drinks it?'

'Valladolid,' said someone with a shrug; and we realised, proudly, that we had indeed found the proper wine for our Spanish omelette.

In 1944, when Philip was a war correspondent in Italy, I met him a little while before the fall of Rome, and having no transport of my own, begged a seat in the car that he shared with Cecil Sprigge, the *Manchester Guardian* correspondent.   On the night of June 3rd we slept in a barn, not far from the city, and the following day watched the Americans fight slowly forward.   Philip was critical of their cautious tactics, and declared impatiently that he could see

no reason for delay. We drove past a company of dusty, unshaven infantry, and had some conversation with an angry officer commanding a squadron of tanks. From a village church nearby came a wedding procession in rural finery, the bride and bridesmaids in their white frocks ducking and wincing as shells burst in the field beside them.—We drove a little farther, past the city boundary, and then a pair of field-guns opened fire on us at embarrassingly close range. We studied the situation from a ditch, and quickly decided that the road to Rome was not yet open to traffic.

It was early morning when we went in, to the welcome of crowds who were enthusiastic but not carried away by enthusiasm, and Philip and Cecil Sprigge at once began to look for a shop where they could buy ready-to-wear civilian suits. All the shops were shut, but in a quiet street we found a man who was persuaded to open a side door and do business discreetly. I waited outside, and a small crowd gathered round me. A busy little man pushed his way through its ranks, and spoke to me, with some excitement, in German. I could not understand German, I told him. He was obviously annoyed by my ignorance, and the difficulty of dealing with a new set of foreigners. His hands made angry gestures, his eyes shone greedily, and his words came so thick and fast that I could make nothing of them. He repeated what he had been saying with passionate insistence on one explosive word; and the crowd murmured sympathetically.

'Francobolli!' he screamed. 'Ne avete *francobolli*?'— And from an inner pocket pulled a wallet such as stamp-collectors use, and opened it to show an array of brightly coloured samples.

Rome had been liberated, and the enemy driven from its streets. But my stamp-collector had no interest in politics and war, he welcomed the relieving armies with the simple hope that in their pocket-books they carried Penny Blacks, old rare Colonials, or mint sets of the Columbus quater-centenary issue, all eager to sell or swap.

Philip and Cecil Sprigge came out wearing purplish-blue trousers, tweed jackets of a vulgar, improbable cut, silk ties, and imitation Panama hats. Their uniforms were rolled up and pushed into a corner of the car, and we drove to the Vatican. They had changed into civilian suits—they could not be called plain clothes—to enter the Papal State and ask for its news. They were immediately admitted, and in the Vatican heard confirmation of a current rumour that in March, in the Ardeatine caves, three hundred and twenty Italians had been murdered in reprisal for the throwing of a bomb in the Via Rasella and the death of thirty-two Germans. There was a dark malignity in this subterranean massacre that raised goose-flesh on one's imagination, a fear of unnatural evil, as if the priests of Moloch had come back—to sacrifice innocent stamp-collectors.

But we lunched well, on macaroni and veal, in a restaurant on the Piazza del Popolo where people were noisily drinking toasts from table to table, and exchanging ebullient kisses. A blue-chinned, self-conscious little man came in wearing a Sam Browne belt, too big for his meagre waist, and carrying a rifle. He looked about him, expectant of applause, and was greeted with cheers and hand-clapping. He was a waiter in the restaurant, and the rifle, one gathered, was evidence of a martial spirit rather than of martial achievement. He was given half a dozen glasses of wine, and having become rather drunk, was persuaded to go away. But in five minutes he returned, carrying now a light machine-gun; which caused some alarm.

Philip showed me the despatch he had written, in which he said that the Fifth Army's capture of Rome was the fruit of the Eighth Army's hard fighting in the Liri Valley. He got into trouble for this, and his privileges as a war correspondent were suspended for fourteen days. The Americans, though extremely generous in a material way, were jealous of fame, avid of renown. A few weeks later Philip was in an aeroplane that crashed in Yugoslavia. Among its passengers were Evelyn Waugh and Randolph Churchill, who, with Philip, escaped the wreck. Most of the others were burnt to death, and Philip inherited a nightmare that plagued him, recurrently, for the remaining years of his life.

Now, seven years to the day after our luncheon in the Piazza del Popolo, I had come to London to do some shopping that reversed his practice in Rome. I was to be re-commissioned for my journey to Korea, and I had to buy khaki drill uniform. I had grown somewhat stouter with the years, and the second-hand tunics I bought had previously been worn by a Major-General. I was to receive temporary promotion to the rank of Lieutenant-Colonel, but my figure had done better than that.

The long summer's fishing that I had hoped for dwindled to a few days; but every day was full of interest. On the Hill of Nigg, above and behind my house, there is a small and shallow loch between tumble-down cliffs and a wood of twisted pines. Fulmars nest on green ledges of the cliff, and above the wood, where roe-deer harbour, a pair of buzzards can usually be seen, slowly cutting the air with their broad wings and mewing confidentially to each other. The land along the coast is the property of one of my most redoubtable friends, a short and burly man with eyebrows that look like hedgerows newly cut-and-laid, and a stammer that he sometimes uses with great effect.—There was a lady at a wedding, enthusiastic as ladies often are on such an occasion, who waved her champagne-glass at him and said excitedly, 'Oh, Mr. Robertson, doesn't the bride look lovely?' 'B-b-brides always look lovely,' answered Peter morosely. 'I often w-wonder where all the p-p-p-plain wives come from.'

He had found good natural feeding in his little loch, and stocked it well, and made spawning places for the trout by tipping loads of gravel along the more accessible bank. The fish multiplied and grew, and acquired a curious, individual character. It was almost impossible to catch them in favourable conditions—when the air was mild and the wind blew gently from the south-west—but in harsh inclement weather, when the sky came snarling from the north, they rose to the fly with alacrity.

It was a week or two before I left home, and a day of unseasonable cold for June, when Peter asked me to fish; an arrowy rain blew in from the sea, and in a couple of hours we had had enough of it. But in two hours I had caught four fish weighing a pound, a pound and six ounces, two pounds and one ounce, two pounds and nine ounces—in that order. Two came to a grouse-and-claret, two to a Peter Ross. 'Better stop now,' said my host. 'You're bound to be disappointed by the next one.'—The arithmetical progression was unlikely to continue, indeed, but Peter himself, the year before, had taken a three-and-a-half pounder; and though the seat of my trousers was coldly wet, and my fingers white and nerveless, I left with a certain reluctance.

Then I flew to Orkney, to fish water that I had known for most of my life; and the exquisite impatience to be afloat, that had been the master of my moods when I was twelve, was undiminished at fifty-two. It was, if anything, aggravated by memory, and as I pulled a boat down a green bank and into shallow water that sparkled above a stony floor, I knew precisely where I should make my first cast, and how I should manage my drifts.—Except for an occasional five-pounder, the fish in the Harray Loch are not large, but there are plenty of them, and for strength, and speed, and a dashing spirit they are unsurpassed. Within their silver coats, rose-speckled and tinted with gold above the belly, every ounce is an ounce of swift pugnacity—and delectable again when it comes upon the table. The transcendentalism of the hunter—the ultimate oneness of the hunter and his prey—is realised most pleasantly, and most practically demonstrated, when he and his well-cooked victim meet again at dinner, and the relish of the chase is renewed in appetite. A trout of a pound or more, of the Loch Harray sort, makes a most admirable dish when baked and served with a sauce Rémoulade; or it can be boiled and eaten cold, with such addition as a cold salmon gets. Smaller fish are exceedingly good if split, spread, boned, and fried in oatmeal; but there should not be too much oatmeal. And little ones of six ounces give great pleasure if, in the manner of herring, they are rolled and soused in vinegar.

It was a morning of bright sun and dancing wind when I pushed out my boat, but slowly-sailing clouds threw

shadows on the water, and by lunch-time I had caught
fourteen fish, the biggest a pound and a quarter. In the
afternoon the flaring sky burnt every cloud, burnt up the
wind; no fish would stir beneath that brazen vacancy.
And at night, when I fished without success a smaller loch
where only sulky big ones swam, a sudden frost and draughts
of biting air drove me home.

I returned the next day to Harray, and felt uncommonly
foolish. The sky was cloudless, the sun a blazing daffodil,
and the loch as calm as a looking-glass except for ruffled
lanes where passing zephyrs blurred its surface. No sensible
fisherman would have gone afloat—no other did—but I
had long loved, and loved so deeply, that bird-quick,
dancing water in its frame of gentle hills that merely to be
alone upon it was delight; and I had promised some trout
to a woman who, though bedridden, had a greedy appetite
for the delicate, untamed flavour and pink flesh of the little
fish it nurtured in translucence. My word was at stake;
and resolute in folly, I pushed out my boat.

I fished hard for six hours, and caught five small fish,
none of them much bigger than half a pound. There were
no natural flies on the water, and, in consequence, no fish
were rising, despite the mildness of the day. The sudden
hard frost of the night before had killed the hatch of fly,
and the fish knew it. But some years before, my friend
Nick Roughead and I had discovered that in the early
months of the year, before the sun had warmth enough to
bring out the flies, it might be warm enough to lead into
very shallow water the little snails that are a trout's best
feeding; and by fishing in the shallowest of water, over
a pebbled shore, we had sometimes taken home a good

basket. So now I fished over the stones in a few inches of water, slow and gently, where the light reflected from smooth pebbles gave the dead-calm loch a doubled brightness; and in these impossible conditions I caught enough to redeem my promise to the bedridden woman whose lively appetite so stoutly contradicted her incapacity.

Nick Roughead is a better fisherman, and far more knowing in the art, than I. Burly, thick-bodied, and bald as a stone—as bald as I am—he played Rugby for Scotland for several years, and captained the best team it has had this century. Then, for some inscrutable reason, he became a literary agent. But when the 1939 war began he joined the Navy as a rating, and as a rating served in Malta convoys and in the bloody assault on Walcheren. The sort of author he admires—his idea of what an author should be—is Hilaire Belloc, and when the war was concluded he found, among the young authors of the day, none likely to grow up in Belloc's shape and temper; so he abandoned his trade as a literary agent, and took seriously to fishing. I got much benefit from his teaching and example, and once in his company saw a kind of water-ballet—a heliotropic ballet—of uncommon charm.

We were fishing, in warm bright weather, a bay of the Harray Loch called Tenstone, when the soft wind died and the water, above a floor of green moss, became a still transparency. We leaned over the side of the boat to look down, through a dark clarity gleaming with golden bars, at the soft carpet below; and in the unmoving water saw, floating upward, a flock of bright little hard-shelled beetles, about the size and colour of lady-birds. They were motes of amber in the green water, but tawny gold when one caught the light, and there were so many that their flight to the sun, their heliotropic ascent, was like a tribal migration before the terror of hostile cavalry.

Then from the south-west came a catspaw of wind, a wider flurry, and a steady ripple. In thirty minutes we caught half a dozen fish, and every one of them was stuffed like a mince-pie with golden beetles. The last we took, a fish of twelve or thirteen ounces, was marked on both sides, a little behind the gills, by crinkled yellow scars : it had once been the captive, in its smaller days, of a shag or heron, and still showed the wounds of that hard beak.

It is a loch of great enchantment, rich and erratic in its rewards. Often I have come ashore white and haggard with cold, often scorched red by the sun. I once lost a fish—the biggest I ever hooked there, no less than six pounds—on the very last day of the season, when a quickly rising winter squall drove my boat ashore, blew off my cap and the spectacles from my nose, and thrashed and staggered me with hailstones as I stumbled about a stony beach and tried to net my great fish. But I could hardly keep my feet in the wind, I was half blind, and I struck its gaping jaw with my landing-net, and broke my cast.—I remember a happier occasion, and a Sunday morning when my wife said, 'Will you take the girls to church?' But I, looking at a prettily broken sky and smelling a soft west wind, said, 'Not to-day, I think. I'll take them on the loch instead, and show them how to catch a trout.'

Within twenty minutes I had hooked a good fish, and lost it. I cast again—I was using an old rod gone limp at the top and a light trace that was beginning to fray—and almost at once there came a ponderous head-and-tail rise, I

struck, and my line went screaming out. My two small
daughters, side by side, were at the oars, and with excellent
self-control and steady discipline they obeyed my orders.
They recognised an occasion, they were silent and shared
my anxiety as with infinite care I played the leaping fish.
Again and again it threw its great gleaming shape into the
air, and twice they rowed in desperate pursuit as it took out
all my line. At last it began to yield, it lay dour and heavy,
fighting still but no longer strong enough to leap in fury,
and presently I netted it and took it home at once. It was a
brown trout, a cock fish in perfect condition, weighing four
pounds and seven ounces. 'Sunday morning on the Harray
Loch', I told my wife, 'can supply its own verses to *Bene-
dicite, omnia opera*.'

And once I pulled a young man from its waters. That
was on a day which began with infinite melancholy; for
storm and sunshine are not its only moods. There are times,
indeed, when the lovely loch is hideously ugly, and the sky
comes down in shame and sorrow to conceal its beastliness.
This was such a morning, and the gloom of the outer scene
lay so heavily on my spirit that I had no heart to shave and
dress, and tie a necktie in a decent knot. I stood in a dressing-gown at my study window, and looked at nothingness.
A mist had risen from the water, and the colourless weight
of a miserable sky had sunk to meet it. Fog or cloud
obscured the view, and condensed in blubbering tears upon
the window-pane. Somewhere in the grey obscurity there
was a droning noise.

This was during the war, in 1943, I think, and I was at
home on leave for a few days. The old familiar noises of
the loch-shore—redshanks whistling, snipe drumming, and

a red-throated diver hallooing from the farther side—had been much reinforced by war; and we had learnt to distinguish the harsher notes of aeroplane engines. The noise in the fog, growing rapidly louder, was unmistakable. It was the innocent and homely sound of a Walrus: the slow and sturdy old amphibian that the Navy used. But the Walrus was flying unusually low and uncomfortably near my house. I opened a window, and leaned out anxiously, and could see nothing. Nor could the pilot, I realised.

The noise receded, traced a half-circle through the viewless air, came close again, and turned away. It was very low, it could be only a few feet above the water. Then, abruptly, it stopped; and there was silence in the fog.

I ran upstairs, put off my dressing-gown, and pulled on coat and trousers above my pyjamas. I hurried down to the little jetty where I kept my boat, and pulled out into the fog. I knew the narrow channel between the nearer shoals like the lines on my hand, and I thought I knew where the noise of the engine had stopped so suddenly. I pulled hard for eight or ten minutes—breathlessly hard—and saw upon the water a grey shape that seemed in the fog as monstrous and inordinately large as some primeval beast. Waist-deep in the water, two figures were shoving at a wing-tip, trying to push it off the shoal on which it had grounded. They had come down just south of a little island called the Holm of Kirkness: on one of my favourite fishing beats.

I rowed up to them, and asked how I could help. The fog was thinning now, and a light wind blew from the west. If I could tie-up to the other wing, they said, and pull athwart the wind—to the south, that is—we might swing their Walrus clear; for the hull was not solidly grounded, but rocking on the stones. So I made fast with a rope I had, and pulled, and pulled till my throat was dry as a rotten floor and my eyes were drowned in sweat. They, at the other end of the wing-span, shoved and shoved—and then the wind freshened and blew the hull clear. I slipped my rope, they climbed aboard, and started the engine. They went past me in a fan of rising water that blinded me, and when I had dried my spectacles I saw the Walrus with drumming engine, poised, as it were, for the accelerated run and the take-off into a quickly lightening sky. But it was pointing to the north, to shoals on which there was only paddling depth, and plain disaster.

I shouted, and bellowed, and rowed with furious speed towards them. I told them there was only one way to safety and deep water, and a little sceptically the pilot turned. It was shallow on every side—an excellent place for fishing, but not for a seaplane to come down—and the navigator had to jump into the water again to push a wing round. But then they pointed in the proper direction, and for a hundred yards or so I led them through the safe channel. The navigator climbed onto the starboard wing, and the pilot opened his throttle. The Walrus roared past in a cloud of spray, and blinded me again. I wiped my spectacles a second time, and saw the seaplane six or seven hundred yards away, not running straight for its take-off, as I had expected, but aimlessly, as it appeared, zigzagging. And as I stared, failing to understand its manoeuvres, I saw between us a little blob on the water. Something about the size of a football.

I bent to the oars again, and now it was harder work, for the wind was quickly freshening, and to increase discomfort it had begun to rain. I felt a little frightened now, and pulled with the strength of fear. But when I came within shouting distance of the navigator, he told me he was un-hurt; though he looked extremely uncomfortable. He had fallen off the wing as the pilot turned to face the wind, and he would have been safe enough in the loch if only he had been able to inflate his Mae West. But something had gone wrong with the system by which air should be pumped into the life-jacket, and he hung in the water, in a flying-suit half full of water, and was kept afloat only by as much air as might fill a bicycle tyre. He was fairly calm, though very pale.

He tried to climb in over the side of the boat, but when I said it would be safer to come in over the stern, he replied at once, 'Of course! I should have remembered.' There was a lot of weight in his waterlogged suit, the wind was stronger now, and I had some difficulty in helping him aboard. He thanked me, with the utmost courtesy, and said they were both sorry to have given me so much trouble. And then I had to row again.

The Walrus was half a mile to windward, and the pilot had no intention of coming back into shoal-water. I was getting a little tired, for the wind—no, it wasn't really strong; it was only what is properly known as 'a fresh breeze'. But my sodden passenger was a heavy load, and when we drew near the Walrus, and I had decided that the only way to transfer him was to back-down on the nose of the seaplane, the pilot complicated my task by charging me amidships. After avoiding him several times I persuaded him to accept my plan—my voice, though not tuneful, is loud enough—and after some delicate watermanship my passenger returned to his own vessel. Then the Walrus headed to the west and took off into a sky that was ugly still, but clear enough for two or three miles ahead.

I turned my boat and rowed slowly home. The bottomboards were afloat in several inches of water, I was soaked to the skin, and very tired. It was three hours since I had run upstairs to put on a pair of trousers, and I had been pulling hard for much of the time.—But I have been usefully employed, I told myself, and in due course, I dare say, I shall have something handsome to show for this. A parchment from the Admiralty, in flowing script, to thank me for my arduous service in preserving from destruction one of His Majesty's Walruses, and saving from the Harray Loch one of His Majesty's navigators. The Navy, I assured myself, shivering and weary as I rowed for the shore, is never remiss in courtesy, never laggard in its gratitude. Many years from now, I thought, my son will still treasure the parchment, if I have it suitably framed for him—as, of course, I shall.

I went back to my duty, such as it was, and awaited with lessening hope the acknowledgement that was my due. But no acknowledgement ever came. No one ever gave me a word of thanks for helping to save a Walrus, and for rescuing from the fish-fraught waters of the loch a pleasant and self-possessed young officer.—But the silence was not hard to explain. The young men who had ditched their ship, and got it safely away, had decided to say nothing about their misadventure, and so avoid the tedium of a court of enquiry. They assumed that I too would be discreet—as I have been, until now—and why complicate their war by tiresome, unproductive, judicial proceedings? They had, I imagine, an extra pint or two of beer that night, and said to each other, 'I expect the old basket's been in a jam himself, once or twice, and he won't talk. My Christ, we've been lucky! Same again?'

I have not told the story, after nearly a decade, to complain of their neglect; but as a fisherman I cannot omit from the game-book one sub-lieutenant of the Royal Navy. In his waterlogged flying-suit, as I netted him, he must have weighed at least two hundred and fifty pounds; which raises my average appreciably.

## IV

## THE PIPERS' TUNE

'Everyone has the adventures he deserves.'—André Gide has said so, and though I doubt the originality of his discovery, I am inclined to admit the truth of it. Before I left home there was news of a possible truce in Korea, and the prospect of a peaceful visit suited me very well. I like soldiers, and I admire their virtues; but I have no great share of them myself. I am more truly pacific by temperament than many a tetchy pacifist by conviction; and my high regard for the soldiers, and the Royal Navy, is largely a consequence of my recognition that whatever we have had of peace in this century is due to their bravery, rather than our rulers' sagacity. They have, moreover, very good manners.

My destination, on the first stage of my journey, was Singapore; but I got no farther than a Royal Air Force station in Wiltshire, where an officer, whose real interest in life appeared to be gardening, told me that the flight had been cancelled for lack of an aeroplane. All transport planes had been grounded, and their crews expected to go to Persia at any moment. There was trouble brewing in the damp heat of Abadan, where the Persians, it was said, had suddenly been filled with patriotic ardour by their tardy discovery that the Anglo-Iranian Company was making a very good thing of the oil-wells which its engineers had sunk; and in Teheran the Prime Minister had skilfully aggravated the crisis by bursting into tears and retiring to his bed. No one knew whether the Royal Air Force was preparing to carry troops for protection of the oil-fields, or to rescue employees of the Company from the wrath of Iranian patriots; but the courier service to Korea had certainly stopped, and on the following morning I returned to London.

In the Savile Club, by agreeable hazard, I met Stephen Spender. He was brown as a dish of walnuts from Italian sun, and sitting in the midst of a huge untidy nest of letters and discarded envelopes he looked like a large and exceptionally handsome bird preoccupied with incubation. He was, indeed, engaged in good works. He had been soliciting help for distressed poets in England, or displaced persons from Central Europe—I forget which—and his periphery of letters was the response to an appeal he had written. I promised my small support, for whatever benign purpose it was, and provoked a response of typical generosity. He spoke of Shelley, and proposed that each of us write, in friendly competition, a novel about him, and his marriage to Mary Wollstonecraft, and their life together. They were both endowed, he said, with peculiarly tender sensitivities, and their misfortune was that their sensitivities were mutually exclusive. Percy, because his own feelings were always so intensely engaged, was incapable of sympathising with Mary's apprehensions, or even admitting their existence; and Mary, with all her mind's antennae quivering to private gossip of the universe, had no time for the secrets that Percy was distilling from it.—He himself, said Spender, had some experience of that sort of delicate but resolute exclusiveness. It could be wilful, he thought; or half wilful. His own subconscious mind had developed a most ingenious defence against, not only contrary argument, but irrelevant or noxious information. What he did not want to hear made him dizzy, and so incapable of listening to it.

The Shelleys' domestic life was not, I thought, a subject to which I could happily give my whole attention for the long months of novel-writing; but I was very well pleased to hear Spender talk of it. The felicity of his conversation is that it seems both casual and open-handed, unpremeditated and unfenced—as if a lonely man, about to dine, should throw up his window and call to the first passer-by: 'If you're not engaged elsewhere, why not join me? I don't know what's for dinner, but do come and take pot-luck.'

New orders were sent me, and better orders than the old. I was to leave the following morning, not in the meagre comfort of a flying troop-ship, but in the luxury of an air-liner; and for that large improvement I had to thank the Persians. Fortune was with me—that was evident —and my unexpected day of grace in London was well spent. Nobly spent, indeed, for much of it was devoted to loving and reverent memory of a great and greatly burdened man.

I met Bernard Fergusson, who had lately been commanding the 1st Black Watch in Germany, and at night we dined with my friend Doyne Bell, who was so thoughtful as to provide a magnum of Meursault for the occasion. Thus agreeably stimulated, we spoke long and warmly of the late Lord Wavell, whom Fergusson had known intimately for many years. My own acquaintance with him had been small—he was elected Chancellor of Aberdeen

University when I was Rector—but his greatness was easily recognised, and to my immense respect for what he had done was added an ever-growing affection for what he was. In the living world he was such a man as the innocent and trusting mind of childhood believes great men to be.

In childhood, with good luck, we may live surrounded by greatness. The Argonauts and kings in armour throng our reading, and breathing the same air with us are living champions, far voyagers telling tales of distant islands, and great voices that speak with confidence of mighty issues. But as we climb the years, and mount upon a little pedestal of time, the greatness of our living elders is diminished; and looking round their narrowed shoulders we are tempted to perceive a shrinking even of our legendary heroes. We lose belief in greatness, and the world becomes a poorer place, more meanly peopled, than in our innocence we had supposed. The power of vision lessens with the view, and we accept a slow impoverishment of our estate; or turn away from men to seek consolation in religion, in the arts, or the shrewd fantasies of science. But then, it may be, when we are resigned to mediocrity and disappointment, we hear of someone whom the common frame of our experience cannot accommodate, someone whose deeds declare, and whose presence makes credible, the sort of existence we accepted when first we took delight in the resource of Ulysses and the long endurance at Roncesvalles. We are forced to admit, against the current of our thought, that greatness may live in mortal air, and history cannot always be explained by economics, but may require from time to time an epic poet to preserve its truth. Our brighter vision is renewed, and the world expands again.

Such was Wavell's effect upon the mind, for knowing him, and something of his deeds, it was impossible not to believe in greatness. In that square figure was housed a spirit of antique grandeur, and with his massive heroism went gentleness and modesty, even humility. He had, of course, no need to proclaim his virtue; for history would be his spokesman. He had stood like Atlas with a shaken world upon his shoulder, and while he listened to the guns, heard also in his mind the lyric choir of English poetry. His face, graven deeply as if by desert storms, could hold long silences, forbidding as the Sphinx; but when he spoke, it might be, with easy magnanimity, to take upon himself the faults and weaknesses of lesser men. He had lost an eye in battle, but laughter twinkled in the other. Against huge numerical odds and an unknown strength he had fought, in close succession, two victorious campaigns; in the pomp of Delhi he had ruled all India as its Viceroy; and he came home, unwearied and unspoiled by pomp and victory, to speak and work for little causes, to help where help was needed, as willingly as if some local charity were the greatest burden he had ever known. His own regiment had his love and duty to the end, and the red hackle in Wavell's bonnet meant as much to serving soldiers in the Black Watch as Fontenoy or any honour on their colours.

I had seen him with his soldiers at Duisburg in 1948, when he and I were Bernard Fergusson's guests at the Highland Brigade Games: it was not as Rector of Aberdeen University, in attendance on my Chancellor, that I went, but to satisfy Fergusson's sense of humour, whom it pleased to see, together at his table, the Colonel of the Regiment and a former private of the Watch. And my visit began so badly that I felt, for a little while, as unhappy as a private being marched in disgrace to the Orderly Room.

We flew from London, and I fell asleep in the aeroplane. An hour or two later I woke feeling miserably sick—the plane was bumping and lurching—and before I could recover equanimity we landed somewhere in Holland. A Dutch guard of honour, very handsomely dressed in dark blue and silver, was waiting for the Field-Marshal, and he, with mistaken kindness, made me walk with him when he inspected it. I was still faint with sickness, and the colour of cheese. Fortunately I was on Wavell's blind side, and unseen by him; but I was painfully aware that my company did him no credit.

Then, preceded by Dutch soldiers on motor-bicycles, we drove into Germany. It was not the legendary Wavell who sat beside me—silent and unresponsive as some rough headland frowning above a chattering sea—but a man eager for conversation and argument; and the subject he chose was Rudyard Kipling.

Now my knowledge of Kipling's work is respectable enough, and I had no need to simulate admiration. But Kipling is a difficult subject and cannot, I think, be properly judged except against the background of northern India in the heroic decades when our imperialism was evangelical in essence, and a man's work was regarded, by the evangelists, as his necessary act of worship. But except under some compulsion of the soul, or as stepping-stones to a large purpose, work is not widely recognised as desirable in itself; and when Kipling came home he found only a minority who shared his faith and the vision of the dedicated soldiers and civilians of the Empress of India. Being disappointed in his fellow-subjects, he grew embittered; and in his later years his thwarted hopes, now harshly repressed, sometimes made his writing obscure. . . .

But Wavell would hear nothing against him, and out of his prodigious memory drew quotation after quotation that refuted my criticism. From the Lama to Mr. Pyecroft, from Hobden back to Mrs. Hauksbee, he summoned his forces and loyally maintained that righteous anger, such as Kipling often showed, could not be described as bitterness, which was an impoverishment of the spirit; and what I called obscurity was in fact the natural expression of an ever-deepening understanding.—There was nothing over-bearing in Wavell's manner, nothing really combative. He had had so much pleasure from Kipling that gratitude was bound to speak warmly, and a genial delight in argument played robustly on the surface of old affection.—I began to feel that it was ungracious to look for weaknesses in so good a poet, in so rare a story-teller; and before we reached Duisburg I had gone back to the generosity of boyhood, and there was no visible fault in the author of *Kim* and *Kaa's Hunting*, of *The Last Chantey* and the *St. Helena Lullaby*.

At Duisburg that night there was a ball that might have become—or so one thought, with a morbid fascination, at the time—as famous as the dancing in Brussels on the eve of Waterloo. The Russian blockade of Berlin had just begun, and Russia's further intentions were quite obscure; though one could hardly doubt that they were unfriendly. But in the meantime the Highlanders and their guests were dancing, and the lifting kilts and the tartan sashes made a very gallant spectacle. A little gallantry, one reflected, was

almost all that Europe had to defend her, should Russia
move; and the leaping gaiety of the reels, at such an hour,
was a comforting reminder of many occasions when pride
and gaiety had saved the day.

Then, for a little while, the dancing stopped. We heard
a farther and more numerous music, and from the broad
steps of the house we saw the pipers of the Black Watch
and the Gordons, with an escort of torch-bearers, come
marching through the green darkness of a pine-wood.
The red tartan and the green, white plumes and gleaming
drums, the beat of drum and the fierce delight of the pipers'
tune.—There was an absurdity of pride in their tune, the
whole-hearted swagger of the old centuries when men knew
no larger enemies than the hands and courage of their
enemies, and fear had hardly been discovered. Fear lost its
meaning against that tune. So long as the spirit lived and
the tune was good, the end of the day would bring no
difference, whatever had befallen. A salute for victory, a
lament for the dead: that was all the difference, and all that
mattered was the goodness of the tune.

Gaiety endured until the night was almost done, and
quickly reappeared at breakfast-time. I had never break-
fasted with a Field-Marshal before, and thought a stately
silence would prevail. But the Black Watch is not as other
regiments. We are amateurs of history, we dabble in
literature, and in conversation we can be nicely allusive.—
There was a sergeant of the 2nd Battalion who, speaking
of the desperate and bloody sally from Tobruk, in 1941,
declared: 'We drove the Jerries afore us, sir, like Christ
clearing the money-changers out of the Temple!'—And
now, at Bernard Fergusson's breakfast-table, the coffee-cups

and toast-racks were pushed aside to make a space for rhyme
and iambic pentameters.

Wavell, coming straight from his Chancellor's duty and
academic ceremony, had discovered that some of his toilet-
gear was missing. He had told Fergusson: 'I left my
shaving-brush at Aberdeen'; and Fergusson, quick to catch
the sentence's iambic flow, had promptly seen what could be
launched upon it.—'What about the *ballade* you were going
to write, sir?' he enquired. He had made a beginning, said
Wavell, but as Fergusson had suggested it, he thought Fergusson should help to finish it. He read a stanza or two, and
some half-made lines. He gave his manuscript to Fergusson, who found a few missing rhymes and gave it back.
They completed it before the coffee was cold, and the last
stanza and the *envoi* read:

> My chin, once glossy as a nectarine,
>    Now looks like holly on a Christmas card,
> Or straggly hawthorns in a woodland scene
>    Such as is deftly drawn by Fragonard;
> No R.S.M. would pass me for a Guard
>    However much I titivate and preen.
> My luck would daunt a Roland or Bayard:
>    I left my shaving-brush at Aberdeen.
>
> Pity me, Prince: the water here is hard,
>    Hourly my tongue inclines to the obscene,
> Full of strange oaths and bearded like the pard
>    I left my shaving-brush at Aberdeen.

Laughter on the face of greatness has a moving beauty.
Wavell wiped a tear of laughter from his wounded eye,
and across the breakfast-table he seemed to recede and grow
in magnitude in the perspective of history. In the distance
were Delhi and the black-bearded troopers of the Viceroy's
Bodyguard; Ethiopia lay beneath his arm; swift and secret

in the darkness the Army of the Nile moved out against the vast imposing structure of the Italian Empire, and O'Connor, for our first taste of victory, rode his armoured columns westward through Cyrenaica. . . .

We spoke of all that—over a magnum of Meursault—and Doyne Bell remembered an evening when Wavell had dined with us at the Savile Club, and startled our table with his comment on some excesses of the time. There had been talk of authority's growing taste for authority, of the concentration of power in political hands and the politicians' excessive demand for power. It was not, in essence, a political debate, but rather a moral discussion : it was no political doctrine that was deplored, but only political excess.—And Wavell, leaning forward, heavy-shouldered, listened in silence until, by infection, silence grew general. And then he spoke.—Kipling, he said, had noticed such a tendency in our times, and deplored it. He had, indeed, propounded a drastic remedy for it. Did we remember *Macdonough's Song*? he asked. And in a very gentle voice, with a gentle smile on his desert-graven cheeks, he recited :

> 'Whatsoever, for any cause,
>   Seeketh to take or give
> Power above or beyond the Laws,
>   Suffer it not to live !
> Holy State or Holy King—
>   Or Holy People's Will —
> Have no truck with the senseless thing.
>   Order the guns and kill !'

Silence returned—but only for a moment—to our table. It was, indeed, more than ordinary silence, more than mere lack of words. The little currents of thought and apprehension that usually chatter in worn runlets through the mind were stilled as if by a sudden frost; and in the hush of a winter morning we looked, and blinked, at the ice-glare on that cold conclusion.—It was Wavell himself who broke the silence and found an easier topic. Golf, I think. He was going to St. Andrews. . . .

# V

## CONVERSATION IN SINGAPORE

A SULLEN refusal to work with sufficient vigour, by one of
the port engines, delayed our start in the morning, but when
at last the Constellation took the air, and steward and
stewardess moved so easily up and down the central aisle,
bowing for conversation, I thought how strange and re-
assuring it was to see a tradition adopting new ways of life.
B.O.A.C. had found a different element, but in style and
mannerism it was very like the great shipping companies,
the P. & O., the Cunard, and the Orient Line. Comfort
and politeness had found their sky-legs; dignity had
migrated from the sea, but wore the same bland surface of
reliability. It was very pleasant to be flying, so far, with
such assurance of well-being; but the earliest landmarks
on the road to war were quite incongruous. Brighton,
Dijon, Rome, and Capri signposted our way.

An acquaintance with the beauty of clouds—with the
upper surface of clouds in the deeps of the sky—is one of
the benefits that aeroplanes have brought us. Our fathers,
if they took the trouble to climb a mountain, could look
slantwise down on the curling mists that gather in a valley,
but we are the first of mankind to see the great continents
of the air, its enormous prairies and fantastic archipelagoes,
in sunlight from above. And what beauty there is, what
light and splendour, what heights of loveliness and brooding
fear, in the landscapes of the clouds! The south of France

lay hidden under pleated canopies of clean-combed wool, and vaporous high curtains; but the Mediterranean was a deep-blue field in which were planted, row upon row, ten thousand little flocculent clouds like lettuces. And the day went out behind a wall of smoky rose that cut off the immeasurable farther view of an apricot sky, an upper sky of yellow plum-skin.

We slept in Cairo, and in the morning recognised the first signals of the East: ants on the bathroom floor, buzzards drifting in the still, bright air. Then the desert: Cairo's hideous, nonsensical, suburban sands, and the larger desert beyond, veined and wrinkled into gigantic lizard-shapes. The savage crust of Sinai, the red Arabian desert, a flatness scored by mammoth feet, then dust and dissolution of the view, and darkness. The two Russian passengers who had come aboard at Rome lay sleeping, asprawl in their tilted chairs, but their responsibility had not been forgotten. This was an oblong package, about the size of a shoe-box, sewn up in heavy canvas and sealed with brown, portentous seals.—They were short and stocky men, pale of face, apparently identical in build, whose heads looked as if they had been set upon their shoulders without the intervention of a neck. They wore dark suits and drab overcoats of similar cut, but not, one would say, made to measure. They gave no response, except a distrusting stare, to any attempt at conversation; but in Cairo, with a minimum of words, they stubbornly refused either to be separated from their canvassed parcel or to have it examined by a Customs officer. And now, while they slept, the sealed box was fastened to the right ankle of the younger one by padlock and a thick steel chain.

The flight from Cairo to Karachi lasted nine hours, and in Karachi, with buzzing ears and surprised by oven-heat— the darkness was like a thick felt, preserving within it the smouldering heat of the day—we idled for a couple of hours before taking off again to float across India, all unseen, and land in Calcutta for breakfast. (Little pale-yolked eggs of India, white butter, flabby toast, sugar-bowls under beaded net, and fragments of skin in the boiled milk: the lonely men in dak-bungalows, whom Kipling sang, broke their fast on these, and so to-day do the skyfarers.)—Then a nacreous mist above the Hooghly, and some new passengers to consider: a youngish, glossy-haired, handsome man, uneasily smart in the exaggerated, brittle smartness that suggests, but often unjustly, an association with night clubs or black market; and his wife, a yellow-skinned, lacka-daisical woman, taller than he, of melancholy aspect and slovenly beauty. Her cheeks were lightly pock-marked, she was heavily pregnant, and to accommodate her belly she had sewn, very roughly, a long gusset of pink flannel into an ill-made skirt of red, artificial silk; but in repose she had a slackened dignity that quite belittled her husband's assertion of importance. She paid small attention to him, but occasionally made large and tender movements of affection about their two black-eyed, gaudily dressed children. Her arms were lemon-hued, scarred by vaccination, and bare to the shoulder; they made rhythmic patterns, slow and deliberate, when she handed sweetmeats to the little girls.— She and her husband carried Israeli passports, and if his back-ground was emancipation from the ghetto, hers, one might suppose, was reluctant expulsion from the tents of Kedar.

Seven or eight hours of flying took us to Singapore,

green below a purple rainstorm, and we circled the island till the rain had passed. I was driven to Changi, at the eastern corner, and relaxed after my journey in the hospitality of the Royal Air Force. I had, however, only a few hours of relaxation. I swam in a warm discoloured sea, I smelt the curious muddy smell of mangroves, I let the tropic sun encourage the pallid tissues of my northern skin; and then I had to go and buy a white dinner-jacket and thin black evening-trousers. For my service was to begin with a series of dinner-parties, and my host was an Air Vice-Marshal of robust physique, of cheerful temperament, and a reputation for late-sitting. But I am a late-sitter myself, and suffered no inconvenience from that.

Officers' wives enjoy their life in Singapore, and the wives of other ranks like it no less. They have Chinese or Malayan servants, and appreciate the comfort they give. They are, moreover, so honest as to admit their enjoyment. 'We come out here for three years,' said one of them, 'and for three years we never get up on a winter morning, we never feel cold and we don't wash dishes, we can do our housekeeping in an hour, and wear nothing for most of the day but a shirt and a pair of shorts, if our knees are all right. Oh, we'd be fools if we didn't appreciate it! For we know quite well that we're going back, when our three years are up, to a London suburb and the kitchen sink.'

'That,' said another, 'is what we have escaped for a little while: the tyranny of the kitchen sink.'

'How can civilisation,' demanded a husband with irritation in his voice, 'survive without domestic servants?'

'Perhaps it can't. Civilisation was built on division of labour; and nowadays, when professors of Greek have to make their own beds, and neurologists get up and light the fire, and Cabinet Ministers dry the dinner-plates their wives have washed, we're pointing back to the general squalor of the Stone Age. Back to hugger-mugger,' I said firmly; and let a Chinese butler refill my glass.

'It's so important to be tolerant,' said someone, 'but how can you feel tolerant when you've no time to *think*?'

'Civilisation depends on a leisured class.'

'Enlightened slavery may be the answer. There are several million Asiatics who would be infinitely better off in decent households, as temporary slaves under indenture, than they are in their own villages.'

'I couldn't bear it!' exclaimed a woman. 'To have a slave in the house would be unbearable. It's bad enough to have a dog to look after, and to be utterly responsible for another human being—oh, no, I couldn't do it!'

'Well, we needn't worry just yet. We're in Singapore, and in Singapore we do have leisure, and we can enjoy ourselves.'

'And we're very tolerant!'

'And truly civilised?'

The palm-trees shrugged their leaves against the grape-skin dark. The air was warm as a conservatory, and smelt of frangipani. Under a new moon, only a finger's-breadth from its nether arc, Venus shone large and brilliant on the calm of the sky. And someone began to speak of the latest operation against bandits in Malaya.

North of the island, throughout the long peninsula, there were planters in their lonely bungalows, forbidden to go abroad after dark, who sat with loaded revolvers beside the whisky on their tables. Their night was warm as Singa-

pore's, and Venus shone as near the moon; but their peace
might be broken at any moment by a rattle of gunfire or the
crash of a bursting grenade. Into the peace and luxury of
the island, over the narrow Straits of Johore, came tales of
ambush and murder, the echoes of Communist revolution.

The city of Singapore had some resemblance to an overcrowded raft afloat on a dangerous sea. . . . It was a pleasant
city to look at, with broad streets and pavements reasonably
clean. In the kind and sunny equatorial air—the sun's heat
modified by half-encircling sea—the people were agreeably
casual in their demeanour, genial of temper, as it seemed,
and on the surface life looked easy. There was no great
need, in that climate, for expensive clothes or elaborate
lodging. But the population was too numerous. Behind a
façade of solid buildings on the waterfront the city was a
gigantic bazaar, and the oriental bazaar seems to oppose, to
its horde of customers, almost as great a horde of shopkeepers. The human pressure, one felt, was too high for
safety—if the weather broke. If the climate turned hostile,
with political gales and economic ground-swell, the city
would be very like an overcrowded raft on a sea where
rough-skinned sharks swam in bloody expectation. There
was great wealth in the island, mostly in Chinese hands,
and the political sharks would also be Chinese. . . . There
was a poet of the IVth century called T'ao Ch'ien who
had a lute without strings. When a critic derided it, he
answered: 'But it's quite unnecessary to go to the trouble
of plucking strings if your ear is good enough to hear the
possibilities of music in such a lute as this!'—As an influence
on the oriental mind, T'ao is outmoded. But how infinitely preferable he would be to Mao!

C

I spent four or five days in Singapore, and dined one night with General Sir Charles Keightley, whom I had known in Italy during the war, and last seen in Duisburg, at the Highland Brigade ball, when I watched him dancing an eightsome reel. Red as a foxhunter and leaping as strenuously, he charged his partners as if they were an Irish wall—and the same exuberance coloured my memories of him in Italy. As a Divisional General he was for ever racing forward in a little armoured scout-car, and in the last great battle of the campaign he announced the imminence of victory, with the utmost bonhomie, by a back-handed blow that knocked the wind out of me.

It was a morning I remember with considerable pleasure; for it was truly interesting.—It was, I think, the 25th of April 1945, and the battle for the crossing of the Po was nearing its reward. Charles Keightley was commanding our Vth Corps, in whose area the main action lay, and I had gone to call on the Brigadier of his General Staff to ask what our immediate prospects were. His B.G.S. was a very able young officer called Toby Low—later a Member of Parliament—and finding him alone in his caravan I enquired, rather diffidently, if there was any news. He had begun, very civilly, to demonstrate the course of events on a large wall-map, when the door of the caravan was thrown noisily open, and in strode General Keightley.

'What are you doing here?' he demanded.

'Picking the brains of your B.G.S., sir.'

'Well, you can't pick them now. I'm going to use them myself.'

I retired to the far end of the caravan, and while pretending to study another map, listened to the General's instructions. He had been far forward and seen for himself the wreckage of the German divisions on our side of the river, and now, to exploit advantage, he was issuing new orders, and the orders came in a swiftly flowing but sharply defined torrent. Formations and map-references were named without a moment's hesitation, without regard to notes, and instruction emerged clear and concise. In-formative summary, preparatory warning, and executive orders: terse and quick and decisive.—And almost before the torrent ceased, Toby Low had a pair of telephones like a bridle about his chin, and was ready to transmit all he had heard.

'That clear to you, Toby?'

'Yes, sir.'

'All right, get on with it.'

And then, genial and relaxed, he came to me at the other end of the caravan and asked, 'Were you listening?'

'I'm afraid I was.'

'Sounds good, doesn't it? Now look at this, and I'll show you what's been happening.'—And on the map, as quickly and concisely as he had issued orders, he sketched the course of battle, and showed the final movement by which he proposed to finish it. Then, turning to his B.G.S., enquired, 'Did you get through to them all right?'

Toby Low had been talking, rapidly and quietly, and simultaneously as it seemed on both his telephones. 'Just about finished, sir.'

Charles Keightley laughed, with the unabashed and open pleasure he had earned, and said to me, 'That's how you win battles! Easy, isn't it?' And dealt me a smacking, back-handed blow on the chest.

At the door of the caravan he stopped and said, 'Come and dine with me to-night. I caught a German General this morning, and he'd quite a lot of champagne in his car. I'm told it's a good champagne, so come and try it.'

It was General the Graf von Schwerin who had surrendered himself, and the Graf's champagne was most praiseworthy. *Spolia opima.* . . .

But now, in Singapore, Charles Keightley was in graver mood. He had only recently been appointed to his command in the Far East, and he had just returned from his first visit to the Malayan jungle. He realised that the war was not merely a war against five thousand Communist irregulars slinking through the rubber, but a struggle with the bedevilled minds of fifty thousand simple people. Fifty thousand, or double that? No one knew how many had been terrorised, or hypnotised by the repetition of seeming-simple, lying phrases. Of pious dogma that had no relation to the truth, of promised benefactions that tyranny would grind to dust.—It was difficult for a soldier to fight against a state of mind, for what were the proper weapons to use?

Ridicule, I suggested. The fine promises of Communism were so absurdly remote from its horrid practice, that they stood wide-open to ridicule. If George Orwell's *Animal Farm*, for example, could be translated and robustly transformed into comic strips, would it be useful? The Chinese had a sense of humour, and so had the Malays.—But the topic was too large for cocktail-time.

I went, on the following morning, to a hospital to visit about fifty soldiers who had been wounded in Korea; and felt a little nervous when I introduced myself, and humble when I said good-bye.—I shall not pretend that all were perfectly good-humoured, and spoke of their hardships with careless laughter. But they did, in truth, show a patience and sweetness of temper that were remarkable. They grumbled because they had been left in Singapore, though they had been told they would be flown straight home— the Persian crisis had prevented that—but they grumbled honestly and reasonably, not sourly and from injured minds; and those who had suffered most, who had lost sight or limbs, had least to say.

I sat with a boy who had had an eye shot out. He had been a railway fireman, and his ambition had been the common nursery wish, to become an engine-driver. But now that hope must be put away, because he had volunteered to fight in Korea, and he had been unlucky there. 'But if they give me a chance to get a bit more education,' he said, 'I expect I'll find indoor work. A booking-office wouldn't be so bad.'—It seemed a poor prospect compared with driving an engine from York to London, and his friends, I thought, might call him a fool for leaving a sound job to fight obscurely for a difficult cause in a distant land. But he was patently a good boy, and the good, though they suffer, have resources of their own and their own rewards. It is the ill-made who have no compensation when misfortune comes, and turn to hatred of their world.

# VI

## THE DOORSTEP OF ASIA

A SUNDERLAND flying-boat with a Cockney crew took me from Singapore to Hong Kong. We got up in the dark, and went aboard at Seletar, and roared over muddy water to meet a crimson dawn. We were hardly airborne before someone brought mugs of tea and enormous sandwiches, and throughout the ten-hours' flight we were comforted or drugged by huge quantities of food. The Cockney airmen were not physically large, but they ate like giants: vast, crowded plates of meat and vegetables, dumplings and potatoes, and succeeding plates of various puddings, and presently sandwiches again, and boiled sweets, and another pint or two of dark-brown tea. 'They drew extra rations— for you,' explained their Wing-Commander, who came with us. He was a neighbour of mine, in Scotland, and we had much to talk about; but better than Highland gossip was conversation with the crew. They were all *characters*, and much of their talk was badinage, leg-pulling, familiar jokes.—'He gets away with it every time,' said one of them, pointing to a friend. 'Put him on a charge, and what happens? He goes in to the C.O., and strikes an attitude. Sort of cringing; you know? "Don't 'it me, sir," he cries. "Oh, please don't 'it me! Just give me a good talking-to!"'—Well, what can you do with the like of that?'

It was an excellent crew, highly skilled, of long experience in tropical and sub-arctic weather. But a stranger, a foreigner, might have found it difficult to realise their virtue; and heaven alone knows what inner faith possessed and lighted them. Music-hall and local pub and a warm domestic life appeared to be their background; but out of that had come a talent for skyfaring, the faculty of long endurance, a liking for adventure—the sudden coasts and icy clouds that menaced their winter patrolling from the Shimonoseki Gap to the seas off Vladivostok were no less perils than Hakluyt chronicled—and how the marriage had been made between adventure and the earthy humour of London streets only God and the genius of England knew. And the English genius, like God, is impossible to define; because, though often eloquent, it never condescends to be explicit.

Ten hours in the sky is a long time. I sat beside the pilot, and with him charged the ocean-cloud. We saw, like mountains in a Chinese painting, the coast of Indo-China; and an island, whose name I forget, as closely cultivated as a market garden. I read a little, and wrote letters, and still had time to think. To think? It is too specific, too laudatory a description of the open-mindedness with which I entertained passing ideas and casual sensation. . . . It was ten years ago, I remembered, that I flew in a Sunderland through stormy skies to Iceland. There was a General aboard whose Staff Captain, a man too old for his rank, was handsomely bemedalled from the first war against Germany. In civil life, he told me, he was a Hatton Garden diamond merchant, and two or three years later he went back to his business. He was in plain clothes when next I met him, and taking me to lunch at the Thatched House, he gave me good advice.   Precious stones, he said, were going to be a very sound investment, but unless one had a great deal of money it was rather too late to buy diamonds; which had already gone up in price.   I still had time, however, to buy emeralds.   Emeralds were dearer than they had been, but cheap in comparison with diamonds, and the market was sure to rise.   They were, moreover, very pretty things to have in one's possession.   He took a little parcel from an upper waistcoat-pocket, and unfolding it displayed a few small stones, grass-green in their nest of cotton-wool, and one noble, square-cut emerald that shone like the heart of light in a great Atlantic wave.   What was it worth? About £800, he said.

It would, I agreed, be very pleasant to own a little hoard of emeralds, and I felt—oh, not sad, but disappointed that I could not indulge in so charming a hobby.   Did he carry many precious stones in his waistcoat-pocket?

Not many, he said, but he usually had a few.   If I was interested in diamonds—well, here were two good ones and some smaller specimens.   And from another packet he spilt a scintillation of jewels in whose little symmetrical facets light danced and twinkled, cold and brilliant.— Everybody liked diamonds, of course, but why were rubies not more esteemed?   They were highly regarded in India, and perhaps they looked their best against the lobe of a Hindu ear, or the pallor of a Moslem neck; but surely they were beautiful in any circumstances?—A tiny cascade of rubies joined the diamonds on the table.   A frozen translucency of pigeon's blood, the ice of claret, fire crystallised and carved to let it out on every side.—He had some pearls as well, but pearls were not his business. He was almost apologetic about his pearls.

Now if, I thought—flying at 7000 feet above the South China Sea—I were an author like Arnold Bennett, I might well have found in that gallant and amiable diamond merchant a subject to fill a novel; but I had done no more than take pleasure in his company, I had made no use of him. I had, indeed, no great wish to be a novelist like Arnold Bennett, but I envied him, at that moment, his ability to pursue his vocation in a brisk and business-like way; for my own habit is indolent and laborious too, wasteful of both time and opportunity. I cannot divide my day and give four hours to work and four to amusement. I cannot write in railway trains or other people's houses. I can neither force myself to set down five hundred words in a morning, nor light-heartedly go off to enjoy myself when I have failed to do so—but like an angler fishing a sullen lake, I must sit and wait for the rise. If I am working, I work all day, though often I achieve very little; and when I am idling I can hardly bring myself to answer a letter.

I rebuked myself, above the China Sea. I deplored my lack of method, and grew a little worried to think that after writing, for my pleasure and my living, for more than twenty years, I had developed no economical and efficient manner of writing. I still had to wait for the mood, then drive it till I grew warm. The creative part of my mind is fairly active, but the working parts are sluggish. I enjoy writing, yet bemoan the effort of beginning. *Odi et amo*. . . .

In the Opera Cellars in Stockholm a young man from the newspaper *Svenska Dagbladet* had demanded my reasons

for setting up in trade as an author, and my justification
for so continuing. I had evaded his questions because I was
neither willing nor ready to reply; but they remained
uneasily in my mind, and from time to time I had thought
that some day I must try to answer them. For nowadays
motives are keenly regarded, motives are sought and pursued
as butterflies and big game were hunted when times were
easier and minds were easy with them. Yes, some day I
would say what I had to say; but not this day. Not at 7000
feet above the China Sea. If I cannot write in a train or in
other people's houses, how could I be expected to write in a
Sunderland flying above the Paracel Reefs?

Time passed, the sky clouded, and at last, skirting some
hostile islands, we approached Hong Kong in surly weather;
and Hong Kong in dark-blue curtains looked as if its
architects had set out to find an oriental Glencoe in which
to re-create Leadenhall Street. Among hills that low clouds
exaggerate, the city is strangely solid, and an outpost of
imperial merchants has all the dignity of a capital, though
it has no land to rule. But there were two significant
changes since I had last been there, for the great harbour
looked half empty, and the high-piled, crowded island was
far more numerously occupied. The Americans had dis-
approved of some of the cargoes our shipping brought,
and many Chinese of the mainland, disliking what they
had heard of the Communists, had fled there for sanctuary.
As busy as an ant-hill, Hong Kong was said to be prosperous,
and at night it was fantastically decorated by the electric-
ally lighted alphabet of China. The names of shops and
restaurants and dance-halls leapt from the darkness, green

and yellow, blazing sapphire and incandescent rose, in the beautifully meaningless characters of Chinese writing; and staring, entranced, at the glittering letters which were skeletons of ancient hieroglyphs, one saw them as symbols of the development of all writing : from a simple means of communication to a deliberate form of pleasure. Even the alphabet, in China, was designed as a decoration of life.

I had official calls to pay, and I was committed to a good deal of formal entertainment. When I was young a dinner-party or any elaborate social occasion was fearful torment to my spirit: I was ridiculously shy and idiotically self-conscious. But now, with a little effort, I can, as it were, stuff myself out of sight, and let an impersonalised effigy, endowed with an elementary faculty of speech, go on parade. I do not enjoy such occasions, but I no longer suffer. My happiest afternoon on the island was spent in undress.

I had lunch with a man who had extricated himself, only a few months before, from Communist China, where he had great commercial interests. My fellow-guests were a naval officer and a Chinese doctor. None of them had any sympathy with Communist dogma, but all agreed that Mao's dictatorship was firmly established. The promise of territorial reforms that had prefaced, and for a little while disguised the true nature of the revolution, had quickly been followed by merciless control and harsh taxation of the peasantry; but a numerous, energetic, and fairly efficient army of officials had no difficulty in controlling the angry farmers who, having listened to the Communist mission-aries, were now paying for their mistake and being bled by Communist tax-gatherers. Our host was compelled to pay

the salaries of his many employees in China, though the
new régime prevented him from doing business and had
cut the very roots of trade. But he could, if he received
permission, travel by rail from Canton to Hankow, and
thence to Peking, and arrive in the capital at the hour
promised by the time-table : for Mao, taking his example
from Mussolini, was advertising the efficiency of his rule by
making the trains run punctually. And his achievements
and his gospel, said the Chinese doctor, had had a great
effect on young, enthusiastic, inexperienced minds. He
had attacked, with all possible force, the traditional family
sentiment on which Chinese society had for so long been
built; and many young men had jumped at the opportunity
to deride their fathers. It was nonsense to describe the
Chinese armies in Korea as volunteers, but there were
volunteers among them. He, the doctor, had friends in
Shanghai who were in deep distress because their sons had
left them and gone off to fight for Communism.

We went, in the afternoon, to swim at Big Wave Bay.
The waves were small and gentle, but the sea was hyacinth-
blue and the air was cool.—There were, in our party, two
little Chinese girls of nine or ten years of age, whose infant
figures had a grace that seemed to naturalise the silken
graces of Chinese painting. I have never, I think, seen
humanity in so delicate and lovely shape. They were, quite
certainly, the offspring of an old race that for many generations had esteemed beauty as one of the supreme values of
life : beauty in trees and stone, in jade and lyric, in water-
falls and human beings. But would the Communists who
had conquered the land maintain the vision?—I remembered the two squat and solemn, earth-bound and ridiculous

little men, with a canvas-covered shoe-box chained to a servile ankle while they slept, who had travelled with me from Rome to Singapore : no loveliness nor grace of being would spring from their dull loins.

Nor was beauty, at Big Wave Bay, confined to children. There were some gay parties there, with grown-up girls whose legs and arms of living ivory—their pert breasts and bottoms were flamingo-hued or parrot-bright in silk—compelled us to walk, with apparently a casual motion, to take a nearer view of them; and in their little noses, the deliberate setting of their eyes—in the refinement of cheekbone and the well-turned length of their legs—there was evidence, again, of an aesthetic principle that had influenced even parenthood.—How brutal, in comparison, was Japanese history, if one accepts, as its end-product, a typical group of Japanese girls in bathing-suits.

But my chief engagement in Hong Kong was with the soldiers in the New Territories; and the New Territories are a doorstep to Asia that steeply climbs and becomes a gazebo from which something is visible of Asia's terrible immensity. The noisy wharves and broad streets of Kowloon, then paddy-fields for ever green under rocky hills, and hill repeating hill; a winding road, bright firths of the sea, and a golf-course planted to give a little air of calm and reason to the turbulence and mysticism of the East; then jeep-tracks that twist and turn in dizzy ascent to ridges from which, in endless tautology, the ridges and yellow hills of China, variegated by the green banks of watercourses, recede into the clouds of immeasurable distance. Barbed wire, the symbol of our new intolerance, marks the frontier, and a bridge across a muddy stream is guarded

on either side by rival police.   An unnatural solemnity in-
spires the Chinese constables as they examine the papers of
apathetic peasants who go to and fro: the awful, oppressive solemnity with which Communism, like Calvinism
before it, overloads its servants.   The solemnity of the little
men in the aeroplane, chained to a box full of dreary secrets.

The Middlesex Regiment and the Argyll and Sutherland
Highlanders, though they made no promises and had, perhaps, given little thought to the matter, offered more to
the world than Mao's indoctrinated legions.   They had
learnt, for example, how to live with their neighbours.
They spoke appreciatively, with real friendliness, of the
American tank-crews and mortar-gunners with whom they
had shared a winter campaign.   And that was truly remarkable, for the private soldier, with his private view of action,
often finds it difficult to believe that others—even of his
own kin—are doing as well as he.   To be generous to
allies, to foreigners, was, in my young days, a thing unheard
of.   Nor, in the second war against Germany, was there
much sympathy between our battalions and the American
regiments beside them.   But in Korea, where both were so
far from home, they had felt the unity of their common
plight.

They were, of course, critical of American strategy and
tactics in the first winter of the war.   The headlong advance
towards the Manchurian border, without pause for reconnaissance, had worried them by its neglect of military
principles; the precipitate retreat from an enemy left far behind had angered and perplexed them.   But they exempted
the American soldiers from this criticism of their leaders.
'There was nothing wrong with the Yanks,' said an earnest

corporal, 'except two things : they were badly led, and they hadn't been very well trained. But they were quick to learn, and there was a big difference after Ridgway came out.'—The Americans themselves, in the American way, spoke more severely of their early deficiencies. 'We've got to hand it to your infantry,' said one of their regimental officers. 'I don't say anything against our boys, but the way they'd been trained ! Every damn one of them had his ass screwed to a jeep.'

The Argylls and the Middlesex could afford to be generous. The two battalions that had been sent so hurriedly to reinforce the threatened lines of Pusan had quickly made a name for themselves; and it is not fanciful, I think, to say that their reputation, in the first place, was due to their boots.—The Americans, at that time, wore rubbersoled shoes that merely whispered to the road, but the British were shod with iron and leather, and when they went ashore in Pusan the cobbled quays rang like a thousand anvils beneath their tread. The great voices of the sergeant-majors split the air, the soldiers fell-in and dressed on their markers—boots all together falling with a crash—and the chorus of their marching feet, drilled and decisive, filled the hot air with the menace of their confidence. Boot-leather and drill, on their first day in Korea, won a moral victory.

Their second achievement was also moral. It followed the tragic error of three American pilots who, ordered to support the Argylls in their first engagement, mistook one hill for another and dropped their bombs, not on the enemy, but on their allies. The Americans, when they discovered their mistake, were overwhelmed by grief. The Argylls, recovering quickly from the shock, were stoical.

Blunders occur in every war, and there was a phrase, much used by contemporary fatalists, that could palliate what had been done. 'It's just one of those things,' they said, and comforted their distracted visitors. The Americans, generous themselves, were deeply moved by so much generosity in others.

But the reputation of the Brigade ultimately rested, of course, on its achievements. Its training on the steep-sided hill-country of the New Territories had been ideal for a Korean purpose, and the young conscripts who were half its strength ignored the compulsion of their enlistment and fought like volunteers. The 3rd Royal Australians joined the British battalions, and their vigour and traditional *élan* were excellently governed by several officers of strong character and profound experience in war. The Brigade led much of the advance towards Manchuria, and covered much of the retreat; and such was their competence in action that it was not uncommon, in that first winter, for their American allies to address them as 'you professionals'.

Less than half of them, however, were professionals— and why did the others fight so well? Did they recognise a good cause and strenuously resolve to support it?—It was a good cause. The much-advertised principle of international rule by international law received in 1950 material support that appeared to promise serious intention; and hope, in consequence, re-visited the better parts of the world. But did the soldiers reason, and philosophise, and fight like Roundheads for their convictions? I doubted that, but tried to get an answer.

The Middlesex were non-committal. I had some pleasant conversation with their N.C.O.s and men, and always it dwindled, after we had found a little warmth of common interest, into village gossip.—Or platoon gossip : there is no great difference.—The Middlesex were unwilling to speak of their private feelings. They thought, perhaps, that service with the Die Hards was its own justification. Or, more likely, they found it unnecessary to explain—and foolish to labour to explain—an intuitive knowledge of what was both the proper and the sensible thing to do. In the most trying days of all, when the American estimates of Chinese strength, fantastically exaggerated, suggested that nothing could withstand it—and when the Siberian winds were a torment that no one could exaggerate—I think it likely that a stubborn Britannic contrariness took hold of them, and they fought with the satisfying intention of proving their allies wrong. But they were quite as reticent about themselves as all those travelled Englishmen of the upper classes who, for two hundred years, went everywhere and looked at everything through pale-blue, unrevealing eyes. The Middlesex defeated me, and the Argylls challenged my credulity.

The Scots are more exuberant, more emotional, more talkative, and more serious than the English. The Lowland Scots have never enjoyed, nor envied, the amateur status of their neighbours, and the Highland Scots have not wholly abjured a romantic attitude to life. I was sternly rebuked by two good men of the Argylls when I asked them : 'Did the Jocks know what they were fighting for?'

We were sitting on green turf in a warm and charming landscape. A large garden of lawns and trees confronted us, and beyond the trees a golf-course had been spread, urbane and frivolous between sharp-sided hills of the sort that

Chinese painters had so often turned into symbols of beauty and eternity. 'It wasn't just another regimental occasion?' I said. 'They really felt it was a war worth fighting?'

'Sir,' said the Company Sergeant-Major, in a voice that nearly brought me to attention, 'they knew that Communism's been at the back of most of the trouble in the world for the last six years. They knew it was Communism they were fighting in Korea. And that was enough to make them serious.'

The Sergeant went further. 'There was more to it than that,' he said. 'There's half of them, at least, who knew it was a different kind of war from the old wars. It was a war to keep the peace, or try to. Like the police in Glasgow try to.—I heard them talking about it, again and again.'

My two companions, I repeat, were good men. Sound men, proved in battle, who could understand what one said to them, and whose own words were always worth attention. But this response came too close to what I had hoped for to be readily accepted, and some while later I asked several of their officers, 'How much of that can I believe?'

'You can't *disbelieve* it,' said someone.

'The Sergeant's a bit of a romantic.'

'That doesn't prevent him from being serious,' I protested.

'They weren't showing-off, I'm sure of that. If that's what they said, that's what they themselves believe.'

'And if they believe it, so do a lot of others!'

'Well, perhaps. I wouldn't put anything past the Jocks, really.'

We dressed for dinner. There was a guest-night, and the pipers played. Decorum gave birth to geniality, and geniality put forth enormous flowers. The Chinese hills were silhouettes in black velvet against a starlit sky. The room in which we sat grew larger and larger as remembered time and remembered scenes were added to it. Honour was there, and Honour, unbuttoned, was jovial indeed. Gallantry sat with us also, and Gallantry, who said nothing of her deeds, let down her hair. It was an admirable party, and it went on for a long time.

I remember a story I was told, of a party given in grimmer circumstances, after the first Chinese offensive had been checked by battle. Some officers of the 27th Brigade—British, Australian, and New Zealanders—were entertaining Turkish guests of the Ottoman Brigade that fought so well and lost so heavily. The Turkish officers showed a noble appreciation of all they were given, and one of them rose to make a speech. He said this and that about life and the world, he distributed praise and blame. 'But in the end,' he said, 'it is we, we here, who know reality. We Anzacs!'

It became a great joke later on, but I do not know if they laughed at the time: the British, the Australians, and the New Zealanders. But if they did, it was the laughter of delight, not mean laughter. For there at last, in the unity of brave men, was the victory that no one fought for, but was won, unnoticed, on the beaches of Gallipoli.

We Anzacs!

# VII

## A MOMENT IN OKINAWA

BUMPING over corrugated water in the darkness before dawn, a fast launch of the Royal Air Force raced across the harbour, and ripping the mild air asunder, found, as it seemed, an inner coolness. Between wings of spray we rushed through a palpable aether that broke like the sea in delicious fountains. A glimmer of grey, the Sunderlands slept at their buoys, and the eastern sky was lightening. We slowed abruptly, and went alongside a jetty.

Then, after the enchantment of speed, came tedious delay. We had arrived too early, and a long hour passed before we went aboard. Another crew, another ship, were taking me to Japan; or towards Japan, for the intention was not realised.—We turned up-harbour, and the engines roared for the long take-off. We gathered speed, but not enough. There were ferries and small boats ahead of us, passing between the island and Kowloon, and nearer still, coming very near and looming tall, a rocky snout of land. The flying-boat shuddered in a final effort, but could not rise. The captain closed the throttles, and we settled down again onto the sea with the snout of land unpleasantly close.

We turned the other way—there was no wind to make a difference—and ran for a long time in, as it seemed, a growing fever of effort before we were airborne. And then, a couple of hundred feet above the water, the finger on a dial began to revolve the wrong way, and an engine failed. We were too heavily loaded to go down at once, however, and flying out to sea we lightened ship by spilling—was it eight hundred gallons of petrol? I cannot remember, and perhaps I exaggerate. But it was a vast quantity, two years of motoring at least, and my parsimonious heart shrank to think our safety cost so much.

We went down again, gently enough, and another boat made ready for flight. This was the Cockney ship again, and the crew were in high humour to be going farther, and the captain lifted her without effort, and we headed north. Formosa was a painting on silk, in grey and yellow, on our port side, and beyond it rose steeply the southernmost of the Ryukyu islands; in which until recently, according to report, no lethal weapon had been known for three hundred years, though venomous snakes abounded, and a docile, courteous people produced, for their principal export, vermilion lacquer. But this idyllic tale was spoiled by the late war. The largest of the islands is Okinawa, which the Americans used as a stepping-stone for their invasion of Japan.

We also made use of Okinawa. Because of mishap we had been late in leaving Hong Kong, there was bad weather over the Inland Sea, and we could not reach Iwakuni before dark. So we went down to an American flying-boat anchorage, and after a meal aboard an American depot ship the Wing-Commander and I were driven some thirty miles to a sort of military country-club; where, to the music of a lively dance-band, we spent an agreeable evening.

Now what seemed remarkable to both of us was the contrast between the extreme discomfort of the depot ship and the luxury of the officers' country-club. The weather was very hot, the ship was small and overcrowded, and had no form of artificial cooling: not even fans. We slept aboard her that night—the Wing-Commander and I— and lay drenched in sweat in an iron cell. Meals were served in an atmosphere of militant democracy, officers took what they were given, and if they didn't come in time for it, got nothing.—But in the country-club there was an opulence of space, a capable orchestra and willing servants, and the sort of comfort that travel-agents make pictures of for their advertisements. There were white women to dance with, for the military administration employs hundreds of secretaries and typists who, for social purposes at any rate, are given the privilege of officers. But having been admitted to equality, they were open to criticism. If a young woman, living in the United States, failed to get herself married within a certain time—this is what we were told—she would seek employment in General MacArthur's administration of Japan. As on the frontier in the olden days, men were in the majority there, and women less fiercely competitive than in Tulsa or Decatur: a year of service would give her a very good chance to find a husband. But if, after twelve months in Japan, she was still unattached, she might sign on for a more desperate term in Okinawa. Men grew lonely there, so far from home, and hungry for domestic comfort. Okinawa seldom failed, but if it did—well, she had the satisfaction of having done her damnedest.

Our American hosts looked after us well, and on our way back to the seaplane anchorage, at midnight, they insisted on demonstrating one of the island's peculiar amenities. Our car was stopped at a cross-roads about which the low brown houses of a little village huddled. We stopped, and waited—and within a minute or two, out of the darkness, there came towards us, from this side and that, a drift of women who, when they reached the car, stood mute and motionless. They did not solicit, they were not importunate. They did nothing but offer themselves in a still and horrid patience. They were not beautiful, they were discomfortingly unattractive; and the enervating pity one felt was diminished by the realisation that they must find custom.

We stopped again, at another village; and the same thing happened. The roadside trade was evidently considerable, and one had to assume that the traditional courtesy and docility of the Ryukyu islanders had been extensively commercialised. The Americans, moreover, in the zeal of their revolt against the old Puritanism of New England, were apparently able to ignore the utter lack of—let us not pretend that beauty is always necessary—but of the rudimentary physical attractions that less earnest seekers-after-life require for stimulation. The American war of moral independence has perhaps been a little too violent. . . .

Suddenly, quite suddenly, on the midnight road in Okinawa, I thought of an American officer who had said something of that sort in another country; and he and several others came vividly to mind. It was an Irishman who told me the whole story.

It was a darker night than this, for now the Pacific moon was out, but then we were walking in the deep and narrowly confined obscurity of a mediaeval street. It was a few weeks after the German armies in Italy had surrendered, and by a pleasant turn of fortune my duty had ordered me to Siena. If duty were always as kind, how virtuous we should be! I worked in a requisitioned villa in whose garden cherry-trees bore their ripe fruit, and the Pinacoteca was only a few hundred yards away, full of strange and fastidious beauty, of exquisite pale colours and tormented elegance, the back-water where Sassetta and Giovanni di Paolo and Vecchietta lived. The gloriously medallioned, zebra-striped magnificence of the Cathedral housed the lively inventions of Pinturicchio—a Frith of the Renaissance?—and Simone Martini's proud Horseman rode in the Palazzo Pubblico under the incredibly tall Torre del Mangia. At night the streets were like deep canals, curving between high banks, and over the tiled roofs of the tall houses, playing Romeo to tabby Juliets, prowled insolent lean cats with piercing voices. There was a lack of good wine, and food was scarce; but Siena was one of the great justifications for our gift of life.

Among my friends there, as well as the Irishman, were three or four American officers who were writing the history of General Mark Clark's Fifth Army. They were men who, in civil life, had been lecturers or professors in one or other of the smaller universities of their country, and he would be hard to please who did not find them agreeable companions. It was, by chance, with the most serious of them that the Irishman was walking, in the street where we had walked on the night that I suddenly remembered, six years later, in Okinawa—and it was his seriousness that had made the occasion memorable.

Nothing but footfall and the echo of their tread broke the silence of the street, no light interrupted the level darkness of the tall houses, until, simultaneously, a curtain was torn back from a high window and a woman screamed for help. A male voice followed, interrupting and contradicting her, trying to shout her down. In the yellowish light of the uncurtained and now open window two heads appeared : an elderly woman's head, framed in gesticulating hands, and the head and shoulders of a young American soldier.

'It's one of our boys!' exclaimed our serious friend. 'He's in trouble, I guess. I better go up and see what I can do.'

'Don't be a fool,' said the Irishman. 'If he's in trouble, it's his own fault—he's obviously tight—and I don't see why we should get embroiled.'

'I'm not going to leave him there, all alone. One of our boys! I can't do that, for God's sake.'

'The sensible thing for us to do is to clear out, now.'

'No, sir! I'm going up and bring *him* out!'

Oh dear, oh dear, thought the Irishman, as our good impetuous friend disappeared through a narrow doorway, and other doors in the street were thrown open, and angry citizens emerged, roused by Italian screaming and American expostulation that still came loudly from the tall and lighted window.—Oh dear, what trouble there's going to be!

'Niente, niente!' he said to the little crowd that gathered. 'Americani, solamente Americani.'—His few words of elementary Italian would have been insufficient to explain the situation, had not that sort of situation been fairly common. The Italians were quick to realise what was going on, and though naturally they were excited, he found to his great relief that they were not unfriendly. The bourgeois

Sienese, at that time, were much afraid of the local Communist Party, which had recruited a lot of members from the discredited Fascist organisation, and they hoped that either British or American troops would remain in their city to protect them from their fellow-countrymen. They were, accordingly, disposed to be lenient about our occasional lapses. They had, after all, had the Goums in town.

'Si, si,' they answered, with sympathetic understanding; and to the newcomers who were thickening the crowd they explained, with tolerance in their voices, 'Americani!'

There was quietness in the room above—our serious friend was evidently in control—and presently he appeared at the street door leading a dishevelled boy who had lost his hat, whose lank hair hung across his forehead, whose tunic was unbuttoned. In the lighted window the woman again appeared, and addressed the crowd. She was still voluble, but she had been pacified. She was grateful to the officer who had come to rescue her and her daughter from a very unpleasant fate, and everything had been settled in the friendliest way. She bore no ill-will.—The people in the street were almost respectful as they went on their way, the dishevelled boy walking between the Irishman and his rescuer.

The cause of the trouble was simple. The boy had seen a pretty girl, and because she was Italian had innocently assumed that she was available for his pleasure. When she refused what he regarded as his privilege, he followed her home. He forced his way into a small but respectable flat, and was not at all embarrassed when the girl's mother confronted him. He was merely angry. He told the mother that she must insist on her daughter behaving in a reasonable way. Then the mother had pulled the curtains, and thrown up the window, and screamed for help.

They walked together along the dark and narrow street, and our friend the American officer rebuked the boy, sadly and sternly, for his intemperate conduct. He told him about America's duty to the world. It was to America that the older countries now looked for help, and for example too. An American citizen shouldered a vast responsibility. He had to learn how to behave, not only as a good American, but as a citizen of the world. And Europe, though practically speaking it didn't count for very much nowadays, was a wonderful place for seeing what people had been able to achieve in the dark ages before science came along to help them out. Right here in Italy you could study history and art. The whole place was full of history, and there were churches to look at, and fine pictures too.

'You ought to take an interest in these things,' he told the boy. 'You ought to get a hobby. Find something you like doing, something you're interested in, and that'll keep you out of mischief.'

'I got a hobby,' said the boy. 'And I like it.'

'You have? Well, that's fine. That's just how it should be. What is your hobby?'

'Dames,' said the boy; and with a swift but staggering gait, went off down a side street.

We returned to the seaplane anchorage and found that the tender which served the depot ship had just gone. We had to wait an hour for its return. Another car arrived with a party of officers who were very tired after their evening's pleasure. Several of them lay down to sleep on the baulks of timber that confined and bordered the sloping jetty, and though the timbers were no broader than ten inches—or twelve, at the most—and there was a drop of five or six feet into the water, they entrusted themselves to slumber with a serene confidence that they would not turn over. They must have had a great deal of experience on precarious couches.

There was no night-cap, no last whisky-and-soda aboard the ship to help one to bed, as there would have been aboard a British vessel; and descending to our baker's oven of a cabin, the Wing-Commander and I again discussed the astonishing difference between the luxury ashore and the penitential discomfort aboard.

Sticky and damp with heat, in an airless cell, it was difficult to sleep; and in my enforced wakefulness I found, I think, the explanation of that bewildering divergence. It was General Sherman who was responsible.—The Americans have a profound and reverential regard for certain figures in their history, and for a number of dogmatic statements they made. One of these ironclad assertions is General Sherman's pronouncement that 'War is all hell'. The Americans accept this as an article of faith, and to show their piety make every aspect of military service as unpleasant as possible. If there is no enemy to punish, they make war a penance to themselves. Their country-club had been built in a year of peace, and was therefore immune from Shermanism; but life aboard the ship was active service, and must therefore entail suffering.

When a British battalion comes out of the line and sees a prospect, however evanescent, of two or three weeks' relaxation, it goes energetically to work to build some comfort for itself, to bring a little domestic flavour into its life, and provide its own amusement. But the Americans appear to have no will to create amenities. They prefer to suffer—boredom and discomfort when fear is absent—because war is hell, and it was Sherman who said so. Huddled together, standing meekly in the chow-line, their junior officers lead miserable lives, devoid of the privileges to which responsibility and the forefront of danger entitle an officer; lacking the respect that an officer should receive if his leadership is to be efficient; and harassed by a democratic conscience whispering, ever and again, that officers are anomalous in an army of men born to equality.

American Generals wear a look of cultivated toughness. Their natural expression may be the amiability of youth, a frank and boyish smile; but they face the world with features composed in grimness, the embattled glare of Indian fighters. And this appearance, of frontier warriors against a hostile world, they began to acquire as subalterns; for without such a mask of fortitude no American subaltern could survive.—Both officers and men escape the environment of military life as often as possible, and the authorities provide them, wherever possible, with lavish means of escape. But neither the authorities nor the men do anything to make the inescapable conditions of their service more pleasant. They prefer to be conscientiously and dutifully unhappy.

The Left Wing politicians of Europe pretend, and even believe, that America deliberately threatens the peace of the world. How little they know ! The Americans are lovers of peace, devoted lovers, and passionate in their hatred of war. This is due, in the larger part, to the fact that the better sort of Americans are still idealists. But in the smaller part it is, more simply, the consequence of their profound belief in Sherman's dictum, and their pious determination that military service shall be a constant reminder of it.

'No bacon,' said a steward at the breakfast-table. He was addressing an American flight-lieutenant with open hostility. 'No bacon as late as this. If you want bacon, you got to get up in time for it.'—War is hell, democracy is stern and sacred.

We flew from Okinawa to Iwakuni in blustery bright weather, and one's first impression of Japan, from the air, was of a landscape created solely for decoration. I had been there before, in the early months of 1936, but from the deck of a steamer the theatrical beauty of the Inland Sea was not so immediately apparent as from the air; and my appreciation of it, then, had been somewhat impaired by the sight of ugly barricades guarding the better streets of Tokyo. I had arrived there, in 1936, just after the assassination of the liberal ministers in the Cabinet, that cleared the way for a military policy and the eventual war against America. The barbed wire in the streets was the necessary preliminary to the attack on Pearl Harbour. I shall not pretend that I recognised its specific meaning, but political murder and barricades leave a certain apprehension.—Now, from the serenity of the sky, the coasts and islands looked only like the creation of some artistic demiurge, a fantastic and sophisticated arrangement of colour and design that seemed to have been contrived for the regalement of lordly aesthetes who were sated with common views and demanded a rococo geology, a more elegant growth of timber, that the morning and the evening sun could illumine for their pleasure.—But we had to come down to earth, we had to go ashore, and in Iwakuni stood the crane and launching platform from which the Kamikaze fighters had been hurled against American battleships. The spell was broken, the bright vision was shattered by that sinister mechanism.

The Kamikaze fighters were, in the beginning, a band of young pilots who had sworn to die in the very act of exploding a bomb-laden aeroplane on the deck of a hostile warship. Their name, which meant Heavenly Storms, was borrowed from the traditional gales that had scattered a Mongolian invasion in the XVIIIth century. Their training culminated in a carefully arranged orgy, of some duration, and when they had exhausted the pleasures of Japanese wine and womanhood they set off on their last flight.—But after a little while the supply of volunteers began to shrink and dwindle, and Heavenly Storms had to be conscribed. Their training and their voluptuary reward were unchanged, but their aeroplanes, when they set off on their ultimate mission, were stripped of landing-gear, and the pilots were enclosed in the cockpit in such a way as to prevent any chance of escape.—They were, perhaps, as resolute as the volunteers, but shut in a cabin they had little claim to their proud title. The crane and the launching platform that had darted them to unwilling death had not only a sinister, but a rather meagre, penny-in-the-slot appearance.

The fine weather did not last. At four in the morning I boarded an American troop-train, and when daylight came Japan was as wet and grey as a November dawn in Manchester. But the troop-train was infinitely cleaner than any train that ever ran through Manchester. The attendants were Japanese, who perpetually went to and fro to sweep up cigarette-ends and the wrappings of chewing-gum and pop-corn; and an excellent breakfast was served, that cost, I think, ten cents. We were going to Sasebo, the great harbour thirty miles north of Nagasaki, where the Navy was to take charge of me and carry me into Korean waters.

# VIII

## THE YELLOW SEA

THREE weeks after leaving home I was aboard the frigate *Cardigan Bay*, not far from the mouth of the Yalu River. An hour or two before dark, in a dense fog, we had been moving slowly northward, waiting for the New Zealand frigate *Hawea* to come alongside and receive her orders for the night. *Hawea*, we thought, was astern, but suddenly a light appeared off our port bow, a pale and tiny radiance burning weakly through the mist, and as slowly she came nearer, on a parallel course, we saw a patch of fog thicken, as it seemed, and grow darker, and put on the nebulous outline of a ship.—So might the Flying Dutchman materialise in blowing cloud.—A minute later she showed herself clearly, a pallid vessel of the same sort as our own, and when she was no farther away than the length of a cricket-pitch a line was shot across her fore-deck to carry certain instructions, and our Captain—the Commander of what was called, in the American way, a Task Element—addressed the Captain of the *Hawea* through a loud-hailer.

A word or two of greeting first, a casual reference to the weather, and then : 'I want you to go as far north as you can, and send away a boat's crew and boarding-party to make a search in the area that I've shown in my instructions. I'll be doing the same sort of thing a little bit eastward of where you're going.'

D

The New Zealand captain said he thought the fog might be too thick for boat-work.

'Oh, I don't think so. The moon and the tide are just right, and I believe it's going to clear. But use your own judgement, and if it's too bad, where you are, to send off a boat, well, you might take a little cruise along the coast and see what you can pick up. Don't go too close, of course, but do try and find a junk or two.'

'Ay, ay, sir. That'll be clear enough, I expect, when I've read the instructions.'

'You're quite happy, are you?'

'Oh, yes, sir.'

'Well, do your best, and get a junk if you can. . . .'

I should have been far from happy if I had been told, on such a night, to patrol the blind, unfriendly coast of Manchuria, a coast that extends into long finger-shoals over which the tide rises like a river in spate and falls like the level of a breached dam. But the Royal Navy has acquired the characteristic (and despite orthodox biology, succeeded in transmitting it) of going about its business with a debonair composure. Its manners, even on the verge of action, are often indistinguishable from party manners. It has bland assumptions, it takes a great deal for granted; and it conceals or depreciates the technical efficiency that supports its assumptions. It refuses to be impressed by difficulties and dangers that a less stylised observer would regard as awe-inspiring. With a possible exception for radar specialists, who watch the pale-blue light of revelation with a priestly devotion, it sustains the amateur tradition of England. But when I use the word 'amateur' it must be realised that I do so with no derogatory implication. Nowadays, when meaning is often very carelessly considered, 'amateur' is sometimes used to describe an incompetent fellow, a fribbler. But I prefer its better meaning of the man who does such-and-such for the pleasure and satisfaction of doing it, and will not condescend to professionalise his talent. He does not want to be recognised as a master of his craft, but rather to appear as an artist carelessly adept in his chosen way of life.

The style is certainly agreeable, and to my mind better than that. I find it admirable, and impossible to imitate.— I had begun my service with the Navy by being sea-sick. That was in the New Zealand frigate *Rotoiti*. An hour or two later, it is true, I got up and drank some gin and ate a hearty dinner. I went to bed again, and though twice we rolled so steeply that I fell half out of my bunk, I slept well, in a placid acceptance of high waves. I can discipline my stomach to the open sea, but I could never fortify my spirit to meet its trials. I could never say, with conviction in my voice, that I was proceeding happily, at fifteen knots in a blind fog, to look for blockade-runners on a badly charted coast.

From *Rotoiti*, a most friendly ship, I moved into *Cardigan Bay* in time to share the last act of a small but spirited and important operation. The body of a Russian-built jet-fighter, a MIG 15, had been discovered in shoal-water north-west of Pyongyang, and at some hazard and with great difficulty the wreckage had been retrieved from a sandbank over which the tidal stream ran like a weir, and put aboard a flat-bottomed landing-craft. A MIG 15 was a prize of great worth. This was the first to fall into our hands, and the experts were waiting with tense excitement to examine the secrets of its construction. Two of them, American engineers of massive build, were aboard when we came alongside.—It was a boat's crew from *Cardigan Bay* that had shared the salvage with the landing-craft, and now the frigate had to escort its treasure south along the coast.—I climbed down to look at the wreckage, and one of the Americans drew back a tarpaulin from the unbroken nose of the fighter, and in language too technical for my under-standing told me how fine a piece of work it was. At that moment he was a technician, pure and simple, a fat and genial man so warmly moved by a display of excellence in his own craft that political feeling had no chance to dispute with admiration. The fighter was Russian-built, it had probably been flown by a Russian pilot, but it was a lovely job for all that. Caressingly he stroked a smooth dark rib of metal, that to my untaught eye had nothing remarkable about it, and said with affectionate approval, 'That's better than we can do, or better than we have done. Yes, sir! We're going to learn plenty when we get a proper look at this.'—I felt ashamed because I knew nothing of metallurgy, nothing of engineering, when to him metallurgy and en-gineering so clearly transcended politics and war. I deplored my ignorance because it prevented me from sharing his enthusiasm; which is, of course, the common handicap of ignorance.—He came aboard the frigate and drank neat whisky with gusto. There had been a little shooting during the salvage of the MIG, and he was delighted to have been under fire.

Slowly we went south, and presently delivered the landing-craft and its freight to a strange sort of vessel, a small floating-dock; and turning north again, ran up the Yellow Sea and into fog. We met *Hawea*, and parted from her. We continued our blind voyage at a speed which seemed to me excessive; but electromagnetic waves went far beyond the look-out's view and reported a clear passage to the radar screen. Night fell, and turned the fog to clotted darkness. The sea was calm. About one o'clock there came a report of something ahead that might conceivably be a junk. There was a little incandescent blob on the tell-tale screen. We turned in pursuit, and the blob vanished. We continued on our new course past the estimated position of the junk—if it were a junk—and found nothing. And then, on the screen, the blob reappeared.

At the northern end of the Yellow Sea it is said that radar is not always quite as objective as scientific instruments should be. It may turn whimsical, and play tricks. And some declare that a small wooden junk, running under power, may disappear from electromagnetic sight merely by stopping its engine. For a little while we played blindman's-buff in the thickened darkness, but found nothing, and philosophically went on our way to the island of Sinmi-do.

It grew clearer, and the island was visible as the darkness of something solid against impalpable darkness. We stopped and anchored, and lowered a boat. A boarding-party went away to search the inshore water, and for nearly four hours we waited its return.—A boarding-party was traditional indeed. A score of long-forgotten stories rose to the surface of memory, and romantic tales from boyhood's bookshelves fluttered their pages. Almost one looked for boat-cloaks and cutlasses as the sailors clambered in. But then, in the hours of waiting, the adventure became one's own. Anxiety made it real, and the boarding-party seemed curiously part of oneself: a hand groping in cold water among rocks where cuttle-fish might lurk. One longed to pull it back into the warmth; but the search must go on, though fingers grew colder and colder, till every crevice had been explored.

Eventually the boat returned, safe but unlucky. No prize had been taken. It had looked into a village harbour and seen junks moored to the quay, but its orders had not called for invasion. No blockade-runners had been found moving with the tide, and nothing more could be done; for now the darkness was ebbing. Up came the anchor, and we headed south again into a viewless, weeping dawn. Wet clouds, too waterlogged to float, or a deliquescent fog, lay upon the water, and the Yellow Sea was like a sullen trench beneath a vile miasma. Somewhere to the west, not far away, *Hawea* was on a parallel course. She had been no luckier than we.

These small ships are nowadays almost as crowded with humanity as Nelson's frigates. Within the last few years the twin arts of navigation and naval war have received great addition from radar and the gyroscope, and new equipment requires more men to work it. The mess-decks looked nearly as full as a London air-raid shelter under the blitz. Men lay sleeping in extraordinary positions, tucked into a corner or negligent on a table-top like a half-closed jack-knife. Ramparts built of small suitcases concealed the bulkheads. Hammocks hung neighbourly as guillemots' nests on a bird-cliff. But there was no sickness aboard, nor had been since the ship came into Korean waters. With, I fancy, a little surprise in his voice, the doctor told me how healthy the sailors were. Though at sea, there were many of them who got little fresh air, but all were kept busy and they ate great quantities of very good food. 'It's the food that keeps them going,' he said, 'but what really makes them fit is the fact that they don't want to fall ill.'

They were in good heart; but why that should be so, no one could tell. There was no evidence that the Navy regarded the Korean war as a crusade. It was merely another chapter in their historical duty of watch and ward, and blockade of a hostile coast. But they went about their traditional task with great spirit, and held themselves in high esteem.

A story that I heard half a dozen times reported a scrap of conversation between a rating aboard the frigate *Black Swan* and a sailor in one of America's large aircraft carriers. The scene was the broad harbour of Sasebo, in which lay a large and imposing fleet of battleships and powerful carriers, of heavy cruisers and light cruisers, and a swarm of destroyers and lesser craft. All were American, all save the little *Black Swan* coming quietly in from sea. She turned, and came slowly under the lee of a towering carrier, and made fast to a buoy.

A sailor in the carrier looked down and shouted his greeting to a rating busy on the forward deck of the frigate: 'Hiya, Limey! And how's the world's second biggest navy getting on?'

'Not so bad, chum,' answered the rating—a Chatham rating? He must have been.—'Not so bad! And 'ow's the world's second best?'

We anchored by night in the difficult harbour of Inchon. In the early morning I went on deck and saw a wide expanse of palely gleaming water. It appeared to be an excellent harbour. But when I threw away the end of a cigarette, it went racing past the stern like a wisp of grass on a mill-stream; and a few hours later the bay of Inchon was a desert of shining mud through which a few rivers meandered.

I lived the rest of the month ashore, with the 29th Brigade on the Imjin front, and early in August went back to sea. My instructions were to spend two or three days aboard the aircraft carrier *Glory*, then cruising some hundred miles westward of the land. I had supposed that a smaller vessel would take me from Inchon, but instead of that I was driven to Seoul airport, where, after enquiry, I found waiting for me a modest young pilot and a small aeroplane called a Fire-fly.—He helped me into a Mae West, and then, with some difficulty, I stuffed myself into the after cockpit, and strapping myself tightly to a parachute, attached myself even more firmly, by webbing belts, to the aeroplane itself. I had little hope of remembering which buckles to unfasten first if ordered to abandon ship, but I pretended to be confident and firmly closed the transparent hood above my cockpit. We took-off quickly, and a moment or two later, while the earth tilted absurdly beneath us, there was a crackling din in my ears and I gathered that the pilot was trying to talk to me. Somewhere on my flying helmet was an electric switch. If turned *this* way it should allow the pilot to speak, if turned *that* way, I could reply. To begin with, however, I could not find the switch, and when I did discover it, its function was merely interruption. It prevented either of us from talking—or my handling of it did—and I could only hope that the pilot had no important news for me. We flew out over little islands and a sea like pale-green, polished jade.

Some two or three years before, in Scottish waters, I had

spent a day in the carrier *Illustrious*, and watched a steady
exercise of aeroplanes landing-on and taking-off. I realised
that it could be done—though never before had it been
done with me encased in a homing bird—and if the deck
of the ship should look uncomfortably small when we
arrived above *Glory*, I had only to tell myself that I knew
from experience it was large enough.

It did look small. It looked minute, a mere chip on the
sea. But quickly it grew larger, and in my last sight of it
before hitting, it was agreeably ample, though it seemed to
lie at a fearful angle. I succeeded in finding the buckle
that held my parachute, and undid that. I opened half the
cockpit roof. I pulled the remaining straps a little tighter,
and stickily grasped a couple of hand-holds. And then,
with a monstrous clatter and bang, we hit the deck, and a
wire stretched across it caught our trailing hook and stopped
our further progress with remarkable abruptness. If a little
boy, a little feather-weight preparatory-school footballer,
were tackled hard by a fourteen-stone, furiously-charging
All Black forward, he might, I think, get a very fair impression of what a deck-landing is like. But immediately
after one has been tackled there is a delightful sensation of
comfort and relief.

I threw back the cockpit roof, I undid my straps, and
climbing out, was greeted by a Commander whose hospitality was immediate, whose understanding was profound.
'The first of your duties,' he said, 'is to come to the ward-
room and have some gin.'

The ward-room was as big as the lounge of a country
hotel, and more populous, more animated. But the traffic
of a country road would not create the profound and

startling noises that overwhelmed at frequent intervals the conversation of the naval residents. Aeroplanes were homing, and each came in with a roar, a clang, and a thump as the stopping wires caught hold of the hook and steel decks repeated the violence of arrest. A voyage in an air-craft carrier was going to be unlike voyaging in other ships. More like going to sea in a factory—or a foundry, perhaps—for the bustle and din of mechanical effort went on, with hardly a break, from day-start till dark. By land, at that time, the war was a matter of deep patrolling and long-range gunfire to harass enemy positions or protect a far-flung reconnaissance; but the pilots of the Fleet Air Arm were more closely engaged. Daily they watched the process of Chinese reinforcement in the north, and daily destroyed what they could of the enemy's preparations. The carriers were ocean factories, exporting bombs and rockets, but on the factory roof there was a gaiety unexpectedly reminiscent of older wars—of the many-coloured bunting that used to fly above the dusk of burnt powder—for on the flight-deck a recurrent ballet was performed.

A batsman stood to one side of the stern of the long, narrow rectangle which was the deck of the ship, and by lowering and raising his coloured disks, by signalling and swaying like the conductor of an orchestra soothing a difficult movement, brought in the plane on its proper course, and guided it to its sudden halt on the arrester-wires. Then from the side leapt a fiery *corps de ballet* in skull-caps and blue or yellow clothing, leaning and leaping to their appointed tasks and co-ordinated purpose, and the Firefly or Sea Fury was wheeled and manhandled to its proper out-of-the-way position while the next in the circus swung

round in the misty air, awaiting its call and the disks of the
batsman, the word of the choreographer, to bring it home.

The pilots climbed out, with dull or savage tale to be
told of air patrol over the Fleet, of anti-submarine patrol, of
reconnaissance to Sinmi-do and back by way of Chinnampo.
Some went to bomb bridges, some to photograph the
result of bombing, and some to engage 'targets of opportunity', as they were called, with cannon-fire and rockets.
A pilot might log fifty flying-hours in a month, and see
very little. He might come back with bullet-holes in his
wings, and still have seen nothing: for a company of
Chinese soldiers, it was said, would sit motionless and un-
detected in their slit-trenches, under a coverlet of leaves,
and aim a perpendicular rapid-fire not by eye—for they
kept their heads down—but by ear at the passing noise of a
plane flying low above the floor of a valley. There were
pilots who did not return. There were others who, though
shot down, were lucky enough to be rescued. If a plane,
reconnoitring some mountain route, were dangerously hit,
its pilot would turn at once towards the coast. The mountains were hostile, but the sea was friendly.

There was a Fury that was badly hit. A companion,
flying near, guided it down to a possible landing-place and
called for help. Three Mustangs quickly arrived, and
together they flew in close protection round the fallen plane
while a helicopter landed beneath them and rescued the
wounded pilot. Those in the air could see no movement
on land, but the wounded man, while he awaited rescue,
had been under fire from all sides.—The Chinese talent
for concealment was remarkable, and soldiers as well as
airmen were amazed by their enemy's ability to lie still as

animals and like animals remain unseen. A pilot told me
that once, flying low in a valley, he had passed over an
orchard that seemed to him quite untenanted, and still as an
orchard can be on a drowsy afternoon. But a draught of
suspicion stirred in his mind, and turning a little to look
over his shoulder, he saw the orchard suddenly alive with
running men. He circled, and came back. The orchard
was still again, not a shadow moved. But he sprayed it
with fire, and the soldiers who stood hidden were revealed
when dead men fell beneath the trees.

This officer flew in one morning, while I was aboard,
and told what he had found in a seaside valley where the
enemy was thought to be assembling. At the end of a
village, under the slope of a hill, he had surprised a breakfast-
party: half a dozen soldiers sitting round a table in the
shade of some trees. He had fired with great relish at this
unusual target, and a little farther, at the water's edge, had
destroyed with rockets a half-built junk. That was his
morning's work. In the afternoon he went out again, and
with a companion found a column of fifty soldiers on a
country road. The survivors of the first attack scattered
and found refuge in a nearby hamlet. His companion blew
off the house-tops with rockets, and he aimed cannon-fire
at the remnant soldiers who had been so unkindly exposed.
—But that was an unusually busy day.

While Chinese and American and Korean delegates at
Kaesong began their tedious negotiations for a truce, the
allied air forces made prodigious efforts to prevent the
Chinese in North Korea from gathering sufficient strength
to renew the offensive. From land and sea the light and
heavy bombers, the fighters and reconnoitring planes went

daily northward, and week after week they drenched the few roads of the country with the rain of their loud assault. But they failed to stop the southward movement of men and guns and the provisions of war. When autumn came the Chinese attacked again. Their strength was insufficient to break the allied line, but despite the long, prohibitive assault from the air their strength was formidable.

It was nearly thirty years ago, in a letter to Colonel A. P. Wavell, that T. E. Lawrence wrote: 'Guerrilla tactics are a complete muffing of air-force'. The Chinese moved light as guerrillas, and most of them were as lightly armed. Aboard the carrier *Glory* were twelve hundred men, aeroplanes carrying rockets and quick-firing cannon, and a densely packed equipment of scientific instruments. But superior weapons gave no sensation of easy triumph over a primitive enemy. The Fireflies and Furies went out against a mass of opponents whose redoubtable advantage was that they could elude discovery and continue to fight dangerously though their communications had apparently been shattered, and the country in which they lived had been reduced to ruin and desolation.

I doubt if modern weapons do more damage, in proportion to our condition, than sword and bow in the Middle Ages. The population of the world has grown enormously, and the applied sciences that made growth possible have produced weapons that take, perhaps, as heavy a toll of our larger numbers as steel and string subtracted from the little armies of the past. No heavier, I think; and the relative cost of weapons may not have altered much either. At some time during the last war I happened to read that the bill for arming a knight and his charger to fight at Agincourt was such-and-such. I looked up the price of bacon, wool, and land in the XVth century, and putting a modern value on the cost of a knight, found it almost equal to the price of a Crusader tank.—Perhaps it is only noise, and our capacity for enduring noise, that have grown absolutely. My private tolerance is low, however, and the warlike din of *Glory* at her ceaseless work was wearisome. The ship, moreover, was uncomfortably hot. She had lately gone to Sasebo for rest and re-fit, but because of mishap to some other vessel had had to return to her station without a holiday for the men or repair to tired machinery. And one of her ailments was an almost total failure of the air-cooling system. Her crew were as moist and warm as a knight in full armour riding French fields at midsummer. Perhaps the true climate of war is mediaeval?

It was with some reluctance that I began to think of going ashore again. We were still cruising a hundred miles from land, and to go to Seoul I must fly. But flying from a light carrier is not quite the same as flying from an airfield. The Fireflies and Furies were catapulted into the air, and the action of the catapult was necessarily violent. The forward throw, if my memory serves, was forty-five feet, and in that short distance the aeroplane, from a state of rest, reached a speed of ninety miles an hour. The pressure of so rapid an acceleration was said to be $2\frac{1}{2}G$, G representing gravity. I had never thought seriously about gravity before, but I felt sure that multiplying it by two and a half would make it unpleasant. When the morning of my departure came I watched, with quickened sympathy, the early birds take off. We were running at full speed against the wind, and in quick succession the little aeroplanes were manhandled into position at the fore end of the ship, where the launching-gear took hold of them. Fluttering and bending in the breeze, the deck-crew leapt to work and leapt away again. Its engine roaring at the pitch of its voice, the foremost plane trembled with repressed energy, and suddenly darting to the square bow of the carrier, was thrown into the air. Delicately hovering, keeping station a few yards from the bow, a helicopter watched the take-off with a grapnel ready in case of accident. The Fury leaned, and circled, and climbed the warm air; and a Firefly took its place above the slot in the deck. Crescendo of noise again, shudder and dart, and soaring flight.

I said good-bye to my generous hosts, and nervously adjusted my straps. I pulled them tight, and made myself as nearly immovable as I could. I lowered my head and grasped the hand-holds, and waited with some apprehension and a slightly quickened pulse. The engine roared in a strident crescendo till it reached its maximum voice, and the still-tethered plane shook with impatience. There came a signal from the deck, and with a wild and bounding impulse we were hurled against a soft, but huge and ponderous resistance.

The sensation was quite extraordinary. I felt at first—in the first moiety of a split second—that I was being pushed through the aeroplane. Then, with a swift correction, that it was being pushed through me. An instantaneous photograph would, I am sure, have shown a perceptible flattening of my face and body. But the release from acceleration was delightful. When the fling of the catapult was left behind, and we flew at normal speed, it seemed for a few moments a

motion as calm and easy as the gliding, cliff-top flight of a
fulmar gull.  Gently we turned, and saw the green sea
slanting below; and with the tension gone I felt, as it were,
a retrospective excitement.  An excitement that I had
suppressed before the take-off.

But I was prepared for that.   I had thought it not unlikely
that I would be a little shaken by the mysterious force called
$2\frac{1}{2}G$, and I had with me something to soothe and medicine
my nerves.   It was held firmly under my left thigh, between
thigh and parachute, for nothing may be loose or unsecured
in a catapulted plane.—Easing my straps, I pulled out my
medicine.   It was a copy of *Pride and Prejudice*.   I opened it
and began to read:

> It is a truth universally acknowledged, that a single man in possession
> of a good fortune must be in want of a wife.
> However little known the feelings or views of such a man may be
> on his first entering a neighbourhood, this truth is so well fixed in the
> minds of the surrounding families, that he is considered as the rightful
> property of some one or other of their daughters.
> 'My dear Mr. Bennet,' said his lady to him one day, 'have you heard
> that Netherfield Park is let at last?'

It worked almost at once.   The sublime confidence of
Miss Austen was infectious, and in her company it was ill-
mannered to suffer from nerves.   I breathed more easily,
and gave myself up to the enjoyment of another world.
Style, the refrigerator, by instant freezing of its essence, had
preserved its whole flavour.

We approached the land and flew above charming, toy-
like islands, miniature hills and promontories, and brown
villages and sandy bays.   The tide was out, and on the
gleaming muddy shore the receding water had left great
branching patterns that looked like monstrous fern-leaves.

# IX

## THE VICTIMS

On the night of my first arrival in Seoul there had been a children's party. Some of the war correspondents had arranged it. They were moved by pity and perhaps even by affection for the tough and hungry little waifs of the capital who had survived its ruin and still ran noisily about the hideous squalor of its shattered streets. A couple of hundred had been invited, and perhaps another hundred also came. In long lines they squatted on their heels, like lively but patient frogs, waiting for the doors to open.

The war correspondents' billet in Seoul had been a block of modern flats. It was relatively whole, in a devastated city, but a cheerless and miserable building. Mediaeval castles and mansions of the XVIIIth century can stand up to misfortune, but the modern apartment house very quickly becomes mean and ugly when luck goes against it. It was grimy and depressing, but the walls stood and there was a roof above it; and in a trampled, dusty courtyard where jeeps and shabby trucks were parked, the long queues of little frogs waited for their supper. Barrack-room tables were spread with lavishly filled plates of ham and peaches, cake and bread.

For the first hour or two the children were surprisingly well behaved. They were admitted in relays, and stuffed themselves in a grave, bewildered silence. Many were puzzled by the appearance and flavour of unfamiliar food, but their elders understood that everything was there to be eaten, though they might not like it. Some of the guests were mere babies: roughly clad, darker-skinned Japanese dolls. A few, but a very few, middle-aged or older women had been allowed to bring the smallest infants. Most of those who looked after the younger ones were girls of ten or twelve, who, while they waited outside, had carried their sleeping brothers on their backs. Brothers, probably; but occasionally the older child was a premature mother. All the senior guests went about the business of eating with earnest efficiency, and carried off any spare slices of bread they could put their hands on. With a few exceptions, their appearance was unattractive. The faces of the older women were engraved with lines of suffering and long endurance, and for them one felt a deep but helpless pity. The little ones, the babies and the ten-year-olds, had black and lively eyes in narrow slits of yellow skin, but their features were flat and dull. It was easier to be sorry for them than to like them. But their good behaviour compelled respect, and here and there was a child of an aspect startlingly different from the majority. There was a girl with a wild gipsy-look, wide-open eyes, and a delicate, narrow chin that made the heavy, recessive jaws of her little neighbours seem a very clumsy pattern for human features; and another, calm and poised, a classical drawing, a collector's piece from the Ming dynasty. Heaven knows what mixture of breeding had begotten the one, and what wilder chance of purity had fathered the other.

Presently the surplus of guests began to cause embarrassment indoors, and a growing anxiety without. Food was running short, and a hundred children waited to be fed.

More tins were opened, new loaves were cut, but still there was not enough. In the courtyard, which was now quite dark, good-behaviour disintegrated. There was scuffling in the queues, fierce jostling for position, and a few terribly anxious mothers seemed to use their infants as battering-rams to force their way towards the guarded door. Little girls with minute brothers cradled on their backs—dumb heads lolling—showed their teeth in a writhen grimace of fury and scratched like cats to keep their place or get a better. Grief took charge of them, a ferocious grief, and for a moment or two, after the sad and appalling announcement that there was no more food, a kind of panic threatened. But some of their American hosts came out with great boxes of sweets, and handfuls of toffee, chocolate, and biscuits were given to the disappointed: enough to pacify and quieten them. Slowly, with shuffling and reluctant feet, they turned and drifted away, back to their holes and corners in the dusty ruins of the city.

'I don't know who's going to win this war,' said someone, 'but it's God-damned certain who's lost it: and that's the poor bloody Koreans.'

The ruins of Korea were nowhere so fierce and terrible as the devastation of the Ruhr. Destruction was not as concentrated, chaos not piled so high; because there had been less to destroy. But the enormous extent of drab and petty dissolution settled on one's mind like a blight. From Inchon to Seoul the road ran through dull, treeless country that had been planted with small factories, a sprawling area of suburban industrialism fallen into such dreary and horrible decay that it seemed to have perished suddenly of a violent dry-rot. Seoul itself had been a city of some pretension. It covered a large area between the broad, untidy waters of the Han and a hill that made a good background for some new administrative buildings. There were ancient gateways that remembered a vanished dignity, and wide streets that had presented a pleasant fiction of well-being. Bombs from above and fire-raisers at street-level brought down all but a fragment of both solid and trumpery workmanship, and the sadness of the spectacle was that it did not move one to indignant rage—as did the German havoc in Florence, for example—but only to sickness and disgust. To expose meagre pretensions is, in a way, more cruel than to ruin pride and dignity; to stamp on little things more brutal than to bombard magnificence; but only degradation is immediately visible, not tragedy. Beyond Seoul, north, east, and south, were cinder-patches that had once been snug villages and lively brown hamlets. A few miles north of the capital were the hideous remains of a little town called Uijongbu: a patchwork of charred refuse, of rusty iron and blackened stone, where a colony of bemused survivors scratched a quite incomprehensible living.

The tragedy of Korea was made more shocking by its general ugliness; and to endure the sight of it one required the absolute conviction that what had happened there might prevent a larger war, for the third and last time, marching over western Europe.—The purpose of the Communist attack on the southern Republic was, I believe, purely strategic. It was to secure a vulnerable northern flank before the main assault went in: the invasion of Formosa, that is. But if Communist China had attacked Formosa, the United States might well have gone to war, not as leader of the United Nations, but on its own behalf; and becoming deeply embroiled with China, would have left Europe open to a Russian advance. War is an evil thing, and a persistent thing. We have not yet found the cure for it, but to localise it is empirically a useful beginning to preventive treatment. And I am selfish enough to prefer a war localised in an Asiatic peninsula to a war let loose on my own heritage.

I knew almost nothing about Korea before I went there, and what I had heard of its people could do little to recommend them to anyone's favour. My father, a sea captain, had at one time traded between the ports of China, Japan, and the oriental butt-end of Russia, and I still had a page of stamps he had sent, for my schoolboy collection, from Port Arthur or Pusan : rather dull stamps, some of them casually surcharged, with values in *poon* and a central device called the T'ai Chi, that the South Koreans now carry on their national flag. I used to follow his voyages through the pages of an encyclopaedia, and I remembered, vaguely enough, that Korea had had a much-broken dismal history —hauled to the one side by China, tugged away by Japan— and the Chinese alphabet had crossed, as if it were a floating bridge, to the barbarous islands in the east. Where and when I could not recall—but in America, I think—I had been told by someone with an impressive manner (with the emphasis that people use to advertise their possession of unusual, and often useless information) that the Koreans had been the first to invent movable type. That, if true, must commend them to persons in my trade, but I knew of no other reason for admiration. In recent years, indeed, they had acquired a thoroughly bad name. The cruellest of the prison-guards in Japanese internment camps were said to have been Koreans. That they had been brutalised and degraded by their Japanese masters might explain their beastly practices, but did not make them acceptable.

In the early months of the war they were often guilty of atrocious cruelty; as if panic had released a long-accumulated hatred of life. Many of their soldiers wore a heavy, sullen look that did not quite conceal—or so one thought—a flickering and dangerous malice. Thick-skinned, rough and earthy, with a savage, inflammable spirit: so they appeared, at first sight. But presently one's feelings changed, and changed for the better. It was not pity that brought a kindlier vision, but looking longer and listening to what others thought.—Against a background of gritty ruin and grey squalor one saw from time to time a woman walking in a perfect glory of cleanliness. Her costume was yard upon yard of a gauzy white material, a windy circumvallation of half-starched muslin loosely folded and voluminous: not, I would say, an artistic composition, but a flaunting testimony to industry and self-respect. For only by some miracle of determination and ingenuity could such dexterous laundering have been accomplished in a broken-walled cellar with a bucket of water for a wash-tub.

There were old men, too, who looked like philosophers, a little shrunken by age, and walked slowly with an air of impoverished, academic dandyism. I shall not say that all in fact were scholarly and benign, but even to have the face of wisdom is something; and their meagre clothes were often as scrupulously clean as the skirts of the white-wrapped women.—Their cleanliness, it may be, was the product of a fretful domestic tyranny, of a hectoring temper that lived on among the ruins; but what of that? The women of

Korea have never enjoyed a chivalrous regard. They lived to bear children, and anything else that had to be carried, and tend the fire: that was the scope of their existence. Indeed the costume of the poorer sort had been designed, it seemed, to express contempt for the very shape of womanhood; for the upper part of it consisted of a sort of half-blouse or short tunic that let their pendulous dugs hang down below its inadequate curtain as they walked, in sombre single-file by the roadside, under their evening burdens.

I saw schoolrooms full of wantonly broken equipment, and I was told that the few years of precarious peace, after the defeat of Japan, were clamorous with the demand for education, and the endowment of schools became not only a sign of civic virtue, but among the wealthier sort a fashionable exercise. Ill-governed it might be, but the southern Republic was striving desperately to teach itself and dress its mind anew to meet the dignity of independence.—Warmer than this approval of good intention, however, was the soldiers' opinion of the Koreans as they were, in all their misery. Of the Koreans they knew, that is: of the bearer companies who had accompanied them to battle. No one, I think, could have expected the soldiers to speak so well of their curious allies. They had been sent to the other side of the world, to fight in gross discomfort for a cause that was not easy to comprehend, and the natural or the obvious, the common response would have been to curse the wretched creatures for whose misfortune they were suffering. But the fighting soldiers spoke of their Korean neighbours with surprising generosity, with a genuine kindness in their voices, with a defensive friendship.

'They've been badly treated, of course, and because of

that they're a bit bloody-minded. You don't want to leave prisoners with them, not if you expect to see the prisoners alive again. But what can you expect, after what the Japs did to them? You give the Gooks a fair deal and they're all right. They're bloody good, if you ask me. We've had a carrier company with us, that's never let us down. They'll come up under fire, and do what they're told, and won't grouse about it either. They've got plenty of guts, the Gooks, and they're a cheerful lot of bastards if they get something to eat. We've got a bloody good carrier company, we have, because we treated them proper, and that's what makes the difference.'

There is a sample of what 'other ranks' said. Officers said much the same, but with more purpose, with a professional notion in their minds. 'Don't be misled by what you hear of them breaking under fire. They have, often enough, but why? Usually because they've been put in the line with no artillery behind them—or damned little—and I wouldn't say that we'd always stay put if we hadn't any guns to help us. But the Gooks are good material, and if we had the training of them we might turn them into something almost as fine as the Gurkhas. They're tough as hell, they aren't afraid, they're quick to learn, and they're loyal to people they can trust. They've got some bad habits—damned bad habits—but bad habits can be cured. We and the French and the Dutch know how to handle colonial troops, and if we were allowed to, we'd make a Korean army—with our officers and N.C.O.s—that could hold their frontier till the cows come home.'

The Koreans have national ambitions that would not be satisfied by service in a frontier legion under European

officers; but if a frontier legion is necessary, it would be
sensible to make it good enough to protect the patriotic
aspirations behind it.   It could be recruited, very largely,
from the orphans of war.   Every company and battery
that I saw had adopted a few Korean boys—waifs and
strays belonging to no one—and dressed them in a cut-down
uniform of jungle-green.   The boys responded to good
food and decent treatment like wilderness shrubs trans-
planted to a kindly soil.   They went about their little camp
fatigues with eagerness and pride, and shouted to each other
as they worked.   Their narrow bodies grew plumper,
their listless walk became a swagger step.—'But what the
hell's going to happen to them when we go?' asked more
than one man, with a kind of agony in his voice.   'Look
at that kid there.   He was starving when we picked him up,
and look at him now!   And he's useful, too.   He's a good
kid, sharp as a knife, and dependable.   But we're not here
for ever, and when we pack up, what'll become of him?'

# X

## THE SOLDIERS ON THE HILLS

THERE was little temptation to remain in Seoul, and I hurried from the grimy dissolution of its streets to the order and cleanliness of the soldiers' habitation. Headquarters of the 29th Brigade was a spaciously designed canvas village in a deserted orchard on a plain below the hills that overlooked the Imjin. The country was pretty enough, in July. There was no big timber in the neighbourhood, but the hills were covered with a luxuriant tall scrub, there were swiftly running, clear streams, and convolvuluses and golden lilies flew their summer flowers. Here and there survived little hamlets of straw-thatched houses, and in one of them I met a dozen natives of villainous appearance, all of whom—this I was told with the quiet pride of a host introducing foreign guests of unusual distinction—had been regular cut-throats in private life. With them was a thin, pale-faced, confident young lance-corporal of the Northumberland Fusiliers who, as well as being in command of the detachment, was its nurse and mentor.

As a complement to its strong regimental feeling, our army has a notably fissiparous tendency. It seeks opportunity for out-of-the-way, independent service, it enjoys isolation, it prefers irregular employment.—There was an officer at Brigade Headquarters, known as Beetle, who had recruited a small native force whose duty was to penetrate the enemy's land beyond the river, and bring back informa-

tion of his strength and dispositions.    It was fed, clothed,
and armed by us; but not, I think, paid.    It received, however, a moral and general discipline of considerable value.

Beetle himself took me to see the detachment of his little
force that lived in a brown hamlet under command of a
lance-corporal.    We passed a warning sign-post that said:
DANGER!  *Smallpox!*, and by a winding, narrow path entered
a little secret valley with a green floor of paddy-fields and
lush hillsides.    The half-dozen cottages of the hamlet, built
side by side about a right angle, appeared to have been
designed for the exchange of evening gossip, for each had its
tiny veranda, and the verandas of one side looked across at
those of the other.    On one of them, surrounded by eight
or nine devoutly attentive Koreans, the lance-corporal was
changing his trousers.    It was almost a mediaeval scene, a
well-coloured, stiffly designed picture in an illuminated
manuscript of a young nobleman at his toilet with his cour-
tiers about him—his jester, too, for one of the Gooks was
clearly a natural.

He received us with dignity, and having laced his boots,
put on his beret with its red-and-white plume, and con-
ducted us round his estate.    It was remarkably clean.    He
had been giving his cut-throats lessons in sanitation and
hygiene, he had had them vaccinated, he insisted that they
wash themselves.    He was twenty-one, and only two or
three of his command looked older than himself.    'How,'
I asked, 'do you make them do what they're told?'

'I keep them in,' he said in a simple, serious voice with a
Northumbrian burr in it.    'They get leave to go out in the
evening, usually, but if they haven't done their work I keep
them in.    And as an extra punishment, if that's necessary—

they get a bit excited sometimes—I make them stand on their hands.'

I did not ask him how he compelled obedience, when he commanded them to stand upside-down, or how he had persuaded them to accept his sanitary rules. He had, apparently, the gift of perfect confidence, and an elementary knowledge of Japanese in which to phrase his orders. The Koreans watched him, as he talked, with admiration in their eyes, and perhaps they gave him no trouble merely because he never expected trouble. There was another hamlet, on the other side of the valley, to which he took us. Ten of his bandits were quartered there, who received him with smiles and deference. There was no jester in this section, but one who looked like a sadistic gaoler. They had all, we gathered, been behaving in a quite exemplary fashion, though they still grumbled at the wastefulness of European conventions, that put cleanliness above profit to the fields.

'It isn't everyone who could handle them, of course,' said Beetle, as we walked away. 'It isn't everyone who'd feel comfortable, living all alone with them. I had two or three failures before I found him. But he took to it at once. He's even learnt to eat their food, and food's a thing the ordinary soldier's rather particular about.'

'If empire-building weren't so unfashionable,' I said, 'he ought to be given a bag of sovereigns and told to go out and found a colony.'

So far as I could remember, the only Northumberland Fusilier I had ever met before was a private with whom, in the Kaiser's war, I talked occasionally in a Y.M.C.A. hut. He was a short, brown-faced, serious man whose naturally grave expression had been given a sinister emphasis by a deep, gutter-like wound on his right temple. This, he said, was the result of a blow from a stone axe, which he had suffered in the Mexican province of Chihuahua while raid- ing, unsuccessfully, an Indian village for women. His com- manding officer, at that time, was an ex-mistress of General Villa, who had been compensated for the loss of his favour by the colonelcy of a regiment that she led with great ferocity but little judgement. The Fusilier, left for dead, had been medicined to health again by two old Indian women who had removed the fragments of bone from his shattered skull with their fingers, and keeping him in their hut, had dressed the wound for several weeks with a daily plaster of sodden leaves. He, too, was a simple, confident man who appeared to take for granted the strange and perilous accidents of life. He was self-sufficient, an im- perialist who had found a proper colony in himself.

We have not lost our gift for making colonies. We have been denied the use of it because, in the process of awakening the dormant parts of the world, we woke in them a dormant spirit of nationalism that now dislikes us for what we did; but given half a chance, or half a wilderness, we still can demonstrate our talent for domesticating it. The rifle companies of the Fusiliers stood on the hill-tops, guarding the river plain, but at Battalion Headquarters they had very sensibly made themselves comfortable. I went to call on them by jeep, over a road carved from the hillside by unresting Sappers, and on our rough journey— now tilted like a trawler bucking the waves of an Atlantic gale, now lurching into receding gulfs—we were accom- panied for nearly half a mile by a butterfly of astonishing size and strength. Its wing-spread was broad as a starling, it was dark blue and green with mottling on the rear edges of its wings, it shone like lacquer in the sun, and twice it circled my slow-climbing jeep like a sea-gull questing galley scraps. And then, all green and blue but duller than the butterfly, the next valley opened, and after another jolting mile or two we came to a group of small and pretty chalets built into the hillside. They were made of native material, of small timber and straw, and very pleasantly they seemed to pacify the savage aspect of the country.

So must the earliest colonists, in many a distant land, have built their first habitations when the coastal tribes retreated; and with the genial encouragement of peace—even a tentative, uncertain peace—the Northumberland Fusiliers had followed and revived tradition. But traditional values were not all respected, for after dinner I listened to a resounding attack on popular physiognomy by an officer whose own appearance, indeed, did much to disprove it. One might have taken him, had he not been in uniform, for a rather indolent young don at some easy-going university, an intellectual who found the world and himself equally amusing; but only a couple of months before he had won the D.S.O. for his tactical and moral strength in maintaining, throughout a long night and despite three wounds, the defence of a multitudinously assaulted hill that overlooked the Imjin.

We have seen, in our time, a general increase of sensitivity and the invention of ever more horrific dangers; but gallantry has often shown itself so conspicuously as to suggest that human nature is acquiring new defences against its new perils, and a new bravery to protect its new tenderness of apprehension. Defence, indeed, is learning to meet the attack.—We had, I think, been saying something of this sort, and I had asked if it was possible to predict, from a previous knowledge of men, which men would behave exceptionally well in battle.—The general opinion was negative. It was not difficult to foretell who would be sound and reliable; those who were habitually so, would not lose their character under the stress of action. But no one could tell, like a water-diviner, the source of outstanding gallantry.

And then the officer of seeming indolence, the self-amused and donnish man, declared with conviction in his voice, 'But you can wipe out, for a start, all those chaps who look like bulldogs and go about with a grim stare and a pipe in their teeth. That's what I think, anyway. I suppose I shouldn't pontificate, but if there's a chap I distrust it's the man with a strong, square jaw, and a frank, wide-open gaze, and a pipe in his mouth, and a wholesome, hearty expression.'

'But a diffident fellow, with a rather melancholy look and a slack mouth, and a cigarette hanging to his lower lip?'

'That's the chap for me! That's the man I'd like to have beside me if things got really difficult and dirty. The ordinary-looking chap with a bit of yellow in his eye and the butt-end of a cigarette on his lip. You can rely on him, but damn the pipe-smoker. He's no good.'

The Brigade occupied the same ground as it had held in the April battle, and the road to the Gloucesters' old position was, geologically, a very suitable introduction to the vehemence and grandeur of their story. It turned to and fro through a highland glen, a blind, steep valley whose walls sharpened, here and there, to sheer rock. It was brightly picturesque in summer weather, but in April the green slopes had been a wintry grey, the rock had looked more naked, and there was no colour on the hills save the flush of dwarf azaleas. It was the proper road to a desperate occasion. It was country that geology had made to echo the drum-major's long reveille on that last morning when the Gloucesters, weary with three days' fighting, parched with thirst and their wounded thick about them, stood up and charged again. It was not a romantic music, they were the harsh and sombre echoes of a voice that was brazen with pride because its body was gaunt with endurance. The Gloucesters were not reckless soldiers fighting for way-ward glory, but steadfast and resolute men whose purpose was a military obligation : they were the flank guard on the road to the south, the old invasion route, and they held their ground because their training had made them good soldiers and their temper made them stubborn. In the early days of their Korean service they had been nicknamed The Gloomies; and their April courage was less, perhaps, a dancing fire than a smouldering heat. But it broke into flame before the end, and the memory of it is a light upon the hills, and the drum-major's bugle echoes like the proud and bitter voices of the paladins at Roncesvalles. It was chivalry that began our history, and chivalry has dignified its record down the years.

It should be said, however, that the Gloucesters' sacrificial gallantry has a little unfairly obscured the good behaviour of their neighbours in the battle of the Imjin. The Northum-berland Fusiliers, the Royal Ulster Rifles, and a high-spirited Belgian battalion under command of the 29th Brigade were in positions, at the onset of battle, much nearer to the vital

road; and therefore they could fight until the tactical value
of resistance had spent itself, and still, with the devoted
and dashing assistance of a squadron of the 8th Hussars,
secure their retreat. The obligation of self-sacrifice—the
tactical obligation—lay less heavily on them, and as their
loss was lighter so their renown is less. But their share of
the battle may not be ignored, and certainly there is none
of the infantry who will accept, as just, any praise but the
highest for 'C' Squadron of the Hussars, whose tanks
brought out the last weary foot-soldiers from a valley
swarming with the enemy.

When the days grew longer and more peaceful, the
Hussars also revealed their domestic talent and a taste for
colonial architecture. They were not content, however,
with mere comfort. They had built, for the ante-room to
their mess, a sort of rustic pavilion behind a great hedge or
screen of brushwood, to protect it from the dust of passing
traffic, and the avenue that led to it from the road was
lined by bunches of wildflowers in gleaming shell-cases.—
'The flowers?' said the Colonel, when I congratulated him
on the display. 'Yes, they look very well, don't they?
My Provost-Sergeant does the flowers.'

Of the several things that I shrank from, when the sug-
gestion was first put to me that I should go to Korea, one
was the prospect, as I thought, of finding the soldiers sour,
embittered, and blackly disappointed by the apparent stale-
mate in their war. But fear had played me false, and they
were, on the contrary, in remarkably high spirits. They
had done well, and they knew it, and their virtue had been
recognised by their more numerous allies. They had almost

E

nothing to amuse or distract them in the luckless and un-
peopled land where rough fortune had set them down, but
they were well fed and on most days of the week the Naafi
brought them a bottle of Japanese beer.   The rifle companies
lived on hill-tops which they had carved into redoubts and
encircled with barbed wire.   The wire was American, and
from a distance the thick entanglements that closed the
narrow valleys between the hills shone like fields of blue-
bells.   The soldiers were brown as hazel-nuts, down to the
waist, and in the heat of summer as lean as greyhounds.
The hills were as steep as a roof, and fat ran off like rain in a
gutter as one climbed them.   Even my lax figure began to
look respectable again, though I nursed my years and halted
as often as I found an excuse.

Once it was to look at a bird in a mandarin's dress of
yellow silk, a golden oriole; once to listen to an oriole
singing, in a leafy glen, as richly as a nightingale; and once
to eavesdrop on a group of soldiers coming noisily and
disputatiously down the hill.   They were a mixed party,
Scots and Irish—Scottish Borderers and Ulster Rifles—
and they had evidently been talking politics and finding a
robust disagreement in their views.   I stood aside to let
them pass, and a tall, black-avised, raw-boned corporal of
the Ulsters turned to those about him and denounced the
Scots in ringing tones and the poignant accent of Belfast.
'Them's the buggers,' he declared, jerking an indignant
thumb at the half-dozen Borderers who had gone ahead,
'that pinched the —— Coronation Stone!'   And added,
with deep feeling in his voice, 'A —— insult to Bruttain!'

A few days later I was reminded of a deeply embarrassing
Irish occasion when, climbing yet another hill, I met a

subaltern of the Ulsters whose family I knew well. He, surrounded by deadly weapons and with a loop of the Imjin gleaming below, appeared to be ideally happy, and his first question was about a dainty little lurcher bitch that his mother had given me some three or four years before.— It was a family that lived, not merely in the company of dogs, but, as it often seemed, for the sole purpose of keeping their dogs well exercised and happy. Yet it was not a family that had been reduced to kennel topics by the shallowness of its intellect or the narrowness of its interests. There were dogs on every chair, but bookcases spilled their contents on the floor, and Captain M. was a serious and pertinacious reader who would, for example, find common roots in Sir Walter Scott for both Proust and Conrad, and wonder why their views of life were so irreconcilable. And Mrs. M. had a wild, poetic fancy that made all her stories seem like fairy-tales, or something filched from a Norse saga, or a mislaid theme for Wagner.

I spent a week-end with them once in a small house they had rented in County Down. There was a big house near-by, with whose female owner they were on difficult terms: there had been a tiresome dispute about some pedigreed hens that the dogs were said to have killed; the lady of the big house supported a local pack of harriers and was prejudiced against coursing, and being a strict Sabbatarian she objected very strongly to coursing hares on a Sunday. But Sunday afternoon shone bright and fair, and the dogs needed exercise. There was an old and cunning greyhound called Snipe; there was a massive and splendid hound whose grandmother had been a pointer and bequeathed to him a noble head; there was the swift and graceful little lurcher bitch that was later given to me; and a terrier or two.  So off we went, but only for a walk; for Captain M. said sternly that we must respect our neighbour's prejudices. But the dogs were full of the joy of life, and Captain M. had a daughter of eighteen or so, who was almost as swift in movement as a hound, and Mrs. M. was never one to spoil anyone's sport.  It happened, then, that after walking quietly and respectably for a couple of miles, we spread out a little, quite casually and without premeditation, and presently Snipe gave tongue.  The greyhound with the noble head leapt into the lead, the lurcher briskly followed, and the terriers added to the chorus.  It was a fine strong hare, and it chose to run across an open hill.

'You can't let the dogs go off on their own!' cried Mrs. M., and broke her way through a hedge.  Her daughter was already far ahead, and Captain M., forgetting his earlier injunction, began to shout directions.  We must go right, he said, for the hare would surely turn that way and with good fortune we might cut its course.  We had a long run across a windy hill, and met the dogs again in a turnip-field. They had lost the hare, but their interest in the field was still lively and they would not be called in.  Snipe went off on her own, and in some gorse at the end of the field, found again.  The same hare, or another?  No one knew, though everyone had his opinion.  The hounds cried, and gave chase.  We followed breathlessly, and on a little rise Captain M. cried in despair, 'Look where they're going! Head 'em if you can, oh, head 'em if you can!'  They were swinging right again, and we ran on a chord of the circle to cut them off, but arrived too late.

They galloped up the drive of the big house, and the

hound with the noble head killed his hare within sight of the Sabbatarian lady. She had been walking in her garden, and just before the hare appeared, had found another dead hen. She had it in her hand when we arrived to offer our apology for disturbing her. She showed a remarkable self-control, and with a condescension that was coldly gracious accepted our explanation. But we were sadly ashamed, and even the dogs appeared to be low-spirited that evening.

# XI

## WHEN THE RAINS CAME

AFTER coming ashore again, so abruptly, from the carrier *Glory*, I spent some time with the 28th Brigade, and I was in the tent that served its Headquarters for a mess-room when the rains began. They came with a lurid glare, in tropical abandon. After an hour or two the sandy floor of the tent was channelled by running streams, and intermittently, to the cannonading of the clouds, its canvas walls were lighted by a sinister brilliance that seemed to pulsate against the sky. On one of the hill-tops that night a man was killed by lightning, another blinded.

In sixteen hours of rain the broad Imjin rose seventeen feet. The ferry cables in the British section were swept away, and on the American front, immediately to the right, a massive wooden bridge was torn from its foundations, broken, and carried out to sea. On the far side of the river there was a large mixed force—American armour, King's Shropshire Light Infantry, Ulsters, a company of the 3rd Australians, and Belgians—that had been reconnoitring deep into the enemy's ground, and now was cut off. These troops had no shelter, no protection from the rain, and rations only for forty-eight hours.

In the morning I drove across a countryside that was strange to the eye and curious to the attentive ear. No longer dusty, but sparkling with water-courses. No longer mute and still, but full of the rushing, surging, pebble-

chinking sound of streams. We drove across a wide, untenanted section of the front—at the hinge of the line, where
it turned sharply to the north—that was alleged, somewhat
doubtfully, to be protected by mine-fields. Its emptiness, a
few days before, had seemed to invite attack; but there was
no risk of surprise now, for the swollen river was an im-
pregnable guard. I wanted to look at a ford in the Hantan,
the largest tributary of the Imjin, and had to walk the last
mile because an unexpected river halted us. A party of
Filipinos were trying to haul a sunken jeep from its swirling
waters, and one of them very obligingly carried me across.
The ford in the Hantan was lost in a brown, dizzily-racing
flood that carried tossing logs and bright plumes of broken
water.

I turned back, and went to visit the Australians. The
main supply route was broken by streams so broad that
it looked as if the sea was coming in, and 3-ton trucks stood
stranded in rushing torrents while brown, half-naked
soldiers, laughing like a Blackpool holiday, struggled with
ropes and cables to haul them out. But the Australian
officers were quiet and apprehensive. They had a company
across the river, and they could neither bring it back nor
go forward to help it. They had, most of them, a tough,
soldier-of-fortune look; but anxiety showed more plainly
in them than in milder-seeming British officers whose
soldiers were in the same straits. I sat and talked with the
Colonel's batman, an old soldier who had served in the
siege of Tobruk. He was unperturbed by Korean misadventure, for his mind was still occupied with the perils
and stink of that beleaguered stretch of desert, and its horrid,
graveyard harbour full of sunken ships. The hills were a

flaring emerald-green under a watery blue sky, and the afternoon sun shone hotly. I went back to Brigade Headquarters, and heard that General Ridgway had suspended the truce talks at Kaesong; and that did nothing to relieve anxiety.

The field-guns were putting down defensive fire in front of the isolated troops, and about midnight I went forward again with a brisk and friendly New Zealand Colonel to visit one of his batteries. He drove his jeep, unlighted, with rollicking speed over a very rough and quite invisible road, and when by inexplicable good luck we arrived safely at the battery, he generously invited me to fire a gun. I let off a 25-pounder, and twice, barking histrionically at the microphone, gave orders for three rounds gunfire.—This I did with the utmost satisfaction, for I have no doubt that war is a very wicked thing, though often necessary, and if any guilt should attach to the soldiers in Korea, I thought it only just to share it. Then we drove back to Brigade as boisterously as we had come, and in the danger of our passage the guilt I had acquired was probably expiated at once.

Unni Nayar. . . . I was on my way to the 60th Indian Field Ambulance when suddenly I remembered Nayar. He and Christopher Buckley had been killed, just a year before, when their jeep ran over a mine. He was a Maratha, a tough, gay, serious, and gallant man. It was he who was really responsible for the discovery, during the war in Italy, of all the great pictures of the Uffizi Gallery and the Pitti Palace in their hiding-place at Montegufoni; for he had asked me to visit his battalion, in the 8th Indian Division, and it was his battalion that occupied Montegufoni. I remembered Nayar's shrill cry of delight when some peasants pulled down the shutters at the far end of a great room, and sunlight fell on Botticelli's *Primavera*.—That night, as we sat talking in a party of Indian officers, Nayar had suddenly protested against the common British habit of regarding India as a complexity of problems: political, economic, religious, and ethnological problems. 'But we are people, not problems!' he exclaimed, with passion in his voice. 'Can you not see that we are people?'

No one, I suppose, whose task is the administration of millions dare look too closely and see humanity in each; but in Korea, where Indians were few in number, it was easy enough to recognise them as individuals. Their Field Ambulance was clean and tidily ordered as if for a General's inspection, and despite the muddy roads its vehicles shone immaculate in their lines. Drivers, clerks, and nursing orderlies had that good pride in their jobs, that sense of responsibility, which, working together, come near to looking like complacency—a justified complacency. They had all been trained for parachute-dropping, but in spite of physical hardening the fingers of the doctors and the orderlies —so said their patients—were curiously light and soft of touch; and even the drivers, according to admiring report, cushioned the fearful roughness of the roads by the tenderness with which they steered.

We spoke at lunch of the Korean people, and in the sympathy of the Indian doctors there was a subtle difference from the tone of voice to which I had grown accustomed in talk about Korea's plight. Nowhere had I heard comment that lacked sympathy, but whereas we spoke with a foreigner's pity, the Indians were moved by closer understanding and a feeling, not deeper perhaps, but more neighbourly. A section of the Field Ambulance cared for civilian patients, somewhere in the southern part of the peninsula, and many children had been examined in whom there were already signs of malnutrition. But more serious than that, they said, was the loss of their winter clothing by thousands, perhaps tens of thousands, of the refugees who had fled from the north. No one could survive the Siberian winds of a winter like the last one who had not proper clothing; but where could so great a multitude find blankets and quilted coats? 'Let us hope for mild weather,' said someone, 'for that is their only chance to survive.' And winter, when it came, was mild indeed in comparison with the previous year.

Some short time ago a firm of publishers [1] in Bombay sent me a little collection of anecdotes and sketches, called *My Malabar*, that had been put together from notes for a book that Unni Nayar had planned to write before he went to Korea. There are delightful memories in it of his childhood in southern India. He tells of a timorous crocodile that lived in a tank at the end of the garden, and lay quietly at the bottom of its pool while, twice a day, the family took their ritual bath. He describes a domestic priest, a 'genial, slightly deaf Brahmin', who 'cooked delicious dishes when he was not actively serving his God', and 'was fond of quoting the irreverent verses of the Malabar poet Venmani', an unusually dark nobleman who flippantly wrote:

[1] Hind Kitabs.

Brahma the Creator, absent-minded
or in his cups,
while making me,
spilt the entire bottle of ink
into the clay,
the Wretch!

Evil spirits were still held responsible for illness, and had
to be appeased. 'For indigestion a tray of vermilion water,
with a dozen leaves of the jak-tree in it and a burning wick
on each leaf, was waved in front of me in clockwise circles.
The water, with the leaves and wicks, was taken to the end
of the garden, then thrown away. With it, the influence
of the witches was also said to leave.'

Now Unni Nayar was a young man when he died. It
was not much more than thirty years since his childish
attack of indigestion had been treated with an array of little
flames bobbing about on leaves of the jak-tree in a dish of
pink water; and thirty years later the Colonel of the
Indian Field Ambulance in Korea dropped by parachute
across the Imjin with a surgical team and all the parapher-
nalia for blood transfusion, all the technical skill that contemporary science demands for a major operation. The
Wheel of Dharma, that decorates the Indian flag, has been
turning fast.

Later that day I met the Brigadier commanding the 28th
Brigade, and with him crossed the Hantan on a tall railway
bridge that had survived its bombing for no purpose until
American engineers, working fast in emergency, gave its
metal road a wooden surface that let road vehicles use it.
It was approached on either side by a steep and muddy,
tortuous ascent; it stood high above the water on bomb-

scarred concrete piers; it had neither parapet nor guard-rail.   But a stream of traffic was crossing, and after a rough drive through hill-enclosed country we came to one of the ferry crossings on the Imjin.   The river was going down and sappers were setting up a shear-legs to carry a new cable.   But lesser streams still ran swiftly over the military roads that bulldozers had carved from soil that had no history of traffic, and on the way home, crossing a broad and turbulent flood in a 3-ton truck, we were stopped half-way over in a gully that was engine-deep, and had to wait for another truck to haul us out with a winch.

On the following day I went to a ferry near Gloucester Crossing to see the return of the battalions from the northern bank.   The Imjin was still broad and running fast, but it had dropped five or six feet and the wire ferries were working again.   The day was hot, and here and there on the river-bank the air was foul.   A lot of Chinese had been killed there in April, when they crossed the shallow stream that ran where now a flood was running, and against continuous shell-fire launched their attack in moonlight.   Grass grew lush and long on the high, curving bank, and its roots had human nourishment.

Beyond the river rose a chaos of empty hills, green with woods and growing though neglected fields on their nearer slopes, but barren in the middle distance, and receding beyond that into lilac shades and a blue mist that seemed to curtain yet taller heights.   In all that vast landscape there was no sign of human habitation—though villages there were, still inhabited, in hidden valleys—and for two or three hours we searched the hills, through field-glasses, and saw no movement.   The soldiers had had to remain in their forward positions to guard the American tanks which had bogged down, and though the Chinese had been avoiding action they might be tempted to intercept or obstruct the retreat to the river. It was not a likely prospect, but it was not impossible; and as we waited, hour after hour, impatience grew a little anxious.

Then at last, on a bald hill-top, we saw a group of tiny figures, so small at first that we could not be sure if they were men or a crest of rocks that we had not previously observed. But the number grew, and a little movement—a minute, slow movement—was visible. They disappeared, and twenty minutes later came into sight again on a nearer slope. There were more of them now, and their movement could be clearly seen. Over another height a second group slowly advanced, and gradually increased in stature. They vanished once more, behind a brown ridge, but presently a long thin column, obviously marching now, came round a shoulder of the ridge, and on a downhill diagonal approached the river. Trees and a small sharp-pointed hill concealed them, and then through the fields, both groups together now, they came to the bank and gathered at the crossing.

The ferry consisted of three pontoons bridged by a light decking and attached to a cable by a wire bridle. It swung out onto the river, the cable sagging downstream, and lying at an angle to the current, took it on the beam and drifted over. The soldiers clambered aboard and stood close-packed as if in an Underground train at the rush hour. They came ashore and silently, with weary faces, climbed the steep southern bank of the river. The first arrivals were a platoon of the King's Shropshire Light Infantry, nearly all of them young. They were heavily burdened, as infantry soldiers always are. They were tired, but not exhausted, and all but two or three had shaved. The ferry went back athwart the stream for its next load, and down the northern hills the columns were still marching to the river.

Some of them arrived at Brigade Headquarters in time to attend a performance by an English concert-party. The Americans had sent professional entertainers to amuse their troops, but these were the first English artistes to visit Korea. They were lively and agreeable people, and they roused their audience to enormous laughter and loud applause. The soldiers, closely seated in a coign of the hillside under a sky that threatened more rain, leaned back and tumbled in their seats, rocked with delight. So much pleasure, in such a land, was a very moving spectacle. There was an adept, gay comedian in the party, a good conjurer who convincingly sawed an officer in half, and two attractive young women, one of whom played the piano. The comedian and the conjurer were applauded and laughed at, but the young women woke a sort of rapture in the soldiers. They sang their songs and played their pieces well enough, but their great appeal was that they seemed to be thoroughly 'nice girls'. There was adoration and longing in the soldiers' voices.

A few nights later, when I was staying with the Canadian Brigade, an entertainment of smaller distinction provoked an even noisier response. A couple of hundred yards from the Headquarters mess there was an open-air cinema-show. We could hear from time to time a snatch of music, a woman's voice that had been canned in Hollywood, and the muffled crack of a blank cartridge. And then, sur-

prisingly, a real, a genuine shot. It interrupted our conversation, but before anyone could say more than 'What
the hell!' there came a ripple, a rattle, a fusillade of shots,
and most of the officers who had been standing round the
bar—all, indeed, except myself and one other prudent person
—ran out to investigate.

Except for some angry shouting there was no further
disturbance, and presently they returned with an explanation.
—A soldier with some experience of the films (or so one
assumed) had taken the precaution to go armed. He had
watched the picture with increasing dislike, and half-way
through its story, shouting a rude remark, he fired at the
flickering face of the hero. But a single shot did no notice-
able damage to the screen, or the hero's offensive smile, so
he gave it a burst—and when his companions expostulated
he threatened them, held them at bay as he retreated into the
darkness, and took to his heels.

'Let me defend him at his court-martial,' I asked. 'He
may not be a good soldier, but the chances are that he's a
good critic—and such people are badly needed.'

He was, however, not only a sensitive man, but alert and
self-reliant, a man with initiative, able to look after himself;
for he was still uncaptured when I last enquired for him.—
The Canadian contribution to the Commonwealth Division
was impressive in several ways. Here and there, in the
ranks of their three battalions, there was a frontier wildness,
an ebullience, a recalcitrance to discipline; but the frame-
work of discipline was strong, and the soldiers carried themselves, in general, with an air of burly pride. Their Military
Police were tall, robust, and admirably drilled. They
looked like men chosen for ceremonial guard in a nation's

capital city. Their build and demeanour were a striking advertisement of Canada's new strength in the world, and Canada had shown its independence of judgement—its awareness of the changing purpose of war—in raising its Brigade to serve, explicitly, the United Nations.

The French-Canadian soldiers, the Royal 22°, or Vandoos, were commanded by a youngish man, thin-faced, quick of speech and movement, and of very decisive character, who maintained an exceptionally high standard of health in his battalion by a method which, despite its success, would possibly upset a psychiatrist's equanimity. I dined with him one night in unusual decorum and with exceptional speed. We dined *à deux*, in the open air, within a little shelter of trees that guarded his caravan. An immaculate white cloth covered the table, a simple but well-cooked meal was deftly served, and within forty-five minutes the Colonel was at work again and I was driving back to Brigade. But in those forty-five minutes my questions had all been answered, and the Colonel had talked with engaging freedom. I wanted to know, among other things, how the Vandoos avoided venereal disease. In the other battalions in the Brigade the incidence, at that time, was 14 or 16 per cent, but in the Vandoos it was only 1·7—or was it 1·4?

'It is because I talk to them,' said the Colonel. 'I myself, I talk to them all. I am like a father, I am severe. I tell them, in the first place, what it is like, this business of making love. I describe what happens.'—His description had the candour of a farmyard, and as little sentimentality.—'And what happens next? Well, ten to one, I say, you were drunk at the time, and when you are drunk you only meet girls who are not clean. So you catch a disease. But what does it matter, you say? This is an age of science and the doctor will cure me with penicillin. So you go to the doctor, and it is true enough: he cures you with penicillin—or so it seems! But in three years, or four perhaps, you begin to feel ill again, you are beginning to feel old, you have rheumatism in your shoulder and a pain in your heart. And then you are not so sure that penicillin has cured you after all! And maybe there are worse things that will happen in ten years, or twelve, when one of your children is blind, or an idiot. And that is because it is not so easy as you think to cure a disease. No, it is not easy. And if you don't want to have rheumatism or go on crutches, if you don't want to have children who are idiots, you will take care not to catch a disease. Don't make love at all, not in Korea or Japan!

'That is what I tell them,' said the Colonel smoothly, 'as if I was their father. And so there is no V.D. in my battalion; or almost none.'—He looked at his watch.—'And now I must go, because my Adjutant is waiting for me, and I have a lot to do.'

Briskly we walked away, and met the Adjutant: a short, square, broadly-built man who looked as if he had learnt his trade in the Foreign Legion. Little groups of soldiers sprang nimbly to attention, and saluted with alacrity. The lines were clean, and discipline wore a high polish. Perhaps the Colonel was a better psychologist than some of the psychiatrists—and certainly he was a good economist. For venereal disease can make shocking waste of an army's strength.

My driver, at that time, was a leanly-fashioned Cockney,

with a gentle, rather melancholy expression, who before he joined the Army had been a barrow-boy. He was a good driver, but on the following morning we got into difficulties in one of the truant streams that still channelled the country, and after jolting for several hours over horrible roads under a hot sky, and climbing a hill to visit the platoon that sat on top of it, and talking to a company of Sappers and persuading my sun-battered mind to record what they told me—after all that, though it was the common pattern of my days in Korea, I felt a little tired—I had been writing notes till midnight—and I told my driver to find a place where we might bathe, because for that afternoon I could digest no more tales of the war. So presently we halted beside a disordered river where one could swim for a dozen strokes, swiftly downstream in a fast-running current, or idle in shallow water at the edge.

I was engaged to dine with General Cassels, and I had in my haversack a clean shirt, a towel, and a piece of soap : for one must observe the conventions when dining with a General. I shared my soap with the barrow-boy, and because the water was muddy it made a coffee-coloured lather, and perhaps we rubbed in as much dirt as we rubbed out. But then we swam in the fast current, and sat in the sun to dry, and the barrow-boy told me about selling lino in the streets of London. Sometimes he had sold fruit, and sometimes nylon stockings, but lino was the most profitable. He had had a partner who did the talking, a quick-tongued and witty fellow; and both of them kept a good look-out for the police. The rolls of linoleum were pieces that had been rejected by the factory because of faults in their fabric or design, but usually they found ready customers who did not stay to examine what they bought, and the profit on a week's hawking might be as much as £40. It was a good life, in its way, nice and independent. You hadn't got a boss and there was no one to order you about—no one but the police, and they weren't so bad if you acted reasonable.

'Are you going back to it, when you're done with the Army?'

But no, he said. It was about time to settle down, he thought. He had been in the Army for six years, and before that, as well as being a barrow-boy, he had had a milk-round and worked in a factory. He had, he admitted, been something of a disappointment to his family, for if his mother had had her way he would have become a priest. 'She had me serving at the altar when I was seven,' he said. His father had been less ambitious, however. His father was a good, easy-going man. In his last letter he had written : 'The worst news I can tell you is that there's a serious shortage of brown ale down here'.

I called again on the Canadians, and in one of their caravans heard a voice, sharp-edged with excitement, say into a telephone : 'This thing's like a snowball ! It's getting bigger and bigger. They've got the story at Corps now, and they're pretty tense about it there. They think it may be important.'—The thing like a snowball was a report that the Chinese troops beyond the river were suggesting an immediate armistice, a local truce to be arranged without reference to their official representative at Kaesong. A company of the Royal Canadian Regiment was north of the Imjin, and a Korean woman had given a patrol a letter from a Chinese Colonel who was apparently willing to make peace at once, and celebrate the occasion with a party. Such was the story, and that evening, at Headquarters of the Commonwealth Division, I saw the letter.

It was laboriously inscribed in printed characters on two pages of foolscap, and the paragraphs were numbered. The language was a stilted, *babu* English, and the signatories described themselves as a Colonel and a Private of the Chinese People's Volunteer Army. The letter referred, with seeming impatience, to the failure of the politicians at Kaesong to agree on terms for an armistice—though at that time the negotiations were only a few weeks old—and mentioned, with formal indignation, the hardships and suffering of the soldiers who must keep the field while their leaders wasted time on idle talk. Then it was proposed that the soldiers, of both sides, should make their own armistice on the simple guarantee of a soldier's honour, and the Commonwealth Division was invited to send envoys, under a white flag, to consider how this could most quickly be done.—The apparent naïveté of the document had, at first sight, inspired a wistful hope that it might be a genuine offer of peace from troops weary of the war; but after a little reflexion it was more wisely decided that the letter was not evidence of the enemy's moral weakness, but merely an attempt to find weakness, or create division, in the allies.

There was a curry for dinner that had been cooked, I believe, by a driver borrowed from the Indian Field Ambulance. It was so fiery, so pungent with turmeric, so tearfully compact of spices and peppers and burning fruit, that for a little while it altogether prohibited conversation, and officers of respectable seniority sat glistening with sweat, red-eyed, and breathing like Vesuvius. The General's mess lay at the upper end of a pretty highland glen, and a tinkling stream guarded the tent. The sound of running water, brightly flowing in a rocky bed, tormented our blistered tongues, our scorched palates.—General Cassels had been brought up in India, and to dine with him was a reminder, not only of the glories of empire, but of its ardours.

We drove by moonlight, through the nightmare ruins of Uijongbu, back to Seoul, where Tom Laister, who was Public Relations Officer to the Commonwealth Division, had found a better billet than the dilapidated block of flats in which I had slept before: a neat little house, almost undamaged, with a garden where an owl cried as if demented from a pine-tree. The weather broke again, I spent a day putting my notes into sequence, and then Tom Laister drove me to Kapyong, in the middle part of the front, where in April the 28th Brigade had fought among the mountains.

Beyond Kapyong, and north of the 38th parallel, the road lay in a cloud-hung, rain-swept valley of desolate magnificence. The surly crests of the hills were dark blue against a wet grey sky, and the sound of rushing streams was unceasing. In several places the road was visibly dissolving under cascades of water that tumbled from the lush hillside, and the jeep threw fountains of spray as if it were a motor-boat. Most of the country seemed quite untenanted except by swallows and white-fronted wagtails, but presently we met a drenched company of American engineers and learnt that we could go no farther. The river was running too high over the ford we had meant to cross—and by now, we were told, the road behind us was probably cut.

We stood under a ponderous rain that filled the air so closely that to be drowned in it seemed not impossible; and ate sodden bread and a well-watered cold chicken. A bulldozer on caterpillar tracks was tearing the steep hillside —uprooting trees and tangled creepers—to get rock for a new road-bed, and a file of Korean porters moved slowly towards the dangerous ford. They were meagrely built, bandy-legged fellows, with no appearance of strength, but they carried straw packs heavily laden with rice for the 6th Republic of Korea Division, that held the line in front of us and now was dependent on coolie transport for its rations. They approached the river, chattering shrilly, and were reluctant to cross. After a lot of argument four of the tallest and strongest went first, and stood in the deepest parts; and slowly the others followed. They waded waist-deep, chest-high in places, feeling their way with long sticks. Now and again one lost his footing and momentarily disappeared in a turbulence of brown water; but the tall men standing in the flood would stoop and haul him up again, and roughly push him on. No one drowned, and the rice went forward.

The rain stopped, and a brilliant sun filled the valley with sudden heat. Flounces of cloud hung on the hillside, white shawls draped the ridges, and tiger-lilies and flowers like yellow hunting-horns shone in a jungle-growth of glistening green leaves. The road was cut behind us, and we had to wait an hour till the breach was filled. Where the tributary stream that we had been following met the Puk-han the conjoint flood tore at the approaches to a precariously standing bridge, and a gang of women were carrying sandbags in what seemed a well-intended but quite useless effort to stem the waters. Another monsoon shower fell as we left the narrow valley, and twice on the forty miles to Seoul we were drenched through, twice baked dry in the suddenly reviving sun. Labourers at the day's end trudged in single file along the road or huddled in close-packed groups under the eaves of a wayside hut. Raindrops bounced on the large bare head of a child sleeping on its mother's back, it woke, and quickly she pulled it forward under her loose blouse—jog-trotting on, her other hand steadying a bundle on her head—and gave it her breast. Old men, straw-hatted, walked delicately in the mud.

Tom Laister had asked a couple of war correspondents to dinner, and one of them got drunk and revealed the misery of his thoughts. The fearful plight of Korea and its people overwhelmed him, and he shouted against the evil in men's minds that countenanced cruelty and permitted so much unhappiness. He was darkly angry with me when I said it would be easier to rebuild the ruins of Seoul than to repair the havoc that Communism made in the lives and in the minds of those it conquered; and even to myself, in the midst of ruins, it sounded a callous thing to say—but it is true.

I walked in the garden, and under a lop-sided moon the demented owl cried *hoot-hoot, hoot-hoot*. I knew soldiers who had half forgotten their own pain in the remorseless cold of that first winter, but remembered, as a hurt still throbbing in the brain, the agony of the refugees on frozen roads. The refugees were running, not from war, but from the terror in their minds. It was fear of the

Communists that drove them to the roads, and the flight had not ceased, nor the fear diminished, when summer came. For a Mongol conqueror was on the march again—a Mongol with a philosophy—and his philosophy was as cruel as Genghis Khan.

# XII

## THE INLAND SEA

I HAD been in Korea for a month, and though I was by no means confident that that was long enough for my purpose, I had to go. I had engagements in the other hemisphere.

The dusty airport at Kimpo, Arabian heat in Taegu, and frustration at Iwakuni made the first paragraph in my journey. My intention was to return, as I had come, to Hong Kong and Singapore; but because of some failure of communication, because of some hole in the administrative net, the Flying Boat Squadron at Iwakuni had received no instruction to carry me south, and there was no ship to take me. The young officers of the Royal Air Force were kind and helpful, signals were made and requests for help sent out, and to pass the time I went to see Hiroshima.

How charming was Japan after the desolation of Korea! There, the drab traffic of war, the ruins, the poverty of the landscape, the plodding misery and hang-dog, bewildered look of war's survivors; but here a green and busy land, populous wooden villages beside a sparkling sea, and plump faces that all looked genial because peace had blessed them. —I shall not pretend that Japan was truly happy, but in comparison with the wretched country I had left, it wore the complexion of happiness. It had been cured of war, and its skin was healthy. Shining-healthy in contrast to the symptoms of malignant disease in its poor neighbour.

Humanity, while it retains the will to live, has a power

of recuperation as rich and determined as a tropical jungle, and Hiroshima had put forth a secondary growth that almost entirely concealed, from the casual eye, the ruins of atomic blast and the wild fire it started. A crowded, briskly living shanty-town covered the dissolution of the old city. Under a transparent blue sky it had an air of gaiety—impermanent and cheap, but lively as a fair—and with bland effrontery, with the sublime indifference of one who offers his father's corpse to an anatomist, there was, at the point of impact of the bomb, a little nest of shopkeepers selling photographs and souvenirs of the tragedy, curios to decorate one's mantelpiece and remind one of Hiroshima. The ragged skeleton of a large building stood here, that had been an exhibition hall, and beside it were a brightly coloured pavilion in which sat a huge and brassy effigy of Buddha— brand-new, of vulgar workmanship—and a graveyard where monuments of polished marble had been eroded by the heat of the blast. A smooth attendant in the pavilion spoke earnestly about the necessity of peace, and tried to sell me photographs of charred and mutilated victims of the explosion. The little shops opposite were as cheerfully decorated as a shooting-gallery at a country fair, and the choice of souvenirs they offered might equally have served as prizes for Saturday night marksmanship. One of the epicentres of the world's guilt had in six years become an attraction for tourists—as, of course, did scenes of martyrdom in the Middle Ages. Perhaps it is biologically better to take a little profit out of tragedy than to sit and brood over it.

My companions were two officers of the Flying Boat Squadron, and from Hiroshima we went, by a ferry-boat full of Japanese family parties, to the thickly wooded, high-pitched island of Miyajima. It is a place of pilgrimage as well as a holiday resort, and an extensive commerce appeared to cater almost entirely for children. A covered bazaar led inland from the pier, a long, long street lined by little shops that offered for sale an infinite variety of articles, of no intrinsic value whatever, but confected with guileless ingenuity for the passing amusement, as it seemed, of the most unsophisticated sort of nursery. An endless array of gewgaws, knick-knacks, pottery, paper ornaments, artificial flowers, fancy vases, mechanical toys, children's trumpets, drums, and bric-à-brac. A million baubles, a vastness of frippery in all the colours of a simple palette, rose and green, sky-blue and buttercup yellow. Here and there, it is true, was a shop that sold furniture and pictures, or printed silks, but the general display had hardly more substance than soap-bubbles. It would have made a pretty setting for a ballet, a Japanese ballet of dainty nonsense, but there was so much of it that I grew perplexed and worried about the economics of inanity.

Nature, I thought, was over-fanciful in Miyajima. There was too much decoration in the trees and the rocks, the whole landscape was rococo, and after a week there I should have been hungry for the naked moors of Caithness. But for a day it was pleasant and amusing. We swam in a mild sea, we looked at a temple, we took off our shoes and drank a bottle or two of beer in a small hotel in the midst of which some bushes, growing profusely from an artificial rock pool, created a green shade and the oppressive atmosphere of an aquarium. A middle-aged woman of subdued appearance sat with us to fill our glasses. She wore a grey gown and a black sash, and made no attempt to talk. There were several women in the place, one of whom from time to time did a little sweeping or dusting, and through the open door of an inner room I could see a girl, with her knees drawn up, sleeping comfortably on the floor. Another girl, wearing only a petticoat, walked slowly past her and in a tin basin delicately washed her face. We were expected, perhaps, to ask for some larger entertainment than a bottle of beer—but the ferry was due, we put on our shoes, and the speechless women bowed farewell.

I hoped to get a seat in a courier plane to Hong Kong, but when we returned to Iwakuni we heard that the morning's news of bad weather in the south had become news of prohibitive weather. A typhoon, previously uncertain of its course, was now heading for Okinawa, and the American flying-boats stationed there had been ordered to leave and find a safer anchorage at Yokosuku in the bay of Tokyo. The progress of the typhoon had already excited the imagination of its observers, one of whom reported water-spouts eight hundred feet high in the Yellow Sea; but whether one believed in water-spouts or not, there would be no courier to Hong Kong that night.

In the morning the meteorologists declared that Iwakuni was now in the path of the typhoon, and would be closed to air traffic until the skies had cleared. The squadron of Sunderland flying-boats must go to Yokosuku, and because it was useless for me to stay in Iwakuni, I decided to go with them. We took off about eight o'clock, and flew along the north shore of the Inland Sea. Islands harshly shaped lay darkly on ruffled silver, and in the light of a windy morning Japan was gravely beautiful. To the south the sky was a menacing dark blue, and the wind was increasing. Above the land, near Osaka, we plunged into cloud and climbed sharply, with a roar of opened throttles, to gain height above the hills. For some time there was no visibility, no true visibility, but between one great island-cloud and another the air was less opaque, one could see a fine rain falling, and watch the approaching darkness like a monstrous wave rearing its wind-blown crest.

Then the sky grew thinner, and with an astonishing sensation of height one looked down, past underlying cloud, at the steeply descending sides of a profound green valley. The view opened, and in the valley were three little towns. It was absurdly over-populated. An arm of the sea came brightly in, and between the higher clouds and the hills beyond the bay there was clear sky. We went down on a quick slant to slip beneath the clouds, but they were closing fast upon the hill-tops, and turning to starboard we flew down the bay, but met swift-coming cloud again. We were quite enclosed, and climbed with a sudden roar to seek a view.—What's the safe height? About 5500.—Up through rain and darkness, lurching a little and bumping in rough air, we flew into sunshine, and presently above a rolling sea of cloud saw something small and dark and manifestly solid beyond that unsubstantial ocean. It looked like the crown of a top-hat, and was indeed the top of Fuji-yama. We flew past at 7500 feet—the crest of Fuji 5000 feet above—and all its upper half, in the elegance of perfect symmetry, showed brown and bare save for two ribbons of snow against the east. There was no trouble after that, and gently we came down to the calm waters of Tokyo Bay.

I was, however, no nearer New Zealand, and my urgent

desire for conveyance through the clouds was momentarily dulled when a captain of the United States Navy, pouring gin with a heavy hand, told me that the present radius of the intervening typhoon was two hundred and eighty miles, and the storm of which it was the centre filled a front, from east to west, of twelve hundred miles. The day, moreover, was Friday, and before the imminence of the week-end it was difficult to find anyone who had the leisure to pay much attention to my demands. I was offered a billet in the Maranouchi Hotel, in Tokyo, where officers on short leave from Korea customarily stayed, and after driving for an hour through dull and shabby scenes of suburban industry I acknowledged a temporary defeat, and admitting I was tired, went early to bed in a room that looked out at tram-lines, an elevated railway, and a large grey building whose nearer wall was harshly patterned by a zigzag fire-escape.

The weather was hot and heavy, as before the breaking of the Indian monsoon, and in the morning I listened to ominous talk about the innate and persistent arrogance of the Japanese, that would show itself again as soon as they had signed their treaty with the Americans: my companions were a newspaper-man whose professional cynicism matched his professional interest in disaster, and a couple of robustly pessimistic old-hands in the Far Eastern trade who had no doubt that the recent docility of Japan, its complaisance in defeat, was nothing but oriental guile and a bland cover for unsubdued ambition.—Saddened by the prospect, so quickly seen, of returning from the simplicity of military existence to the hurly-burly of civilian life, I tried, in the late afternoon, to write some notes for my New Zealand lectures, and was frustrated by the moist, oppressive heat

of my bedroom.   I went, in despair, to a public lounge that
was air-conditioned but noisy with the loud conversation of
several score of young officers, all briskly enjoying themselves, and there, in despite of clamour, in the comfort of
artificial coolness, I assembled without difficulty the ideas and
notions that I had pursued, but unavailingly, in the hot-
house quietness of my room.   A temperate climate has some
advantages.

More conversation followed, but not of the political
sort which had depressed me before lunch.   A gay and
charming subaltern told me, with evident triumph, that he
had spent about £80 in his five days' leave, and so in some
degree got his revenge for six months in the barren wilds
of Korea where there was nothing to buy and very little to
enjoy.   He had, he admitted, not much to show for his
spending, and a fairly large sum had bought him only a
puzzle that he could not solve.

In a night-club called the Cheer-oh! he had picked up a
Japanese girl who told him a distressing tale of her family's
poverty, of increasing hardship, of a domestic unhappiness
so painful to observe that she had decided to relieve it, or try
to, by becoming a dance-hall hostess.   This was her first
night as such, and indeed, said the young man, she appeared
to be not only respectable but wholly without experience of
modern life.   One of the attractions of the Cheer-oh! was a
strip-tease act, and this so shocked the girl, or seemed to,
that she covered her eyes and would not look at the per-
former.   She consented to go with the young man to an
hotel, but in a cab, on the way there, began to weep.   The
young man sensibly told her that he would do better to take
her home, but this she refused to allow, and wept more

bitterly when he said that he could see no point in making
love to someone who didn't want him.   She continued to
weep, but wouldn't leave him.   They spent three hours
together, but when morning came the girl's virtue, if virtue
she had, was technically untarnished.   The officer, moved
by gentlemanly consideration as well as by pity for her
distress, insisted on paying for his white night, and provoked
another crisis.   Oh, what embarrassment she showed at the
offer of money, and what embarrassment he felt at the idea
of insulting a respectable girl, so gently nurtured—especially
if he should pay her too little!   She didn't know what
to say, or where to look.   She cried yet again, in the thin
light of morning, and he, to have done with emotion and
be unburdened by any thought of meanness, gave her all he
had.   Which was the respectable sum of £20.

He still believed that her grief, her inexperience, and her
respectability were genuine;  but now, after twelve hours
for consideration, he was beginning to think they had paid
her a lot better than professional acquiescence would have
done.   Was it possible, after all, that she had been playing a
part, and he had been had for a sucker?   A quick and
worldly critic would assuredly say so;  but no one could
deny the existence, in Tokyo, of poverty and wretchedness,
and  perhaps  innocence  had  also  survived—and  been  rewarded.   He had had a night, in any case, that he would
remember longer than a night of easy satisfaction.

In Iwakuni, a day or two before, a pilot officer of the
Flying Boat Squadron had shown me a photograph that he
had taken of a Japanese girl who stood, smiling and naked,
in a shallow sea.   She was a virgin—her mother had told
him so—and the freedom with which he enjoyed her com-

pany was tempered only by his agreement to respect virginity. 'She's a nice girl,' he said, 'and it's better than nothing, isn't it? I get on well with her mother, too. She's a good cook, if you like their way of cooking.'

There is a charming passage in Gertrude Stein's *Autobiography of Alice B. Toklas* that reads:

We drove by day and we drove by night and in very lonely parts of France and we always stopped and gave a lift to any soldier, and never had we any but the most pleasant experiences with these soldiers. And some of them were as we sometimes found out pretty hard characters. Gertrude Stein once said to a soldier who was doing something for her, they were always doing something for her, whenever there was a soldier or a chauffeur or any kind of a man anywhere, she never did anything for herself, neither changing a tyre, cranking the car or repairing it. Gertrude Stein said to this soldier, but you are tellement gentil, very nice and kind. Madame, said he quite simply, all soldiers are nice and kind.

And in very truth how many examples one has known that substantiate this fine assertion! War does not brutalise men who are not innately brutal. It exposes those who are mean or poor of spirit, it aggravates the cruelty of those who are cruel by nature; but the ordinary decent man often appears to slough a burden of selfish care when he puts off his civilian clothes, and in the uniform he grumbles at becomes genial, care-free, and humane. The British soldier oversea has, on the whole, a wonderfully mild temper, and it is one of the commonest of observations that in any theatre of war generosity and kindliness shine from mortal lanterns with an ever brighter light as one moves forward from the base to the front line. The Americans say, 'You never find an atheist in a fox-hole', and it may be that the larger fear drives out the little fears that commonly harass and demean us, that blemish our moral complexion; or

F

perhaps the seeming isolation of a battalion, or even larger formations, in their own sector, encourages a realisation of common humanity that the divisions of civil life obscure or deny.   Sympathy, indeed, will even embrace the enemy, as soon as he has been beaten.

In the last days of the war in Italy, somewhere near Padua, I met a wandering man who, having escaped from German captivity, had lived in hiding for about eighteen months.   I took him to an outpost of the Allied Military Government that had hurriedly been established in the town, and tried to find someone who could look after him.   There was a crowd of people in the room, half of them in silent bewilderment, half clamouring for attention, and in a corner sat a family party, sombre and tearful.   The Military Policeman who had brought them in thrust his way to an American sergeant who appeared to be in charge, and spoke, close to his ear, with urgent quietness.   The sergeant, busy and impatient, was less tactful.   'Rape?' he exclaimed, loudly above the clatter of voices.   'We got nothing to do with rape here.   Rape's Civil, not Military.'—The statement was not, of course, intended for an epigram, and as a categorical assertion of culpability on the one hand, innocence on the other, it goes too far.   But if the civil populace and the armed forces of a country were simultaneously arraigned on a comprehensive charge of all the recognised sins of omission and commission, the military might well receive the lighter sentence. . . .

On the following day, at the Embassy, I was kindly treated, given news of the weather, and advised to return to Iwakuni.   The typhoon, after swaying east and west, had

finally set its course for the Yellow Sea—the ships of our
cruiser squadron were rolling fearfully in a mountainous
swell off the Shantung peninsula—and though a southward flight to Hong Kong and Singapore might still be
impossible, there was good chance of a passage to Darwin
by way of Manila.   A liaison officer of the R.A.F. was told
to make what arrangements he could for me, and going
early to bed, I got up again shortly after midnight.  I was
to fly to Iwakuni in an American freighter, and the liaison
officer told me, apologetically, 'I'm afraid it won't exactly
be comfortable.  They make you wear a parachute, for one
thing.  But when you see the slap-happy way they do
things, well, perhaps you'll be glad to.'

For twenty miles or more I was driven through black and
empty streets—feeling, at that hour of the morning, lonely
and shrunken of spirit—and presently found myself in a
large waiting-room where half a hundred American soldiers
and airmen slept in strange attitudes on benches or the floor.
I had arrived unnecessarily early, but after an hour or so a
dozen of us were called into a smaller room and given, by an
American private, what he described as a 'briefing'.   It consisted of an elementary description of the nature of a parachute, and advice—delivered with much more relish—on the
several ways of warding off an attack by sharks, if by ill-
fortune we should be dropped into the sea.   We were then
directed to an aeroplane which was heavily laden with
machinery of various sorts, and the private who had 'briefed'
us commanded us to don parachutes and Mae Wests.   The
American Mae West is as heavy as a horse-collar—a collar
for a cart-horse—and the American parachute seems bulkier
than ours.   There was nothing to sit on, in the freight-plane,

but a narrow strip of canvas between the cargo and the shell; and with my double burden I found it impossible to sit at all. I removed the encumbrances, and so did most of my fellow-passengers. Then, through the open door, the remorseless private, still thinking of sharks, looked in and snarled : 'Put 'em on, I said ! And keep 'em on !' Meekly we obeyed, but as soon as the plane took off we slipped out of our horse-collars, propped our feet on the cargo, and took what comfort we could find.

The captain and crew of the freighter were unshaven men dressed in crumpled, dirty dungarees. Their aeroplane was only a modern sort of tramp-steamer, and like the crew of a sea-going coaster they elaborately despised a smart appearance. Their duty was rough and hard, and their manner consorted with it. At some stage of the voyage, in turbulent air with the engines roaring shrilly, one of them appeared at the cockpit-door and shouted, 'Get back to the tail-end, all of you. And stay there till I tell you different.' Like sheep in a storm we huddled together, for ten minutes perhaps, and then he reappeared with a cigar between his teeth and amiably remarked, 'O.K., boys, now.' In smoother air we returned to our strips of canvas and dozed against each other's shoulders.—Rough they might be, but the captain and his crew were efficient airmen. Smoothly we descended at three or four intermediate ports, and rose again with negligent ease. The sun was up, and its rays threw powdered light into the dirty hull of the freighter before we reached Iwakuni.

The liaison officer in Tokyo had given me a movement order that appeared to authorise my passage to Darwin, by way of Manila, in an Australian air-liner. But two obstacles to this project quickly became apparent, for the movement order was discovered to be invalid, and one of the liner's engines had just been removed for repair. My New Zealand lecture-tour was supposed to begin on the following day, and I was growing worried about it. Then there came to my rescue Squadron-Leader Helme of the Flying Boat Wing, for whose hospitality I had already been grateful, and he promised to get authority to send me south with unexampled speed. I must wait another day, that was all— and for entertainment, in the morning, the pilot officer whose girl-friend was a Japanese virgin told me that he, remaining in Iwakuni when all others abandoned it before the menace of the typhoon, had enjoyed a blissful holiday with his platonic love; and in the evening I was invited to dine with a Group-Captain and a Wing-Commander of the Royal Australian Air Force.

We dined very well, and without controversy until, to gramophone music, our brandy was served by two Japanese maids bent lowly upon their knees. This spectacle of reverence so moved the Wing-Commander that he protested loudly against the insufficiency of the accompanying tune, which came from a record of Cole Porter's *Kiss Me, Kate*, and demanded Beethoven. Preferably a symphony: something majestic. The Group-Captain had a large collection of records, and while one of the Japanese maids knelt again to re-fill our glasses, the other shuffled hurriedly away to seek what our ennobled spirits wanted. A lordly music filled the little room, and filled for an hour our minds. But then, as though by infection of its eloquence, it started conversation again, and though the Japanese maids had gone to bed, the brandy, perhaps by a miracle, still circulated.

It was nearly two o'clock before the party ended, and I had to be up again by half-past five.

The admirable Squadron-Leader Helme had secured for me a passage in a Constellation that would fly without a stop to Darwin. The Constellation had arrived at Iwakuni with a load of New Zealand soldiers who, shipwrecked on a coral island west of New Guinea, had been rescued from the reef-bound vessel and transferred to the air for their Korean journey. The plane was returning almost empty, its only passengers two European wool-buyers whose journey had been delayed by the great typhoon, a New Zealand gunner going home on compassionate leave, and myself. From Iwakuni to Darwin was 3200 miles, and a Constellation, without its normal freight but with a full load of petrol, had a range of 4000 miles. The margin of safety was sufficient unless the weather again deteriorated.

It was a longer flight than any of the commercial passages, but there was no pomp or ceremony about its beginning, no tiresomeness at all except the customary prelude to a voyage in the sky which is the passenger's obligation to be at the airport at least an hour too soon. The New Zealand gunner, who was flying to his father's death-bed, discovered at the last moment that he had not the proper documents for his journey, and asked me to help him. This gave me little trouble, and he thumbed a ride from the northern hemisphere to the southern with no more authority than good will; and reached New Zealand in time to see his father.

We took off at eight o'clock, and flew over a silver-grey sea on which dark islands made pictures heart-achingly pretty—children's pictures of fairy-tale islands with little white bays, toy villages, and fields for Noah's animals—or

rocky islands crested like Napoleon's hat—and climbed
through a shining stream of cloud, that glittered against
dark blue, to a staring white atmosphere between cloud
above and cloud below, where the air had a luminous
quality but no certain light, and over a non-existent world
the nearly empty plane (like a vacant tunnel, aloofly flying)
settled to its long journey at a height of rather more than
16,000 feet.   Sometimes, far below, one saw a glimmer of
the sea, but for eight or ten hours nothing else.

# XIII

## THE VAST PACIFIC SKY

I HAD spent a month in a desolate and comfortless land with soldiers who were fighting, perhaps without much conviction, for a cause essentially good, though obscured in parts, as all human causes must be, by private and political interests; and I was on my way to a rich and prosperous, English-speaking land—a new land, with its history before it —to lecture on some of the recent achievements of English literature. In a light and easy way, on the upper levels of consciousness, I was glad to have seen Korea, I was equally glad to be going to New Zealand. But in a deeper apprehension I was unhappy about my obligation to write of soldierly deeds, unhappy about the prospect of discussing, with unknown audiences in Auckland and Wellington, in Christchurch and Dunedin, our recent literary performance.

Both morally and technically it is difficult to write of modern war : technically difficult because the number of men and the strategy governing them are usually too large and complicated to be brought within a visible understanding of the whole; and morally difficult because it is no longer possible for a tolerably sensible, tolerably civilised person to write of war with relish for its whole course and a hearty assurance that victory will be commensurate with the soldiers' effort. That we had been right in going to war in Korea—morally right and politically justified—I

had no doubt; but I could not describe the campaign with
an heroic appetite for all its scenes, with zest for the wintry
fighting and Kinglake's gusto for a charge.   What I could
do, without effort or obliquity, was to praise our soldiers.
It would be no dishonesty to speak of their bravery, their
coolness and hard endurance and humanity, that made a
garden of great virtue in the very midst of destruction.
Though war was evil, even when it was necessary, our
soldiers had been good, in the antique fashion, when frost
and steel and utter weariness had sought for every weakness
to disprove their merit.   But I could only state their goodness, I could not show it, in the novelist's way, by imagining
and describing the detail of their battles.

I was at one time involved in war, not as an observer,
but as an infantry soldier, and I knew that the truth of battle
could only be told by those who had fought.   I had not felt
the Siberian cold of the Korean war, I had not stood against
a multitudinous night-attack and heard the clamour of
Chinese bugles behind the bursting of grenades—and I
dared not offend the truth by trying to imagine the emotions
of those wild and sombre hours.   The soldier in the midst
of battle can be filled with such an exhilaration as the saints
have known when, void of fear, the heat of the blood so
lights the spirit that the uncared-for body is but a shadow
bearing aloft a burning torch.   But, more often, soldiers are
beleaguered cities wherein the treacherous voices of weariness and terror urge them to yield, and courage, that bids
them stand, seems as weak and irrelevant as a three-years
child.   And no one on the face of the earth has ever been so
tired as soldiers who have fought, and marched, and dug
their trenches, and before morning comes are mustered to

fight or march again.—There is the mystery, or part of it, that forbade intrusion.

I should have liked to be trumpet-tongued and wake, in readers' minds, emotions to complement the soldiers' courage and their suffering, but I did not know the truth of what they had experienced, the unique and savage truth of a Korean battle, and even for a good cause I could not make pretence of knowing. I could only draw up a catalogue of their actions and hope that bare facts, by proper arrangement, would find in themselves a little eloquence. I would be honest by compulsion, not virtue—and yet, how dry and thin might honesty appear!

That was the one source of unhappiness, that I could not write well enough of soldiers, and the other was that in New Zealand I might not speak well enough of writers. I have enjoyed, perhaps more than most people, the work of my contemporaries, and very warmly admired their skill. But those whom the most interesting critics most warmly praise have seemed to me, from time to time, to be practising, with fingers already adept but a little wistful, for some larger performance that they will never essay because their touch is too deliberately delicate for the deeper chords, their sensitivity too closely confined for the broader span. They can embroider a theme with expert choice, but usually the theme is small and often wilfully remote from subjects of a common concern. They are laboriously skilful in the dissection of motives, but the motives they explore seldom provoke action of any great importance, or lively enough to rouse excitement. Action, indeed, in critical opinion, is of little moment: such description of action as there is in the work of the intellectual novelists often fails to convince the ordinary reader that such-and-such really happened, or would be likely to happen, and this is so because the author's primary interest was not the creation of viable characters and the narration of what they did, but some theory of character and the disclosure of his sensibility in proving it. The consequence is that the general reader, who still quite sensibly looks for a story in his novels, too often turns away from the intellectual writers and spends his evening at home with the latest *roman policier*, the best authors of which are as expert in their own field as the favourites of the serious critics.

Once upon a time, for too short a time, I was friendly with a Chinese poet called Sin Meh. He was a young man of considerable beauty, the smooth pallor of whose finely modelled face was enhanced by a very small, silky black beard, and the elegance of his appearance accommodated a mind both amiable and ingenious: his tastes were too expensive to be sustained by poetry alone, so he edited, for greater comfort, a clutch of slender magazines whose sale was guaranteed—or so I was told—by the decorative impropriety and amusing scurrility of their contents. Sin Meh used to take me to the Inner City, the lively old Chinese heart of Shanghai, and once, entering a tea-house, we found a casual audience of some thirty or forty people listening intently to a tale told by a professional story-teller. We sat down, still talking, and then a word or a phrase caught Sin Meh's attention and suddenly, with uplifted hand, he asked me to be quiet. His dark eyes shining, the shadow of a smile on his ivory cheek and his lips parted— his lips, above his little black beard, were faintly mauve— he listened with a child's attention to the story-teller, and when at last the old man's tale was done, he turned to me and said—but now in a different mood, now with the proprietorial air of one who displays to a stranger the riches of his native place—'That was most interesting! We came at a good time, for the story he was telling, and you saw how closely the people listened and how pleased they were, was a story about my own great-grandfather, who was a famous judge.'

Or was it his grand-uncle, or his great-grand-uncle? That I cannot remember, but the story was of a judge, of high rank and widely respected for his learning, who in the ripest years of his life, in the glowing autumn of his career, sat in judgement on a young woman accused of having murdered her husband. There was no slightest doubt that the charge was true, but the young woman's beauty was remarkable, her voice was like an old tune heard in the twilight, and the questions put to her she answered usually with engaging modesty, but sometimes with enchanting wit. The old judge, it was observed, paid less and less attention to the evidence, but more and more to the prisoner; and when the case was concluded, and her guilt clearly established, he pronounced her innocent.

The scandal was enormous; it came to the ears of the Empress herself, but though the judge could be punished, the murderess was immune. The law had found her guiltless and restored her freedom. She returned to her own city, and presently the judge was publicly disgraced and dismissed from his high office. But to the surprise of his friends he showed neither shame nor regret, he appeared to feel that he also had been set free—and promptly following the lovely assassin he wooed her hotly, wed her quickly, and lived happily ever after. . . .

There, in the tea-house, I saw the beginning of literature; and, if our civilisation is unfortunate, its end. A story was its overture, a story may be its finale—but in its prosperous middle-age literature and its critics have neglected and depreciated story-telling, and that is probably unwise. A story is the bond between literature and life, for a story must have a beginning and an end, and those are the dominating terms of life. The novel is an expansion, a refinement, a deepening and glossing of a story; and these additions, the junior parts, give importance to the story—but should respect its seniority.

In the novels of a period, moreover, there should be some reflexion of the prevailing temper of the period. I do not mean that novelists should be governed by social obligation, or condemned to what is sometimes called social realism. Society is more indebted to the novelist than the novelist to society, and freedom, which is his proper condition, is also his desert. But within that freedom he should be exposed, from time to time, to infection from the characteristic spirit of his age; and the more intellectual English writers appear to have been regularly vaccinated and thoroughly protected against infection. They have done much, and done it admirably, but they have not admitted the prevailing germ. They have learnt a scrupulous, professional exactitude of thought and statement, they have acquired refinement and sensibility, but in their revulsion from all that is hearty and commonplace they have adopted—there are exceptions, of course, but a general statement must take chances and risk unfairness—an anti-heroical view of life, when life in our century has demanded and been given, to retrieve its blunders, a dominating character of heroism.

I do not know when the XXth century began in Britain. History does not confine itself within exactly counted chapters of a hundred years, and perhaps the XIXth century lingered here until the Liberal victory of 1906 closed a gentle door upon it. Perhaps it was the Post-Impressionist exhibition in 1912 that shocked and finished it. Perhaps it endured until the battle of the Somme, in July 1916, when sixty thousand fell on the first day, all of them volunteers for war, and with their death or disablement the age of the volunteer came officially to its end and the epoch of conscription began. But conscript soldiers saved us, in that war, from the physical and spiritual humiliations of a German victory, as, twenty years later, they preserved us from the ignominy and torment of conquest by the Nazis. The heroism of our century has in Britain been a little reluctant, but its quality is proved by our survival. We have survived, and lived in tolerable conditions, behind a rampart of good though unwilling soldiers. We have made our scientific advances, our political experiments, behind a great wall of soldiers. We have painted our pictures, written our poems, devised our operas within the mortal protection of the Navy, the Army, and the Air Force. Children have been born, love has had its day, houses have been built and gardens tended while young men—conscripts in name but voluntaries in action—warded off the destroying waves of the enemy. Everything we have and are is ours, and still exists, by grace and courage of the soldiers. They are the men of the century, because without them we should no longer be numbering its years—or numbering them only to curse the wretchedness of our survival in it.

Now the intellectual writers—let us simplify, and say

the better writers—have not shown much appreciation of the soldiers' importance, and that diminishes their significance; though their failure is easy to understand and not impossible to condone. They have seen and been sickened by the general squalor, the massive stupidity of war, and because they detest the whole thought of it they have not looked through its horrid envelope to discover the virtue of the men who, in the front of battle, control their equal hatred and their greater fear to keep us alive and allow us, if we will, to make life a little more sensible, a little more agreeable. We have suffered in our century from an insufficiency of wisdom, but we have had bravery enough; and bravery should be acknowledged because we are indebted to it. In an age when much has failed and much been broken, only the soldiers have not been insufficient.

But the writer can only do what he has a mind to do, and what the best writers have done is to prepare a way and elaborate a method—to furnish a technique—that some author of to-morrow, if he can re-establish the primacy of story-telling and see in the perspective of time the unregarded heroism of our half-century, may use to create an ironical masterpiece in which, behind the enduring rearguard of the soldiers, a renewed capacity for action was being forged by those who distrusted action.

In the long and almost empty tunnel of the aeroplane flying so high above the vast Pacific I found a double comfort, and perhaps an answer to my problem, in, as it were, a biological faith and a well-used platitude. I was eating Army rations, and platitude seemed appropriate. 'It has been a time of experiment', I shall tell my audiences. 'Not of absolute achievement—except in Ireland, where

Joyce wrote a comic nonesuch—but of delicate trial and scrupulous exploration. A time of doubtful but conscientious authors with no great stomach for life (and who shall blame them?) but very sensitive fingers and sad, percipient gaze.'—Then I remembered a girl in Sweden, in the spring, a great golden, laughing girl who described a literary party to which she had been taken: 'And there were all the little poets looking at me with frightened eyes!' And that, unfortunately, broke my train of thought. . . .

In the late afternoon we dropped to within a thousand feet or so of a small, flat archipelago near the western neck of New Guinea, and saw a wrecked ship lying with her nose to the surf on an islet called, I think, Masela. This was the *Wahine*, the New Zealand troop-ship that had run ashore and whose freight of soldiers was being flown to Korea in the air-liner that carried me in the opposite direction. She looked, poor ship, unspeakably desolate, being so out of place with her stem pointing to a barbaric shore clad in wind-blown palms and her stern-rail level with the shark-swimming sea. A few hours after she was abandoned, the natives of the nearby islands had begun to pillage her.

About half-past eight, in a tropically rich darkness, we landed at Darwin and were driven over roads half-visibly lined by what seemed to be quite irrelevant houses to a well-ordered hotel for passing travellers, where the curious fatigue of a long voyage through the air was medicined with ham and eggs; and then a hospitable man took me to his house, a half-furnished bungalow raised on concrete stilts above the ant-infested soil, where he and his wife talked of their life in that paradoxical place—so far from anywhere, yet busy all through the day and night with traffic—in the uneasy manner of maroons. Of spiritual maroons, for they had the trappings of civilisation, such as a refrigerator and the telephone, but little of the companionship and normal comfort of civilisation. I wish I had seen Darwin by daylight, but I went through it as though passing an invisible man. An English commercial traveller of the globe-trotting sort told me a few days later that he had arrived there in the early morning, and while walking in search of a lodging had been startled by the sudden ejection, from a door immediately in front of him, of a violently resisting drunkard. The poor fellow had fallen heavily, his head meeting the curbstone like a blacksmith's hammer, and collapsed there, insensible and still. A little before nightfall, returning from his day's business, the traveller was surprised to see him in the same position, apparently none the worse for his fall, but now sonorously sleeping off the effects of his debauch. Whether that curious mixture of tolerance, brutality, and robustitude is typical of life in Darwin, I cannot say, however.

Shortly after one o'clock I boarded another aeroplane that was, in contrast to the empty Constellation, very briskly full, noisy and genial with coatless men and thinly clad women and children who were being vainly cajoled to sit still and go to sleep. A plane with a bus-load of family passengers, a domestic conveyance with a heap of cargo at the forward end. We flew through the darkness and were wakened by the ruddy blaze of dawn to see below a desert-floor as rough as crocodile skin. A flat and empty land, seemingly interminable, that acquired at last the distinction of wire fences, so that its vastness, though otherwise undifferentiated, was measured and divided; and here and

there, beside a group or line of trees, was a lonely cluster of
farm buildings of unpainted, corrugated iron.   Then the
Blue Mountains, but plateau and chasms were all invisible,
for the sky was full of cloud; and after a rough crossing of
the highlands we landed in Sydney a little before noon.

I had a bath, I ate a beefsteak, and twenty journalists
asked what were my impressions of Australia. . . . I have
been a journalist myself, but the nearest I ever came to putting that sort of question was to enquire the price of some
photographs which a man from Syria had taken after the
suppression of the Druse revolt in 1925.   The photographs
were all of rebels hanging by the neck from lamp-posts, and
I got them cheaply.   We published the best of them in
*The Times of India*, for which I was working at that time,
and they made a very good impression.   The people of
Bombay said the British raj was a great nuisance to them,
but thank God it was less drastic than French rule.—I had
no such guidance, however, to the conditions of life in
Australia, and the journalists, who were tolerant and cheerful people, agreed that twelve hours in the sky might be too
small and frail a foundation on which to build a reasoned
criticism of their life and land.   We drank a lot of tea, we
gossiped for an hour, and then I walked till darkness fell,
and saw the great bridge across the harbour rise in a soaring
curve to meet, as it seemed, the impending sky.   But I was
feeling a little tired, I was in no mood for enthusiasm, and
from what I saw of Sydney that afternoon it looked to me
like a city that was still waiting, resentfully, for its architecture.

At half-past ten I went aboard a flying-boat bound south
and east across the Tasman Sea for Wellington, and slept

uneasily through a lurching night till morning raised a
window-sill of gold beneath a pyramid of rosy cloud, and
the rising sun set half the sky on fire.  On the other side
were the white crests of unseen mountains, and after crossing
brown hills, green valleys, pale inlets of the sea, and lace-
edged islands—a sturdy and charming exercise in carto-
graphy—we circled above what seemed to be a nursery-
town of tiny coloured houses on grassy slopes, and found the
shelter of Wellington's intricate and lovely harbour.

It was half-past eight when I went ashore.  In forty-
eight hours I had flown from Japan to New Zealand, from a
little above latitude 34° in the northern hemisphere to latitude
41°, or thereabout, in the southern; and now, my journey
finished—except for an afternoon flight to Auckland—I
admitted a sensation of weariness.  I went to an hotel and
said, 'I want two large whiskies and soda, and then I'm
going to bed till it's time for lunch.  Will you see that I'm
not disturbed?'

There are licensing laws in New Zealand that restrict the
sale of alcoholic liquors to some trifling period about tea-
time, and I was told that I could not possibly be served with
whisky before breakfast.  But dully and persistently—for
though I was weary I was resolute—I repeated, and went on
repeating, 'Two whiskies, two large whiskies, and soda-
water, in my room.'  I was still in uniform, and perhaps I
appeared to be shell-shocked and dangerous.

I got my whisky.

# XIV

## THE LONG BRIGHT LAND

On the following morning I was sitting at breakfast in the Northern Club in Auckland with two elderly members whose friendliness to a stranger was easy and gentle. But at that time of day their thoughts were a little inclined to melancholy, and one of them said : 'I remember when Mark Twain came here on a lecture-tour. I went to hear him, and I was disappointed. I was terribly disappointed. All he did was to tell a lot of stories. They weren't very good stories, and he didn't tell them particularly well. And I knew them all, anyway. It was just a waste of time going to hear him.'

'I don't agree,' said the other. 'I heard Mark Twain in Dunedin, and I thought he spoke well. He certainly wasn't as bad as you say. But what struck me very much was how old he looked. Unexpectedly old, and tired. I saw him getting out of the train, and there was no one to meet him. He had to carry his own bag, and go and find an hotel. I was sorry for him. He looked awfully lonely, and oh, so old !'

These reminiscences were interesting, but in the circumstances I did not find them encouraging. Recollection of the past, however, was well suited to the atmosphere and furnishing of the club, which was placidly Victorian. The dignity of the furniture had been mollified by long use, the cutlery was solid and expensive, and on the walls hung steel engravings of the great Queen's Diamond Jubilee.

After flying fast and noisily across the circumference of the world it was very pleasant to rest for a day or two in a place so calm, so sturdily confined and comfortingly static. I began, too, to learn a little about the temper and *mores* of the land.

The night before, within an hour or two of my arrival from Wellington, I had been introduced to New Zealand politics. A General Election was in progress, and Mr. Holland, the Prime Minister, had just addressed a large meeting at which the opposition to him was organised and rowdy. In a struggle for authority between the Government and the waterside workers, the Government had lately been successful; and sober people, deeply relieved, were grateful to Mr. Holland for his judicious firmness. But the dockers and their friends were still irate, they packed his meeting and tried to shout him down.—Nothing unusual in that, of course, but at the Northern Club they were surprised and shocked. Such things did not, or should not, happen in New Zealand. In less responsible, more intemperate parts of the world, why, that sort of behaviour was expected nowadays. But not—good God!—not in Auckland!

There is indeed an air of respectability over all, or nearly all, the country. It is a land of unusual beauty : unusual because in a little compass it may show pastoral grace and mountain grandeur, rivers winding through deep woods, and long white beaches—and because the general aspect has so little to spoil it. There are no large scenes of industrial squalor, no excess of human ugliness, and the rural view is hardly ever less than pleasing. There is, in the North Island, a sterile heath which is called, ostentatiously, a desert, and about Rotorua are upland moors which under rain-clouds wear a sombre hue; but they lend a difference to the scene, they please by contrast and make the incredible green pastures under their myriad sheep seem all the brighter. Much of the rural scene is hand-made, smoothed and coloured by hand, for the native bush that covered it a hundred years ago was rough and dark. And the houses of the inhabitants are small and trim and tidy, surrounded by careful gardens: evidence, beyond doubting, of prosperity, of a thoroughly domesticated way of life, of respectability.

It is indeed remarkable that a land so young should appear so mature, in the agricultural sense, and wear so well-kempt a look. To see it, and then remember how brief is its history, is to feel a profound respect for the pioneers who cleared the land and the farmers who have made it so rich and seemly. It was only in 1840 that the New Zealand Company's first settlers arrived in Port Nicholson to build a town called Wellington; Auckland was founded a year later, Otago and Canterbury were settled in 1850. For twenty years the settlers in the north were harassed by war with the Maoris, but schools were built as fields were tilled, flocks multiplied as the bush was burnt, gold was mined, roads were made, government evolved—and when the first New Zealanders born in Christchurch and Dunedin had begun to count their grandchildren, the country was already a self-governing dominion with a bold reputation for social experiment. As an act of creation New Zealand is testimony, not only to the craftsmanship and strength of its settlers, but, more remarkably, to their prevailing wisdom.

Circumstances, however, have not encouraged such an architecture as the landscape deserves. There are broad valleys and generous loopings of tree-lined rivers that mutely, but how insistently, demand for their perfection the deliberate serenity and proportion of a fine Georgian mansion.  Turn the smooth corner of a hill, any one of forty hills, and there is the unrealised situation for a Cotswold manor, or abbey church with flying buttresses and a tall spire soaring thinly to the clouds and a rose-window flowering in the sun.  Here could be a corner for the blazoning of Elizabethan beams, high chimneys, and many-glinting panes of leaded glass; and about Christchurch there is room for the full majesty of the Palladian style.  But elsewhere in the South Island some Scottish modes would be agreeable: the exuberance of Craigievar, or even Glamis, the bleak strength of Hermitage or the simple challenge of Coxton Tower. . . . This grows too fanciful, however, and fancy is hooded, suddenly, by a recollection that both islands suffer from a lack of good building-stone.  Fancy, however, was prompted by the landscape—so gracious, so exuberant— and social theory and economic policy may not always shut out a rage for excellence.

In the long northern peninsula, from Auckland to the Bay of Islands, there has been in recent years a rapid growth of population, a development of some clinical interest.  As in the United States, where California takes immigrants every year from colder parts, the movement, in part at least, is heliotropic.  The migrants go north to seek the sun, and sheep in their heavy clothing, and dairy cattle, graze contentedly on warm pastures newly won from bush and scrub. Pampas grass and cabbage-palms decorate the scene, gorse and the golden *kowhai* gild it.  The land and a bright sea are neighbourly, with long beaches like a braid between them, and tree-ferns stand as signposts to a kindlier latitude. Arum lilies grow wild, mangrove-swamps declare the warmth of the Pacific; and the new settlers express their wonder that anyone should live under a less clement sky. The very thought of cold weather makes them shiver, so they say.

It was along this coast, in 1769, that Captain Cook, with his companions Mr. Banks and Dr. Solander, sailed in high spirits and found for promontories and islands the careless and facetious names that still describe them. Poverty Bay had been left behind, round the corner from Cape Runaway, where a war-canoe had turned when a round-shot was fired above it, and fled so fast that spray flew from prow and paddles. A plenitude of shell-fish and conger-eels gave its name to the Bay of Plenty, and Mount Edgecumbe commemorates a sergeant of marines. A small island was christened the Mayor, a lesser group the Court of Aldermen. On the Hauraki peninsula the astronomer, Mr. Green, went ashore to observe the transit of Mercury and so find his longitude and a name for the bay where he landed; Oyster River and Mangrove River and the Barrier Islands were the products of dull days when imagination made no effort; and a moment of sentimentality named Thames. Bream Bay gave the ship enough fish to feed its crew for two days, and with appetite still lively a group of rocky islets became the Hen and Chickens. North of them are islands that look not unlike Crusaders' effigies, recumbent on stone tombs: the Poor Knights, they were called.

At this sunlit end of New Zealand the *Endeavour* and her complement were always in danger of being surprised by the warlike Maoris, who would put out in their canoes to pelt the English mariners with stones or lie in wait to sur-

round and menace them when they went ashore.   But Cook
was neither aggrieved nor daunted by their hostility.   From
time to time, when a tomahawk too closely threatened, a
native was shot, but even then without animus; and the
voyagers remained calm enough to recognise and admire the
good qualities of the Maoris.   The charm of the story, of
the first voyage at any rate, is in part created by the light-
heartedness that shows so often in a narrative of prodigious
achievement and immutable resolve.   The *Endeavour* was a
bark of 360 tons, about a hundred feet in length, and her
complement numbered ninety-five.   A small ship to explore
the unknown world, and overcrowded, one would say.
But no one, it seems, suffered unduly from anxiety.

I wish, for their pleasure, that Captain Cook and Mr.
Banks and Dr. Solander had found among their larger
discoveries a shell-fish called the *toheroa*.   It is a bivalve that
lives in deep burrows on some of the northern beaches and
feeds on plankton nourished by fresh water seeping down
from inshore lagoons.   It grows almost as big as a saucer, fat
and pearly-white in its shell, and from it a soup is made of
marvellous richness and delicacy, of an exquisite and subtle
flavour that defeated all my effort to define it until, having
eaten two full plates, I realised that if oysters of the best
English sort were fed for a season on asparagus-tips, a con-
coction of them might have such a taste.   I doubt if there is a
better soup in the world than *toheroa* soup, but the poor bivalve has been too much fished, or hunted is the better word,
and now it is so scarce that a law restricts its capture; and
of those that are taken the greater part is tinned and sold to
the United States for dollars.   Though what dollars may
buy, more gratifying to the palate, I cannot think.

It was in a small and good hotel near Whangarei that I found my *toheroa* soup, and Whangarei lies at the head of a gulf that flows into Captain Cook's Bream Bay. It is a little place but prosperous, both port and market town, and because it is a growing town the matter of architecture was again obtrusive. New bungalows were reaching out and covering the nearer fields, and though any one of them looked modest enough—a neat little box of a house, £3000-worth of local habitation and a fancy name—they were collectively extravagant and, I began to feel, an increasing peril to the land. Auckland, with about three hundred thousand of a population, covered an enormous area, and every little town, leaping out in quarter-acre plots, was as prodigal as it could be, and proud of its expansion. Every new house required a quarter of an acre of land, for the New Zealanders, as well as being a sociable people, are independent and like their privacy; and they are all passionate gardeners. But flower-beds and insistence on privacy are eating away the pasture, and when I went to Gisborne, the port of Poverty Bay, I was truly shocked by the rapacity of its trim and pretty streets.

From a hill above the harbour one looks inland, across the town, to a flat alluvial plain of immense fertility and brilliant colour. The central part of the town is pleasantly designed, the river has gardened banks, the business streets are broad and clean. But the growing residential parts are consuming the fat fields, gnawing at pasture, devouring national wealth. Incredible numbers of sheep and cattle can be grazed on those rich and verdant acres. Nowhere except in the yard of a Noah's ark, in some wealthy nursery, can so many animals be seen. A field of forty acres will carry as many as three hundred sheep, and dairy cows need hardly walk to feed, for under their noses the new grass grows while they lie and ruminate. Here is true wealth, a farmer's paradise—and an ever-increasing urban population is covering it with bungalows and rose-beds.

Now if New Zealand's population grows from something less than two millions to rather more than five millions, as many New Zealanders think it should, and all the new arrivals are housed as lavishly as the Gisbornians and Aucklanders, the aspect of the country will be most lamentably changed. The mountains will remain, the tall hills and great alps will survive humanity, but instead of wide green pastures and enormous flocks, prodigious herds, there will be vast archipelagos of bungalow-roofs divided at right angles by navigable channels for a purely urban traffic. And towns so built, even if they discover some wealth on which to live, will never achieve the proper rewards of urban life, which are an intensification of experience and the consequent quickening of mind that living within the pressure of a crowd produces. The growing towns of New Zealand are designed to avoid pressure, they are suburbs gathering about a non-existent *urbs*, and the *urbs* is non-existent—even where some of it has been materially built—because social legislation has decreed that social life must stop at 6 P.M.

Civilisation needs conversation, and conversation requires some help. But in New Zealand the pubs are closed before sundown and the *restaurateur* is by law strangled in his infancy. There are some good hotels, and all I saw were brightly clean; but about the hour when little boys should be put to bed, life ebbs away from their public rooms, as if ashamed to linger. There are no theatres, and the cinema

cannot fill the place of the theatre.   Urban life is poorly
furnished—but *en plein air* life has enormous riches :  there
are rainbow trout in fast-running streams, deer in the woods
and wild pig, mountains for climbing and broad bays to sail
on.   There is grass, moreover, to feed a vast number of swift
and lovely horses, and in their passion for racing the New
Zealanders find an agreeable escape from the prevailing
domesticity of their lives and their egalitarian régime.   They
gamble with the greatest zest :  in the first six months of
1951 a population of less than two millions, of whom many
are infants, wagered £14,534,000 with the totalisators, and
bookmakers, who are popular but not officially recognised,
took an unknown sum in addition to that.—No one has yet
insisted that all race-horses should be born equal.   Horses
are old-fashioned ;  a few are winners, the rest also run.   And
from the order of good government and domesticity the
anarchy of the race-course offers a very pleasant release ;  for
though order is benign, gambling is more natural.

If I were a young novelist born and bred in New Zealand,
I could, I think, find some occasion for satire ;  but as a mere
visitor I must, to be truthful, speak mainly of what is good,
for that is dominant.   I left the country, after a couple of
months, with unusual regret, with a sense of loss.   I found
much enjoyment, though it was incomplete ;  I was filled
with a curiously troubled affection.   I did not want to
leave, though I knew I should be dissatisfied if I stayed.   I
was too old to identify myself with a new land, but I could
imagine the satisfaction of working for it if one belonged
to it.   And there were minor but constantly recurring
pleasures, most of which came in through the eye. . . .

The tawny uplands of the south, rising tumultuously under

miles of tussock-grass to a desolate grandeur like the third act of *Lear*; and the deep black water of Lake Manapouri under mountains freakt with snow. A public garden, clouded with cherry-trees in bloom, through which the glass-clear Avon meandered, and somewhere, beyond a hedge of wild lilies, a flotilla of black swans sailing. Black swans again, an elegant great fleet of them, on a windy lake where I caught a good trout. The rushing, tumultuous little Oto-piri River, and a cliff near Dunedin where a dozen most ex-quisitely groomed and sublimely solemn penguins clowned on slippery paths. The placid small towns of Hamilton and Cambridge, and the majestic sides of Ruapehu. Alpine heights with frosty lances impaled the sky, and wild horses bolted across a moor. Cowmen, roughly mounted, gathered their herds on steep hillsides, and in snug houses—the domestic theme insistently recurs—women vied with their neighbours to whip a stiffer, richer cream. It is a land of fat-ness, and in white silks and muslins fatness decorates, in every town, the photographers' shop-windows. Wedding groups abound, and oh, what brides and bridesmaids broadly smile beyond the glass!

Though the apparatus of living is up to date, though aero-planes are used to spill fertilisers on high pasture and elec-tricity milks the cows, there remains a simplicity of life, and one may still encounter the independence and singularity of mind that were common form before society became con-tinental; when it was still insular.

I was taken one day to meet an elderly farmer in whose sitting-room hung a brightly coloured picture of Charles Edward Stuart, and beneath it a moth-eaten sporran of the XVIIIth century, a Highland dirk that had been fashioned from a Hanoverian bayonet. His father had left Lochaber a hundred years before, and in his speech was an echo of the gravity native to those who are bred in soaring and desolate places. He had lived according to the dictates of his own mind, and the black cattle in his fields were evidence of its singularity. In the fullness of experience he had decided that nature in New Zealand favours the dark in hue—the bush was dark, and so are the Maoris—and to win the favour of the sky he had sold his red-coated Herefords and bought black-polled Angus. He had, moreover, theories about the dinner-table, which is ruined nowadays, he said, because animals in public slaughter-houses are killed in a state of fear, and that distastes their flesh. When he butchered a sheep of his own he used it tenderly before the knife touched its throat, and its flesh was sweet. But the general public had to eat terror-stricken chops and fear-infected steaks, and was not that the reason why fear was endemic in this generation? In his boyhood no one had suffered from a neurosis, no one had been afraid of life.—He was a robust old man, and his morning draught was rum and milk.

Not far away lived a gruff, slow-moving German, formerly a butcher, now a *vigneron*. In 1914 he had suffered from the patriotic feelings of his neighbours and been stoned out of his shop; so retiring to the country, where neighbours were fewer, he had planted a couple of acres with vines and for several years, being wholly ignorant of his new trade, watched in vain for harvest. But stubbornly he had persisted, and now he had in his cellars nearly a score of enormous, complacent-looking casks that held 800 gallons apiece, a multitude of bottles ready for sale, and customers for every quart. He sold direct to his customers. 'Why should I pay a middleman? Can't he work too?'—He made sherry, marsala, madeira, and port, he said; and sold all his produce when it was two years old, because his clients could wait no longer. He moved heavily on his feet, and with heavy hands uncorked a few bottles and washed some small thick glasses. With ponderous tread he went into his kitchen and returned with a plump cylinder of pork sausage. This he cut, slowly and expertly, with a jack-knife, and sitting on boxes in his cellar we ate and drank. The sausage was admirably seasoned, the wine a little too sweet for my taste, and doubtless because my palate had been poorly taught, I found some difficulty in distinguishing one from another. But they were clearly labelled—sherry and port, madeira and marsala—and the customers could have their choice. Hoarsely kind, wheezing a little, he poured another glass. Once he had been stoned because he was a German, but now he was courted because he grew wine, and need seek no one's favour. He dispensed favour.

In Whangarei, where the fortunate traveller may be given *toheroa* soup, I had been introduced to a self-made scholar : one of those rare men who, early in life discovering some matter that excites their interest, dedicate themselves to its cultivation, or exploration, and let life be shaped by their enthusiasm. The scholar of Whangarei was a chemist by profession, his name was Reed, and his subject was the elder Dumas. He had a library, meticulously ordered, that contained all the known editions of the innumerable works of that prodigal genius, and in carefully bound typescript, translations into English of Dumas' twenty or more romantic plays. Mr. Reed had taught himself French in order to fulfil this duty to his idol. He had spent large sums of money on

his collection, he had corresponded with booksellers and
fellow-scholars throughout Europe. Laboriously he had
compiled bibliographies of the novels, plays, and miscellaneous works, and presented copies of them to the British
Museum and the Library of Congress. He presented me
with a quarto volume, a general bibliography of nearly five
hundred pages, brought up to date since it was printed by
the addition of manuscript notes and inserted pages in
typescript. His enthusiasm had not grown weary, the spell
was still upon him—and for a lifetime of work the reward
was what?

It is an impertinence, I suppose, to say of any man that
he is happy; but when, at seventy-odd years of age, a
lively and ardent mind is discovered behind the placid mien
of a lifelong scholar—when an old man talks with the
exuberance of youth about a subject to which he has been
faithful for half a century—why, there is some reason for
suspecting happiness. That the miscellaneous writings of
Alexandre Dumas are of much importance in the atomic
age may be doubted, and perhaps his romantic plays now
only serve to satisfy an academic curiosity. But why should
a man's work be utilitarian? If utility were the only
standard there would be no true excellence in work, but only
catchpenny toil. To work for love is to set a proper
example, and if happiness is the profit, then the example is
worth our scrutiny.

During this time the General Election was continuing its
course, and though, on the whole, the political oratory was
not distinguished, I heard one speaker who deeply impressed
me. This was Mr. Sullivan, the Minister of Labour in Mr.
Holland's government. I heard him deliver the final

address of his campaign in the little town of Whakatane, and even his opponents had to admire the physique of his eloquence. With scarcely a pause and no sign of fatigue, he spoke for a hundred and twenty minutes, and what he said was without art or rhetorical device, but as purposeful as the in-coming tide and as clear as sea-water in its honesty. As politicians must, he denounced the other side, but always with homely particularity in his charges, and a sort of down-to-earth impatience. He did not claim, but seemed to imply, that administration might be more important than legislation, and then, with no advertisement of its importance, made the remarkable statement that the work of the welfare state must continue, but paternalism could only be paid for by private enterprise and the judicious taxation of its profits.

There, I thought, was substance for a whole speech, but almost casually he threw it out, as though its truth were self-evident, and presently discharged a resounding question that shook my seated ribs. He reverted to the Labour Party's record, and warmly denounced some measure it had suggested. 'Suppose that had become law,' he said. 'Suppose that's the policy New Zealand was committed to. Would that be any benefit to the British Empire?'

A few months later there was a General Election in Britain, but I doubt if that question were often put to a meeting; and certainly it was not often used as a fly-paper for loose votes. Our wild old wicked island in the sea is no longer wild, no longer very wicked, and sometimes a little more parochial than insular. For a larger view—why, go to New Zealand!

G

# XV

## MAORIS AND ISLANDERS

WHAKETANE faces the sun on the Bay of Plenty, and is a place of some importance in the history of New Zealand. One of the canoes of the great migration from Tahiti, in the XIVth century, landed there, and it is said that all the Maoris in that part of the country can trace their descent from its commander. My host, for a morning, may have had an even more distinguished ancestry in a colder region; for though his complexion was dark, his name was Stewart. The early Scottish settlers appear to have contracted native alliances with mutual cordiality, and Maoris and High-landers, indeed, have much in common. Both exercise a solemn respect and a considerable talent for genealogy, and neither use to attach much importance to the workaday side of life. Mr. Stewart's little girls wore, proudly enough, skirts of the royal tartan, and though I had not expected to see that bold red pattern in Whaketane, I had to admit their right to it by consanguinity and congruity too.

I had my first experience, in his house, of an entertainment common throughout New Zealand. They call it *morning tea*, and serve it about ten o'clock; but it may be a formidable meal. It was so in Whaketane. A double-decked trolley appeared, laden with sandwiches both sweet and savoury, asparagus rolls and sausage rolls, and great sponge-cakes the size of a hat-box bisected by a two-inch layer of stiff cream, with biscuits of this sort and that, and buns of many flavours : no picnic nonsense about it, but all the formality of linen, good china, and silver. We talked of Maori ways and Highland ways, and on the walls of the room hung portraits of the four sons of the family who had gone to the war and come home again, and the two who had not returned.

A few hours later I sat down to a rougher meal. I was taken to see a farm settlement where a small tribe, or sept, that had eluded civilisation till some twenty years before, now lived contentedly and worked their land. We were received with antique ceremony by a score of elderly men who, in the working clothes of farmers, sat on benches on an open space of turf before their meeting-house. We took our seats on benches facing them, some twenty-five yards away, and after a little silence the chief of the tribe stood up and with a shout began the traditional *haka*. The old men stamped and shook their staves, and looked fierce enough, and when the war-dance was done there was a hoarsely valorous song, then speeches : first of challenging enquiry, and finally of welcome. A Maori pastor sat beside me to translate, and with some surprise I heard that I was being received as one sent by the King to represent the Church of England. I made no attempt to correct this impression, but replied with what dignity I could summon to my help, and walking slowly forward, pressed my nose to the old chief's nose with a pseudo-apostolic touch.

The long meeting-house, its red timbers elaborately carved, was decorated with photographs of the Royal Family and local heroes. The names of those who had been killed in war, and those who had returned, were inscribed on panels. Except for this adornment the hall was empty. There were no chairs or committee-room tables. The Maoris take their blankets to a tribal meeting, and when they have had enough of formal rhetoric, continue to argue in comfort, at full length. Their conferences usually last all night.

Our dinner, in the meantime, was cooking in an oven of hot stones under a cover of earth and leaves and wet sacking: great gobbets of pork, hens cut roughly in half, and a bushel or so of potatoes. We had an admirable meal, one of the best I ate in New Zealand, for the meat was perfectly cooked and the flavour surprisingly rich. We did not, however, eat it heroically, as we should have done, with bare hands, but seated politely at trestle-tables decorated with paper napkins and bottles of mineral water; and the major course was followed by fruit salad and cream, as if to emphasise the obvious fact that cooking on hot stones was only a ceremony now, like the *haka* of the old men.

I visited several Maori settlements about the Bay of Plenty, and some of their meeting-halls were full of the most intricate carving, every post and panel decorated with formal pattern or genially grotesque effigies with mother-of-pearl eyes and protruding tongues. In all of them were the names of their soldiers who had fought in the two great wars, and here and there a private war memorial had been raised in a cottage garden. The Maoris were good soldiers, and are proud of their dead. They appear also, in despite of critic-ism, to be capable of farming well, and some of them have so far accepted the conventions of their white neighbours as to be house-proud. It is often said, however, that they are incurably idle, and a good many critics of the sort who con-sider themselves hard-headed and business-like complain that successive governments have pampered them and spent unreasonable sums of money on their housing and education. In Auckland and Wellington, admittedly, the Maoris show to less advantage than in country districts. It is not exactly a colour-bar that confines them to the poorer parts of the cities, but lack of thrift or lack of favour, on one side and the other, may have the same effect. In the country they appear high-spirited, of jovial demeanour, and their broad, deep-chested strength is impressive. To the visitor, moreover, their voices recommend them.

The voice and accent of a white New Zealander are not, typically, his most prepossessing parts. People of sturdy build and healthy constitution often surprise the stranger by voices that are curiously thin, bloodless, and without resonance; and a habit has grown of so maltreating the vowels as to create an image, in the listening stranger's mind, not of vocal cords at work, but of a mangle. Such deficiency and misconduct of speech are not a class distinction; they occur in people with little education, and people with more. They are not universal, but sufficiently common to be regarded, at any rate, as a sub-characteristic. The Maori, on the other hand—unless he has been demoralised by urban life—has a voice that comes pouring from the barrel of his chest in a melodious flood, and with pearly precision the vowels bounce and play upon a drum-like resonance. He is a natural orator, and his native language is fanciful and picturesque. There are no sibilants in his alphabet, and a nasal quality in his singing voice acquires generosity from the noble spaces of his nares.

The idleness which is a general charge against the Maoris is sometimes defined: 'They'll work all right, they'll work hard, so long as they're interested in what they're doing.

But when they lose interest, they'll quit.'—Now this may be a criticism of industrial civilisation rather than of the Maoris; and before judgement is made, the climate should be taken into consideration. A good many white New Zealanders of the older generation, with a memory of pioneering days, complain that the younger people of both sorts have lost the will to work. 'It isn't the Maoris, it's our own people who are the problem,' said an irritated man of the business-like, hard-headed sort. 'They're getting too like the Maoris, they're falling into the Maori tempo.' That, I should say, is an exaggeration; but I heard it more than once. And, on the other side, the excellent, dedicated officers of the Department of Maori Affairs were not quite sure whether their proper task was to encourage the Maoris to become better Maoris, or teach them how to live like Europeans. To Europeanise them would destroy their traditions, cut them adrift from their own history; but the old Maori way of life had become an anachronism, and in the modern world they could not justify their existence by dancing the *poi* dance and the *haka*—except, on occasion, at Rotorua.

Rotorua is decried by the more sophisticated New Zealanders, who warn the visitor that he must not take it seriously. But I was delighted by it all, by the natural scenery, the unnatural scenery, and the Maori dances. 'Only a tourist resort,' I was told; but the most profound and terrific forces of our world have shaped it, fantastically and beautifully, for the tourist's pleasure, and I could have spent, very happily, a long time on that wild volcanic plateau, and many hours beside every gurgling pool of mud that pouts and sulks, and blows horrible grimaces as the steam from a subterranean furnace animates the silken-soft, the boiling-hot, the treacherous smooth slime. Sulphur encrusts the firmer ledges on the little peaks that miniature eruption has created: yellow and sinister against a background of spouting vapour, against a roaring tumult of terrene flatulence. Here murder is invited, where a narrow path, bordered on one side by the innocent *manuka*, on the other falls into boiling deliquescence; and murder, it is said, has here and there been done. But then, a little farther on, is a child's playground, and the mud blows nursery bubbles and fattens in sunny smiles. 'Thermal activity', the guide-book calls it, but plastic turbulence is a better description—or a crèche for Satan's young.

This aspect of Rotorua was, for me, set in a most agreeable contrast by a lecture I gave to an audience that consisted, almost entirely, of elderly ladies, invulnerably respectable, prosperous as it seemed, and all very smartly dressed. I talked to them about the problems of the modern novelist, I spoke of Henry James, I laid a light finger on the re-emergence of evil as a literary theme, I mentioned abstraction, I was respectful to Miss Bowen. The ladies listened without a movement of impatience, and without a stir of interest—but in a twinkling, as soon as I had finished, they rose in a susurrus of fluttered silks and linens, and hurrying, bustling, brightly chattering, they brought from an inner room an admirable light supper of sandwiches, both sweet and savoury, of flocculent sponges bursting above an intermediary of cream, of asparagus rolls and sausage rolls and buns in rich variety, with all the dignities of linen, silver, and respectable china. And now, for solid comfort, enthusiasm was uninhibited.—But only a few hundred yards away, in the darkness of the night, a hot and puffing steam rose from the broken earth, the clay of our common substance put on risible and demoniac shapes, and the moist air smelt of sulphur.

I was fortunate again when a distinguished visitor arrived, whose entertainment I was allowed to share. This was Lord Jowitt, then Lord Chancellor of England, and the exhibition arranged for him was of the very sort that my more sophisticated friends had deprecated for its artificiality; but I thought it beautiful and very moving, and doubly moving because it was no longer real. The *haka* stirred the blood, the chorus of male voices beat upon one's mind like war-drums, the *poi* dances were charmingly fanciful and deft as juggling. The men were muscular and handsome, a few of the women lovely, and one or two of them richly fat and comical. A couple of half-caste girls had that delectable, transient, and hybrid attraction that cannot be transmitted or preserved, and one full-blooded Maori woman, strongly built, with an heroic bone structure, wore a look of passionate grief, of epic passion for ever defeated, that made her like imagination's thought of Dido on the shore of Carthage when Aeneas left her for the colder north. They wore their native costumes, more decoration than clothing; a little rueful for progress, one realised that nowadays they only dressed up for a party, but formerly they had dressed up for life.

When the dancing was done, the guests made speeches; and I was rewarded for mine by the prettiest compliment. There were two old, old Maori women, wrinkled and chubby, with blue-tattooed chins, who, uninvited, had come in with the dancers to see the sport, and after the Lord Chancellor and I had protested our gratitude one of them shuffled towards me, accompanied by a half-caste girl who said, 'This old lady cannot speak English, but she has asked me to say that she would like to press noses with you.' Warmly I embraced her, closely applied my nose to hers— the Lord Chancellor had received no such invitation—and cackling contentedly she rejoined her fellow-crone.

The New Zealand Government, I think, does well to be generous to the Maoris. They are a genial and gallant people, and nowadays prolific. Their numbers are small in comparison with the whole population, but their birth-rate is much higher than that of their white neighbours; and generous treatment of a growing minority is statesmanlike as well as charitable.

At the other end of New Zealand, in the extreme south, I met a small community that reversed the general trend and was diminishing. This was in Stewart Island, which is separated from the butt of Southland by the rough waters of Foveaux Strait, that lave and nourish a multitude of very good oysters. Stewart Island was a port of call for whalers before the first settlers arrived in the North Island, and Maoris of the north did battle there, with their cousins of the south, for mutton-birds: the sooty shearwater, that is, of which a quarter of a million are still taken every year to be salted and preserved in their own fat in bags made of giant seaweed. The island's human settlers are decreasing, but its waters teem with fish and its many bays and inlets are populous with birds.

The melodious *tui*, or parson-bird, and the bell-bird that is a flautist rather than a campanologer, are numerous and very tame in the settled parts about Halfmoon Bay; and on a windy beach in Paterson Inlet I saw a great flock of god-wits, newly come from Alaska or Siberia, and another of banded dotterels with black and rufous breasts.  There were little blue penguins, quickly diving, in the sea, and the handsomer, yellow-browed penguins; and black-and-white pied shags roosted on fouled trees that overhung the water.  There were grey warblers cheerfully singing in the bush, and red-billed gulls, like kittiwakes, industriously scavenging the bays.  A picnic party will attract a curious, tawny and black-striped bird, incapable of flight, about the size of a bantam, that is called the wood-hen or *weka*; and in dense bush a company of *kakas*, a plump brown parrot, may be summoned, to crash noisily through the branches and converse in harsh voices, by anyone who is able to imitate—with straining throat and bursting cheeks—their croaking, bubbling cry.

Stewart Island is forty miles long and twenty miles across, and its highest hill is over three thousand feet.  Its tiny population is clustered round a village called Oban, on Half-moon Bay, and within two or three miles of Oban one can lose one's way in the bush.  Among the first stories one hears, indeed, are dismal anecdotes of men, confident in their knowledge of the bush or shipwrecked, it may be, on the farther side, who set out to cross the island and never reappeared.  It is a place of remarkable beauty, with its densely forested hills and broad inland sea studded with islands; but I thought it sinister.  This, however, is not the opinion of the New Zealanders, some of whom profess a cult of it.  In the two main islands the bush has almost disappeared, it has been cut and burnt to make room for pasture, and the descendants of the pioneers regret, a little, the drastic energy of their fathers.    But in Stewart Island the native forest dominates the scene, the islanders live in scanty clearings, and the survival of what-used-to-be excites not only a natural pleasure in a different view, but a sort of piety : a reverence for the beginning of history.

The bush, indeed, has a wild and excessive appeal.    There is a furious, unregulated growth which can produce a surplus of ornamentation within a turbulent magnificence. Big trees abound, and lianas and scrub-growth fill the intervals between them.    There are superb trees, the red pine called *rimu* with its grey trunk and yellow-green foliage, and the stringy-barked, enormous *totara*.    The scarlet-flowered ironwood grows on the edge of the bush, the yellow *kowhai* does not deeply penetrate.    Ferns and tree-ferns flourish, the lancewood perplexingly changes its shape, supple-jack entwines your heels, and stinkwood is garlanded with little dark-red flowers.    There is red or black beech, there is mutton-bird scrub with thick green leaves that have white undersides, there are, perhaps, a dozen others.    If you know where you are, you can sit down and enjoy them; if you are lost, they will embrace and surround you with multiform entanglement and growing fear.    So long as I was within hailing distance of my companions I was enchanted by the bush; but if, for a moment or two, I was beyond their call, claustrophobia threatened me.

There are two brothers there, descendants of a family that had once owned considerable estates in Orkney, who lived what is conventionally called a simple life and taught me, quite unconsciously, how much knowledge and skill a simple life demands.    They were no longer young, but very active in their habit and seemingly of great endurance.

They were skilful woodsmen : they knew their way about the bush, and knew the trees in it. They were discerning naturalists, marvellously quick of eye, apt with a rifle and useful fishermen. They sailed a boat and could repair a faltering engine. They had all the domestic arts, and were good gardeners—but that is no distinction in Stewart Island, where gardening is hardly less than a religion.

I spent a day at sea with them, and they took me up a curious, serpentine river that flowed, black and sluggish, through flat lands densely covered with high *manuka*, until, a long way up, the stream narrowed and we came to an almost imperceptible clearing and a half-ruined hut. We tied up to the bank, and one of the brothers went off with his rifle to try to find a deer. The other sat down contentedly in the little engine-room and took the carburettor to pieces. His wife, and a lecturer from Otago University who was my travelling companion at the time, went ashore to light a fire and rig miniature shear-legs and cross-beam for a cooking-pot. Mosquitoes and midges joined the meal, though a smudge-fire did something to discourage them. It began to rain, but no one was disconcerted. The deer-stalker, though he had failed to find a deer close at hand, felt confident of getting one if he tried again and went farther ; and there was some talk of the likelihood of running aground on the homeward voyage, for the estuary of the black river was tidal, and now the tide would be ebbing. They spoke of it, not with foreboding, but with a thinly concealed relish, and it became fairly evident that they were looking for an excuse to spend a night in the bush. There was a not-quite-ruined hut beside us, there was a rug in the boat that anyone could have who wanted it, the deer-stalker would shoot a deer, and it would be easy enough to light another cooking-fire and more smudge-fires to keep the mosquitoes at bay.—But the rain grew heavier, the sky darkened over the hills before a coming storm, and reluctantly they went aboard again. We had left, in the morning, in clear, calm weather; we sailed back across the inland sea in half a gale.

I returned to the mainland in a small, neatly fashioned, amphibious plane that ran down the beach at Halfmoon Bay, pulled up its wheels, and dexterously rose from an oily swell; circled above a rough-coated peninsula, headed north over Foveaux Strait, and a few minutes later landed near Invercargill.—The distinguishing feature of civilisation is that it makes far fewer demands on one than a simple life in communion with nature.

As a tourist, as a sightseer, I was disabled by an obligation to write, with no loss of time, an account of the British troops in Korea. I carried with me a bundle of notes and documents, and wherever I went I had to work for some hours a day and gradually reduce my untidy dossier to the ordered shape of a plain, straightforward narrative. I was conscientious, and finished my task before leaving. In the early weeks, moreover, I had to give some time to consideration of my lectures.

The university colleges supplied the best and most unnerving audiences. They were alert, they listened closely, and sometimes I was afraid they might believe too deeply. I always quoted Shaw to them: 'It was reading that made Don Quixote a gentleman, it was believing what he read that made him mad'.—To be a university teacher might have great rewards, for the sense of youth in the country sharpens, I think, the appetite of the young. They are insular in habit, but well aware of the world that lies beyond their shores. They live within their native boundaries, but do not appear to be confined by them. A man with a vocation for teaching would not waste his time, but his responsibility would be grave. His students might believe him.

I lectured also, on the war in Korea, to several branches of the New Zealand Officers' Club. The audiences were large, and revealed the pride in military service that is the other side of the national character. A domesticated life is the norm in ordinary times, but when war has spun the coin the reverse shows a military inscription. At one of these meetings a very distinguished soldier quoted with approval a sentence I had once written, and forgotten, in which I spoke of 'New Zealanders who looked like Cromwell's Ironsides, and fought with pride and professional severity'. That was a true description, he said.

For audiences of a mixed sort I devised an exhibition of gossip : not idly, but as a characteristic of English writing. From the *Canterbury Tales* to *Ulysses* the sound of gossip rises above our literature. Spenser and Milton and Sir Thomas Browne are not typical of the shelves they overawe, Byron is a lonely figure, Doughty and Conrad stand aloof. Chaucer's *Prologue* set the style for us, and as soon as a readable prose was elaborated the novelists and the Augustan essayists discovered new inns full of strong characters with curious habits and remarkable features. Sir Roger de Coverley and Moll Flanders asserted a humanism of which gossip is the natural tongue. *Tom Jones* and *Tess of the d'Urbervilles* are ale-house tales writ large. In great books and little ones we find new neighbours, more brightly hued, louder of step and livelier of tongue than live next door, but recognisably of our kind. Dickens nearly spoiled the procession by inventing carnival figures, but still it goes on.

Now this, or something of the sort, I said because gossip is the favourite sort of conversation in New Zealand, and I thought, by relating an audience's familiar theme to literature—by showing that what they talked about, good authors had written about, and done it better—I might encourage them to read, more fondly, better books, and so enrich the style and flavour of their gossip. But otherwise I was guiltless of any attempt to improve, or reform, or to preach. I was tempted, more than once, to say something about cooking, but as a guest in the country I thought criticism would be ungracious, and might even be resented. And yet . . .

The natural quality of the food is so good that it deserves both skill and reverence in the kitchen. What lordly dishes a French housewife would make of it! But the New Zealanders, like the Scots, think that baking is the better part of cookery, and spend their ingenuity, exhaust their interest, on cakes and pastries and ebullient, vast cream sponges. Soup is neglected, meat mishandled. I have seen their admirable mutton brought upon the table in such miserable shape that the hogget—so they call a sheep of uncertain age—appeared to have been killed by a bomb, and the fragments of its carcase incinerated in the resultant fire. But on the lowest depth of all was a fish restaurant in a small town that perhaps I should not name. I was driving with my friend, the lecturer from Otago University, and we stopped there, at the mid-point of a long journey, because there was nowhere else to stop and be fed. We went into a room where six small tables were cleanly laid, and a waitress with an impatient gesture slapt down a hand-written menu. She was an extremely pretty girl, in the Irish way of prettiness, but seemed out of temper. I asked her what she would recommend, and contemptuously she snorted at me.

'I wouldn't recommend a thing,' she said. 'I never touch their fish!'

# XVI

## THE TASMAN SEA

My table companions, in the ship that carried me from Auckland to Sydney, had little conversation. The young purser wore a friendly smile but was otherwise uncommunicative, and there was a girl who admitted, disconsolately, that she never knew what to say; but on deck, one morning, she waved to a passing sailor and in a sudden gush of confidence declared, 'He's a lovely boy!' She was Australian, and for some months had been visiting New Zealand as a sort of working tourist. She had found casual employment, usually in hotels, easily enough, and she was going home with reluctance to tend an ailing mother. She liked New Zealand, but remembered little of what she had seen there. In one town she had had good quarters and an easy employer; in another the food was poor and customers hurried away without tipping.—Such were her recollections, and the only motive for her travels that I could discover was mere restlessness. It is a characteristic of the Australian aboriginal, who will leave a good job, and possibly his family, for no other reason than a suddenly compelling desire 'to go walkabout'; and a good many white Australians seem to have inherited from the land a similar nomadic tendency.

On my other side, at table, sat a neat little, pretty little, shy and bespectacled nurse who was returning to a remote island in the New Hebrides where, in a population of five

thousand Polynesians and Melanesians, the white community consisted of a trader and his wife, two nurses, and two
women teachers in an Anglican mission.   She had no visible
qualifications for so arduous and lonely an existence, and her
holiday at home had been little more than an opportunity
to rebuild her strength.   'I'd had fever and lost more than
two stone,' she said, 'and then the engines broke down in the
little trading steamer I came back in, and we ran short of
food.   I suppose I looked a wreck when I got to Christchurch.   I couldn't go anywhere but mother came running
after me with a glass of milk.'—But it is hardly true to say
that she had *no* visible qualifications for her comfortless and
dedicated life, because when she spoke of its difficulties—
after her shyness had worn off a little—a new light appeared
in her eyes, a modest but dancing light behind her spectacles,
and in deep humility beside her I recognised the gaiety that
sometimes lies on sheer goodness : like a natural bloom in
youth, a polished obstinacy in later life.

   She told me one day of a crisis in the mission hospital
when a native was brought in, bleeding from half a dozen
axe-wounds that an angry wife had inflicted, and she and
her fellow-nurse had realised that before the gaping crevices
could be cleaned and stitched, the patient must be anaesthe-
tised.   But neither of them, at that time, had been trained to
give an anaesthetic, and very nervously they administered
nitrous oxide with one eye upon the book.   A crowd of the
victim's fellow-villagers pressed against the windows, and
were amazed, then angry, when the wounded man collapsed
in seeming death.   The nurses were afraid they would be
attacked, and in desperate haste swabbed and stitched the
maltreated flesh, and just as they had finished, their patient

woke up.  He woke up singing, and the horde of villagers broke into the hospital in exuberant delight to congratulate him on his return to life, while the two nurses added to the noise the half-hysterical laughter of relief.

The silent but good-humoured purser invited us and two or three of the ship's officers to drink with him in his cabin; and again I found some difficulty in prompting and maintaining conversation, till I persuaded the little nurse to tell her story of the resurrection.  She had a great success with it, and I felt very pleased to see modesty surrounded by an audience.

Except at meal-times, when some conversation is necessary to give boiled mutton a flavour, I did not seek conversation; for in New Zealand I had been swimming down an almost continuous stream of colloquy and chatter, and it pleased me, for a change, to be taciturn and solitary.  I had begun, moreover, to write a few notes on what I had seen of New Zealand, and what I thought of its social landscape; and with some perturbation I was beginning to anticipate my visit to Australia.  In New Zealand all my travel had been arranged for me, but I was going to Australia privately, a free agent.  It would be utter folly and a shocking waste of opportunity, I had told myself, to leave the other hemisphere without seeing something of it.  But how much, of so vast a land, could I hope to see in six weeks? How should I plan my journey?

I had decided to move in one direction.  I had less inclination to look at the cities than at what lay beyond them, and my intention was to go north from Sydney, to see some part of the Barrier Reef, and so into Northern Queensland. Then to New Guinea.—But in the middle of the Tasman

Sea I began to wonder why I had included New Guinea in my journey. It seemed, on reflexion, a most improbable destination for a tourist's idle fancy.

I had been writing for several hours that evening, and to assist my hand and memory I had been drinking, in my cabin, a little whisky and tap-water. About midnight, when all the ship was quiet—for the New Zealanders went early to bed—I walked round the tilting deck and with a familiar delight looked at the ebony-black sea, streaming and freakt with foam, that raced astern over immeasurable depths. The ocean-sea at night is a perpetual, awe-striking pleasure— pitch-dark, unfathomable, but conquering ships inscribe their signature upon its surface—and as I walked, round and round again, my delight was reinforced by the lurching, jovial movement of the vessel, and my progress became something of a dance. The weather-side was wet with spray, the deck was slippery, and once, when turning before the wind, I slid and stumbled and leapt for safety to a stan- chion.—But was it wholly the rise and fall of the sea that upset my balance, or was it, in part, the whisky and tap- water I had been drinking? I could not, with precision, decide; and felt no compulsion to do so. For with a marvellous clarity and a robust assurance that the white- crested, black waves appeared to fortify, I perceived that philosophically there was no reason to suppose a state of inebriety less desirable than stark soberness. Morally, per- haps, and socially, yes; but philosophically, no. Inebriety had its pleasures and satisfactions—I danced again round the streaming, lurching, wind-swept corner—and who could say that sobriety had better? Why, even morally—well, men in liquor have been guilty of fearful things, but so have sober men. They were sober men, presumably, who invented the atom bomb, and have drunkards ever done worse than that?

Wet and tired and contented, I returned to my cabin, and as though a window-blind had been drawn from before it, I saw, staring through the glass, the reason for my journey to New Guinea. It was an old, old reason, native to a colder climate and the romantic dreams of youth. But not my youth. . . .

In the southernmost parts of New Zealand I had met several people whose birthplace and relations I knew in Orkney, and while talking to them I had revisited some forgotten places of my boyhood. There was a woman whom I remembered as a red-faced, laughing girl in a farm where we lodged throughout a rain-drenched, blissful summer; and I found her, still rosy of cheek but grey-haired and stooping a little, mistress of prosperous fields all snugly fenced on rich and level ground—wealthier far than ever she would have been at home—but with tear-stained eyes and in a shaken voice she told me that never, in more than forty years, had she ceased to regret the little wind-blown acres of her childhood, a shallow loch below the house, and the waving of wild lupins beyond the garden dyke; and her sorrow in prosperity was an epitome of the exile's pain that holds, like mortar, the building of a new land.—I had thought much of Orkney, and subconsciously, I suppose, already uncovered the reason I was looking for.

In the years that followed the first great war, when I was a medical student, I became friendly with our parish doctor. He was a good doctor, but suffered from the frustration of a romantic nature. He had served in some minor expedition to the Arctic, he had ventured uncomfortably into the upper reaches of the Amazon, he had enjoyed other voyages of exploration; and then, falling in love with a very young but precociously attractive girl, had married and settled into a country practice. He compensated himself for his lost Amazon, his abandoned Polar ice, by shooting grouse and snipe with assiduity, by fishing the Harray Loch with a fine hand; but Orkney winters are long, and when there was nothing to shoot and no fish to be caught, he took to drink. In August and September, in the summer vacations, I used sometimes to shoot with him, and afterwards we would talk about the voyages or marches of exploration that could still be made in the world. There was one in particular on which he had set his heart, and often I heard of the Fly River and its fever-stricken swamps, the fearsome ridges of saw-toothed limestone that rise above its source, and the Sepik that falls beyond them to the other sea.

Until the pedantry of medical education, in its earlier phases, obscured my spirit, I was, in some respects, a fairly enthusiastic student. Once, at some risk to myself, I made a post-mortem examination of a cow that, it was feared, had died of anthrax. In another part of the island the disease had been reported, and the farmer whose prize beast had suddenly expired was very frightened. He called on me after dark one evening, and pleaded with me to come and look at it; so I climbed into his trap and drove away with him. The cow lay under a bank of meadowsweet beside a deep-cut ditch, and first of all we rigged a tarpaulin screen to conceal the light of two stable lanterns. We flayed the skin from the upper half of the body, and with a carpenter's saw I cut out a great section of its ribs. I was somewhat puzzled by what appeared to be a gross confusion of organs lying beneath, but after laborious partition of what, I suppose, were its lungs, I discovered the heart; and then, triumphantly, was able to show a collection of yellow globules about the valves. 'There's no sign of anthrax here,' I said firmly.—I had no idea what the signs of anthrax were, but time had not yet invaded the fine confidence of youth.— 'It's fatty degeneration of the heart that killed her. I told you you'd been overfeeding when I was fishing here last week; and that's the cause of death.'

The farmer was very grateful to me. For several years I shot over his hill and marsh, free of payment, and with a meal waiting for me whenever I cared to stop at his house; and always I congratulated myself on the profits of ignorance, for if I had known more about anthrax I would certainly never have gone near his cow.

It was, perhaps, some rumour of my post-mortem practice that persuaded the doctor's wife, when the doctor pursued his winter drinking into summer, and fell seriously ill, to ask me to look after his practice. She had tried, and failed, to find a qualified locum tenens; and I was the nearest likeness to a medical man for a good many miles around. I had just failed my second professional examination for the second time, I think, but in the liberal conditions of the post-war years I had done some surgery, a little pathology and materia medica, and my midwifery practice. I was given the loan of a motor-bicycle, and accepted my responsibilities without excessive anxiety. The doctor's wife was a self-taught but fairly efficient dispenser, and she knew what medicines were preferred by the regular patients to whom medicine had become a habit.

For a few days I had nothing to worry about—a woman was kicked by a cow, a man cut his hand on a scythe, a child got measles—but then I was summoned to a woman in labour, and dreadful fears assailed me, on my motor-bicycle, of a breech presentation, of twins, of haemorrhage, and a twisted cord. But she, thank God, had neither doubt nor fear. She had had healthy children before, and calmly she gave birth to another. I remembered all I had been taught, I was tolerably quick and earnestly careful. I bathed the child, and left both of them tidy, and with knees still trembling a little went down to the kitchen. Warmly the husband shook my hand, and gave me a tumbler half filled with rum.—The night air was frostily cold, the motor-bicycle steered itself and swiftly ran of its own impulse, and through dark clouds a wild moon sprang to play absurdly with its reflexion in the loch.

I was, perhaps, a little over-confident on the following day, and rode unperturbed to see a difficult case in the northern part of the island. This was an elderly woman who, the victim to a sense of persecution, had begun to suffer also from retention of the urine. Without much trouble I relieved her of physical pain, and several times returned to help her disability. Presently, with most lamentable ambition, I began to think I might also find an exit for the pressure on her mind, and one day after the smaller operation had been performed, I persuaded her to talk about the *idée fixe* that burdened her. She had discovered I was sympathetic, and she was willing to tell me of the danger in which she lived. There was a woman in a nearby farm who for long had been jealous of her, and had tried in various ways to ruin her life; and now was bent on murder. She dragged me to a little window, and showed me the house of her enemy. Her voice grew louder, her excitement quickened as she looked across a pot of geraniums on the window-sill at the greystone roof of a cottage on the hill— and the hard, strong grip of her hands tightened on my arms. She would not let go, and I could not break her hold. Her anger turned against me, and as her voice rose to a scream she shook me till my head nid-nodded on my neck. I decided that her sense of persecution could very fairly be described as mania, and felt some fear for my safety. But her brother came in before she grew really violent, and with gentle authority quietened her almost at once. They were both respectable, good, hard-working people—her normal expression had little resemblance to her maniacal look— and I had seen the rationale of an earlier diagnosis. It would not have been difficult, in older circumstances, to believe that she was possessed of a devil.

But the doctor, who was now almost recovered from his illness, laughed very heartily when I showed him the bruises on my arms and confessed my fright. He told me some gossip of the countryside—in the lonelier places people often had strange fancies about their neighbours—and then, I dare say, we talked of the farther world, and exploration, and the sources of the Sepik and the Fly. He had something which could be called, perhaps, a distant cousin of an *idée fixe* about New Guinea; and it was the interest I had acquired from him that was about to take me there. The motive was his, not mine.

# XVII

## THE CITY OF YOUTH

THERE was a woman in Sydney who worked at the reception desk of a good hotel. She was of middle age, friendly and efficient. She did me a number of small services, and one day while I was talking to her, idly enough, she sighed and said, 'I've just heard we're all to get a rise in pay after Christmas.'

She paused, as though to consider the coming year, and added lugubriously, 'And then we'll all be worse off than ever.'

It was, I suppose, a shrewd comment on the course of inflation; and her understanding, her realism, were typical of Australian thought, which was quite unlike Australian practice. One heard on all hands criticism of the financial or economic structure of the country, and everywhere there seemed to be a curiously tolerant acquiescence in policies that were generally regarded as quite unrealistic. Vast sums of money had recently been made on the annual sale of wool, but no one, it appeared, would be the richer. Either the wool-sellers had old debts and future taxes to pay, that absorbed all their profits, or they bilked the government and bought motor-cars and refrigerators before the tax-gatherers could reach them, and waited to be dunned. Price-levels were determined by this state and that, and this state, in consequence, had no butter or potatoes for its own consumption; while that, which produced nothing but beef, had no beef for its dinner. Labourers in remote and comfortless districts where gold was mined or electric power was about to be elaborately generated were paid enormous wages and gambled them all away. Everything cost more than it was worth, and the only common policy of the several provincial governments was opposition to the central government in Canberra. Perjury flourished, as though in the very tropics of imagination, and in a prolonged enquiry into the state of the liquor trade, that filled many columns of the newspapers while I was there, one simple genius of perjury appeared. 'I am twenty-nine years old,' he told the judge, and when the evidence again and again made his statement ridiculous, he repeated, in approximately these words, 'I was twenty-nine then, I'm twenty-nine now, and I'm going to go on being twenty-nine. It's the best age to be.' Corruption, it was alleged, was widespread, and the salaries of the professors at Sydney University had long been paid—or so I was told—from an overdraft whose only guarantors were Faith, Hope, and Charity.

I cannot swear to the truth of these statements—except the shortage of butter and potatoes, and the singular idealism of the man who claimed to be twenty-nine—but repeatedly I heard them, and never in a tone of complaint. Always in the undertone was the tolerance of people who knew that extravagance of any sort, in almost any degree, could be paid for by the incalculable and hardly-broached riches of their land. Australia is untidy to look at—geologically untidy, agriculturally untidy, and in some of the remoter urban districts a gallimaufry of disorder—but it is the untidiness of ease, of carelessness, the unbuttoned state of people who live well by right of inheritance and care little for appearances. To my primly disciplined Scottish mind there was much, at first sight and hearing, that seemed reprehensible; but one morning in Sydney my criticism was blown all away by a great gale of pleasure.

It was, I think, a Saturday morning. I was, at any rate, in a hurry to do some shopping and small business before office and magazine were closed. But Hunter Street was crowded, Pitt Street was stormy with opposing tides of traffic, George Street was a maelstrom of humanity. It would be impossible, I saw, to get my business done and buy the shirts I needed; and my temper, which is short, began to express itself in words as brief. But then, enisled in turbulence, I had time to look about me, and the crowds that thwarted me, I perceived, were strangely young and uncommonly attractive. Girls beyond counting, sunburnt and laughing, in bright frocks that all looked made for holiday. Young men, bare-headed and bold of movement, with clear skins and confident loud voices. Older men and women, stout and prosperous, genial with good living. But the majority was young, and the smell of salt water mingled with the scent of the girls in their summer frocks, as though their brown arms and legs, dyed by the sun, were perfumed also by Pacific waves; and their finery had not a costly, artificial look, but a natural gaiety like apple-blossom in its season, and like orchard-bloom in a gale of wind it blew about the streets, a storm of petals in Hunter Street, a honeyed chaos in Pitt Street, and in George Street a whirlwind from the Hesperides, where sea-spray tempers the sweetness of the air. I forgot my business, I could do without shirts, I decided, and in a state of wholly unexpected pleasure I let the tides take me this way and that, and wondered why girls in Sydney should be more lightly built, more slightly fashioned, than girls in Auckland and Dunedin. Few of them were distinguished by the challenge or a memorable perfection of beauty, but surprisingly many had the charm of prettiness, freshness, and physical assurance. The young men were unlike the long, lean, heroically statured Anzacs of the first great war—perhaps Gallipoli took too many of them—but they were sturdy, light-footed, and though city-bred had a mountain-glow or fore-shore colour of health.    And their elders (plump and know-ing, with an eye for pleasure and a ready turn at the next bar) were everywhere, it seemed, in the minority.    It was a youthful traffic, the youngest crowd that ever I was caught in; and if indeed corruption and the economics of Cloud Cuckoo-land financed them, their bloom was strangely sweet.    I escaped at last, but carried with me the sensation of having walked through a seaside orchard in a hurricane.

At breakfast one morning I was joined by a man who appeared to be smouldering with energy and enthusiasm. His name, he told me, was Nevil Shute.    He had not, how-ever, come to my table to discuss the proper task of the novelist in a world that—I have sometimes thought—needs more than novelists to set it aright; but to convert me to his own fervid belief in Australia, and in the magnitude of its future.    He did indeed tell me that an author whose revenue came equally from Britain and the United States was, by some leniency or loop-hole of taxation, three times better off in Australia than in England; but that was merely incidental to his theme.    If I used my eyes, he said, I would see for myself that development had so far only scratched the surface of the land.    I would be told that Australia could never support a population of more than twenty millions; but that was utter nonsense. The nonsense of unimaginative people who could not see the riches they walked on. Agriculture was only in its infancy, stock-breeders were little better than nomadic tribes whose flocks took a season's grass and moved on to look for new pasture. Drought was a recurrent menace only because the rainfall was not conserved. Even with such a primitive, casual, easy-going practice as governed the land, it was immensely prosperous; and with hard labour, with management and science, with a controlled and proper distribution of the rain, its prosperity could hardly be calculated. But it must be given a larger population, a much larger population, a population that would work because it knew there were rewards for work. A population of a hundred millions.

'One of the first differences—and it's a big difference—that I found between life here and life in England,' he said, 'was in the sort of story that's told. The story you hear in a pub, the ordinary sort of gossip about what's happened to Old So-and-so. In England, typically, it's a hard-luck story. Poor Old So-and-so's in trouble again. But you don't hear that in Australia. The typical story here is a good-luck story.'

He saw Australia, in the time to come, as the centre of the Empire. . . . In New Zealand one hears talk of *the Empire*, and accepts it as part of the endearing quality of the land; but in Australia it is more like a fragment of the challenge of Australia. Though in our own country faith in it was cool enough, the concept of empire still existed on its exuberant periphery, and under brighter skies it seemed not impossible that our history should have an interesting to-morrow as well as a distinguished past. In air undimmed by Channel haze or the smoke of midland counties, one could almost see it. . . . Canada lay in the other hemisphere, yearly growing in authority and wealth—her soldiers in Korea carried themselves like a Praetorian Guard —and in the south it was by no means unlikely that Australia, carelessly rich, was approaching with a casual slouch the eminence of its future. Britain lay between, and from the vantage-point of a land where confidence was as native as the kangaroo—where the vulgarity of optimism could stretch itself—Britain appeared still to hold some useful cards; and the joker had not yet been dealt. . . . So much in earnest was Nevil Shute, so full of conviction, that again and again, in the next few weeks, I almost heard his voice in my ear, saying, 'Look at that! They could do better than that, couldn't they? That's good land if it was irrigated and properly worked, but they can't work it because they haven't got the people.' As he had done, I saw the challenge of the land, and its enormous invitation; but there was such variety in the scene, such difference of climate, and above all so vast an area to domesticate and use, that the invitation, I thought, was addressed to all Europe. All its races could find a second home there.

The visitor, however, is often more enthusiastic than his hosts, and of my new acquaintances perhaps one in three was eager to expose the weaknesses of their society; for, like the Americans, the Australians take a pleasure in excoriating their faults—or, at any rate, the faults of their neighbours. The best intellects, I was told, leave the country because intellect has so few companions, and eminence of any sort except wealth is resented. A rich man does not excite jealousy—not angry jealousy—because riches are widely regarded as the issue of good luck. In the goldfields a man of no exceptional ability often made a lucky strike, and a fortune won in commerce seems to the uninstructed merely another nugget. Riches might happen to anyone, therefore no one is offended by riches. But intellectual superiority awakes suspicion, and recognition of it provokes dislike.

Another critic complained that Australian society had no cohesion. It was anarchic, and there was a rootless proletariat that recognised no authority and knew no responsibility. It was among those rootless ones that Communism found its adherents. There was no country in the world where Communism, on economic grounds, had a weaker case; for the labourer, so far from being exploited, took a handsome wage, had abundant leisure, and used the value of his scarcity to dictate the terms of his employment. 'They've got freedom, all the freedom there is, and they can't take it. It's too much for them. They have to find someone to tell them what to do, and how to think, and because they've got a chip on their shoulder they choose the Communists. They want something to believe in, and they want to make mischief too. Well, Communism fills the bill. But if Australia had coherence there'd be a natural authority for them to lean on, and they'd have plenty to believe in as well.'

Of the charge of moral rootlessness I cannot speak, for six weeks is too short a time for deep discoveries; but of physical rootlessness, of a nomadic tendency, I met, in so short a time, a good many samples—and the disarming thing about them was that they had thrown up a job in such-a-place, not because they found work there intolerable, but because they expected to find life somewhere else more interesting, or the mere change of interest. Typical of them was a young man whom I stopped in a street in Sydney to ask my way to one of the ferry-boat landings.

'I'll come with you,' he said, and turned about.

'But I'm taking you out of your way.'

'That's all right, I got nothing to do.—You from the old country?'

'Yes.'

'I've only been here a couple of months myself. I come from Adelaide.'

'What's Adelaide like?'

'Best part of Australia, if you ask me. They've got the best government, anyway. South Australia's the only state that has got a good government.'

'Why did you leave it?'

'Well, I wanted to see places.'

'And what do you think of Sydney?'

'I like it. They seem a bit crazy here in New South Wales—compared with South Australia—but I like it.'

And so did I. As a city, of course, Sydney between its Pacific beaches and on the interlocking bays of its inland harbour has one of the most magnificent situations in the world, and though its architecture, in comparison with what it will be five hundred years from now, is only in the wattle-and-daub stage of development, it hamstrings criticism and compels an admiration which is independent of respect, a liking which is indifferent to approval. A cold grey mind could find fault with Sydney, but heart and bowels respond to it.

I was flattered to meet a namesake of my own who was,

H

adding, in a very robust and daring way, something to the
enjoyment of its inhabitants.  He was a young man called
Don Linklater—the prefix was a Christian name, not an
Hispanic title—and to enlarge his hobby of submarine
marksmanship he had established a small factory that made
spear-guns to shoot fish under water, and formed a club of
fellow-enthusiasts for such adventure.  He invited me, one
day, to join the club on an afternoon excursion, and I met
about a score of young men and women in surroundings
which were curiously reminiscent, at one and the same time,
of the lounge in a Highland fishing hotel, an experimental
backyard factory, and the better sort of picnic.  We ate
enormously and drank sufficient beer to wash down chicken
legs and thick ham sandwiches, we appraised catapult-guns
and steel arrows, we were suitably jocular about cold water
and the happy resistance of young women to low tempera-
tures.  And then we drove, not to a sunlit, calm blue bay
such as the Mediterranean fish-hunters use, but to a rocky
coast on which a heavy swell beat with dull thunder and
raised white curtains of angry spray.

The young women decided it was too rough for them,
but the young men undressed and re-clothed themselves in
woollen vests and drawers, in pants and corselets of heavy
rubber, in skull-caps and goggles.  They found intervals in
the breaking sea, and dived into turbulent grey water.
Some had a breathing tube that showed above the surface,
but most of them relied on capacious lungs to give them
hunting time.  Only a few fish, however, were shot at the
first essay, and we moved to a corner of Botany Bay where
the coast was steeper, the sea rougher, but fish more plentiful.
And there someone discovered, lurking sluggishly on the

bottom, a carpet-shark or wobbigong; and asked if I would like to see it. I said I would, and my namesake loaded his gun and dived into twenty feet of water. He failed to find it the first time, but dived again and quickly reappeared with an agitated cord in his hand. He was pulled onto a ledge of rock, and the wobbigong that he had shot neatly in the head was hauled in after him. It was a little more than six feet in length, of a strange, reptilian ugliness: a heavy, mottled skin, a big, blunt head with a tattered fringe like seaweed depending from its mouth, and a thick body that tapered to a long, whip-like tail. Its stomach contained two smaller sharks, partially digested, and two ungainly appendages reiterated its sex and appeared to indicate a very passionate existence on the ocean-floor. How shocking must be the mind of the wobbigong, if one accepts Lamarck's theory of the formative power of the *sentiment intérieur*!

I tried to establish my relationship with Don Linklater, but he was uncertain about the birthplace of his grandfather, and we could not determine it. He maintained, however, the tradition of that Linklater who was a quartermaster of the *Bounty*, and in the mutiny stood firmly by the loyalists and sailed with Bligh in the open boat to Timor. Don Linklater supported his hobby with the claim that, in the case of war, his submarine fishers might become the nucleus of a corps of frogmen to attack the enemy's shipping.

We cannot long forget war—in this age that desires chiefly to be done with it—and I was wakened one day by the telephone and a voice that I had not heard since the retreat of our Fifth Army in 1918. It was a voice that had kept the burr and homely accent of Fife, and with the proper caution of Fife it demanded who I was. . . .

'Linklater speaking.'

'Is that you, Linky?'

'Who are you?'

'D'you remember Joe Haig?'

'*Joe Haig?*'

'The Black Watch.'

'Good God, yes.'

'I thought you'd remember me. Well, can I come and see you?'

'Yes, of course. When will you be here?'

'I'm on my way now. . . .'

He was my senior in those days—he was a corporal—and when I met him I was glad to see that he retained his dignity. His hair was almost white, and his cheeks were lined with the decent responsibility of his years. He looked a good and solid man, and as we talked I found myself slipping back into an old, friendly, but junior relationship. He had been very kind to me, he had looked after my inexperience; and when that war was finished he had emigrated and lived since then, modestly enough but in comfort and respectability, in one of the industrial parts of Sydney. We gossiped in the traditional way of dead sergeants and half-forgotten places, and he told me that he had recognised himself in a book I wrote, where he lived anonymously in a summer episode of an ammunition tent that went on fire when he was sleeping in the midst of it. We delved here and there in time, and suddenly he said, 'I was wondering what you'd be like, when I was coming here, but man, you're just the same Linky still!'

Discount the apparent affection of the diminutive. It is a Scottish habit, especially in the eastern parts from Fife to Aberdeenshire, to give diminutive form to any familiar thing; so much so that a cup of tea, between friends, becomes a 'cuppie'. It was not affection that puzzled me— there was between us the natural kindness of old association —but the charge of *sameness* perplexed me, and when I went to bed that night I could not sleep for thinking of it.

Between myself, at the age of fifty-two, and an eighteen-year-old private I could see no resemblance whatever. I did not feel that my dead self had been a stepping-stone to better things; it only seemed as dead as coral reefs on which, when they have served their turn, new polyps build. I drove memory backward, and I could find no sympathy between youth and me. I knew what youth had been like, but he was no nearer than someone in whom I felt a friendly interest. I could remember mud at Passchendaele and the cutting swing of a kilt whose muddied fringe had frozen stiff; but only as something I had read of in a good convincing novel. I am not the same creature, I told myself. I am only a polyp on its useful skeleton.

But because I had been fond of Joe Haig, and was sentimentally affected by meeting him again, I struggled still to find a link between me and the boy whom he remembered. I returned with some confidence to my student days in Aberdeen, and recollected clearly enough that exuberance of spirit had alternated with the black despair of youth; and in my seasons of black despair, I recalled, I used to comfort myself with two assertions: I have been almost a good soldier, and I am going to be a poet. The second was quickly disproved, and the first was based upon short experience. But that experience had been vivid, and though I could no longer recapture its sensations, I still knew its circumstances.

In a period of some confusion I had become sniper to my company, and often enjoyed a position remote from the others and rather in front of them. The period I recalled— the period I had used for comfort in the black days—was occupied by ragged fighting in the neighbourhood of Zillebeke Lake, or between Zillebeke and Kemmel Hill: an area that had been much fought over. And there one day, from my advanced position, I had halted a small German attack by shooting the officer leading it, who collapsed with his hands to his stomach, and his company, disconcerted, fell back to their trenches. Later in the day another attack made some progress, but was stopped on open ground. Two of the enemy dropped behind a little heap of earth that sprouted coarse grass from the grave of some forgotten soldier, and engaged me with their fire. I had a better position than they had found, and him on my right, who was much exposed, I silenced at once. He on my left aimed well enough to alarm me, but after re-loading I got him too. And for one night—and I think a second night—I lay out in the darkness at the corner of a long ditch, hedge-guarded, and intermittently through the night fired single shots, or little clattering bursts, to discourage patrols who might be trying to creep towards us.—In these and similar affairs there had been, I remembered, a taut exhilaration; but the feeling of it had long since vanished. I had a visual memory, but no sympathetic knowledge of the private who had done those things and answered to my name at roll-call.

I explored the past again, and remembered something

that in my student days, when all this was real in memory, I would have been glad to forget. . . . I was watching the turn of a road, between two and three hundred yards away, across which the Germans were moving, singly and with caution, to develop their fortifications on the other side. They leapt and darted from right to left—my right to my left—and vainly I tried to halt them.   It was early morning, there were wisps of fog moving slowly and close to the ground; and snap-shooting in a bad light is not easy.   But after several misses I wounded a man, and for a little while there was a pause in the traffic.   Then two men ran across together, and I missed them.   A minute, two minutes, three minutes passed; and from left to right came, quite un-expectedly, a slow-moving group of three.   I fired, and two fell; the third leapt into safety.   For a second, or less than that, I felt the wildest exultation, and then, with a realisation of what had happened, I dissolved in misery and tears.   The two men had crossed to save him I had wounded, and on their return I had killed the wounded man and one of his would-be rescuers. . . .

Some five or six years before that, at the age of twelve or thirteen, I had gone out shooting in Orkney with a single-barrelled gun.   It was the first gun I owned, and its balance was very different from the ancient, hammer-triggered, borrowed piece to which I was accustomed.   I missed everything at which I fired, and with the intemperate disappointment of boyhood grew very unhappy at the thought of going home with an empty bag.   And then, between a bed of reeds and the stony edge of a little loch—to this day I remember, within a yard, where it was—I saw a sleeping mallard.   I stopped, and knew a frightful choice.

With self-loathing, I put up my gun and fired. I was so close to the poor duck that I blew her head off, and in utter shame I threw the dishonoured body into the water. That was at twelve or thirteen, and at eighteen, or newly nineteen, I felt the same dissolution of remorse for having shot a wounded German. And at fifty-two the sense of shame was not quite dead.

It was more than pity for the man; it was remorse for having broken the rules. My pity for the man exceeded my pity for the duck, but I felt, I think, no greater sense of guilt. Guilt was equal, because both acts were equal in their shabbiness.

Now this, in my sleepless recollection of time past, was the only event that united me, in feeling, with the boy whom Joe Haig still saw in me. If he was right, and there was still a sameness between us, was it only a sense of guilt? That was an uncomfortable conclusion to a sentimental reunion. . . .

# XVIII

## NORTH TO THE SUN

BEING detained by pleasure, I stayed too long in Sydney and in consequence did injustice to Brisbane. To go from New South Wales into Queensland is something like crossing the Potomac from the northern states of America into Virginia. The atmosphere of Brisbane is not that of Richmond, but it is closer to Richmond than to Philadelphia. People on the streets move more slowly than in Sydney, and there is more leisure in their voices. In Brisbane, in the shade of jacarandas, there may be a graciousness as characteristic of it as ebullience of Sydney; but I cannot be sure, because I did not stay long enough and perhaps my visit was coloured by good fortune. Perhaps my host and hostess persuaded me that their town was so agreeable.

I left Brisbane in a seaplane that took off from a closely curving river, crowded with traffic, and a little more than four hours later, and six or seven hundred miles to the north, landed in a brilliantly dancing sea beside a small island ridiculously called Daydream. Its geographical name is West Molle, and it lies in a group through which Captain Cook sailed on Whitsunday, June 3rd, in 1770. On one of the islands he saw through his glass two men and a woman, and a canoe with an outrigger. For most of the year the population is hardly more than that to-day, but in what is called winter there is a concourse of tourists from the south. I arrived about the end of the season, and on Daydream's

233

fifty acres there were some twenty visitors and the same
number of employees of the company that exploited it as
a holiday resort.   It was often difficult to distinguish one
from the other, for no one wore many clothes and some of
the employees were hardly more active than the visitors,
who did nothing at all.   Of the male population the most
distinguished in appearance was a grey-haired man with the
air of one accustomed to a life of leisure in pleasant places;
he might be, I thought, a fashionable painter who enjoyed
the friendship of wealthy patrons.   And so, perhaps, he was,
for on my second morning there I saw him painting the wall
behind the bar; for a few minutes he brushed on a yellow
pigment with flowing ease, then descended from his steps,
sat down to read a newspaper, and got up to drink a glass
of beer.   We talked lightly of politics, but I did not learn
his status.

Among the female visitors a very tall and rather bonily
slender woman was conspicuous.   She was darkly sunburnt,
her hair was canary-bright, she changed her scanty raiment
three or four times a day, and her voice dominated all
nearby conversation with the high, clear confidence of its
tone and her brisk assurance that all she said would provoke
attention, compel amusement.   Smaller, quieter, and humb-
ler visitors whispered to me from time to time, 'She's a well-
known barmaid from Sydney', and 'Ah yes,' I said, 'I
thought as much'; and listened with respect to her next
remark.   I had spent a morning, with literary persons, in the
great bar of the Australia Hotel in Sydney, and humbly
observed the beauty of one, the dignity of all the young
women who indefatigably drew unending pints of beer and
with the haughty indifference of *croupiers* raking chips from

a roulette table swept from their dark counters the lavish
change that customers left upon them. The barmaids of
Sydney, I had been told, were influential members of the
community, and all were very rich. Only butchers—again
I depend on hearsay—dared approach them with familiarity
or serious attention; for Sydney butchers enjoyed a solid
and abiding affluence that everyone revered.

On Daydream Island there were also some elderly
married couples who took their holiday quietly; one or
two newly married couples who did not stir beyond their
private trance; and a conchologist and his wife who had
lived there for several years and collected either four or
forty thousand shells, many of which they painted in bold
colours and sold to tourists. The beach consisted of very
rough coral, like broken finger-bones, and when the tide
was in everybody swam in a narrow lane close to the shore;
in deeper water there might be sharks. The accommodation
consisted of wooden shacks, of simple design and indifferent
workmanship, and through the hillock of tropical vegetation behind the living-huts ran several footpaths that afforded
a twenty-minutes walk. The reservoir, at the end of the
season, was bone-dry, and all water had to be carried from
the mainland. But above the island was spread a cerulean
roof, the air was the ocean's distillation of common air,
and the sea danced on the rough coral like Chinese jade
upon a Chinese wrist. And from the island a launch went
on little voyages through an archipelago of extraordinary
beauty, past broken cliffs and tree-furred shores, to land on
dazzling beaches where reflected light warmed the very
marrow of one's bones and the emerald sea put one's mind
to sleep. The islands of the Whitsunday group would be

idyllic if they had wells and water-courses; but most of them are dry.

I stayed for two or three days on Daydream, and left in a launch that took me to a little port called Cannon Vale, where I boarded a bus that went south again, for a hundred miles, to Mackay. The bus was nearly empty, and light upon its springs, and the road was abominable. It was ridged and corroded, like corduroy, and we were not driven so much as bounced towards the south. But the sparsely populated country was very interesting. A harshly sculptured land, at the beginning of the journey, opened into valleys roughly cultivated for pasture, where many horses ran, and corrugated-iron shacks stood on stilts above the sun-browned earth. The bush had been burnt, and cattle pastured among a secondary growth of slim, anaemic, finger-thin trees and the leprous statues of dead gums. Over the taller hills in the distance hung a threatening, thunder-blue sky, but no rain fell to relieve the long drought. We drove through a dismal, sun-shattered hamlet called Bloomsbury: it had a railway station, some cottages built of corrugated iron, a cow disconsolate in the hot foreground, another stealing sugar-cane from a loaded wagon, and a few lean and slatternly inhabitants somnolent in the heat. Empty creeks channelled the country, most of them dust-dry, but some holding pools of water. All this territory had the look of *colonial* country: of country that had been claimed and roughly settled, but was only in the first chapter of development. There were hills in the background, cloud-compelling hills, and if the creeks had been dammed they might all have held water. It was pleasant to see dust again—dust rising from a road as corrugated as the iron shacks beside it—

for dust is a rarity in Britain now; and through its amber clouds shone the flowers of bougainvillea and poinciana.

I had decided to stay for a few days in Mackay, primarily to repair ignorance; for I had never heard of it until I landed in Sydney. I found accommodation in an hotel whose public apartments consisted of a dining-room and a lobby which looked like a stage-set that had been designed for comedy. There were four doors and a staircase, there were some tables and chairs down-stage, and in the left rear stood a quarter-circle of office-desk behind which youths and maidens in the employment of the hotel loudly flirted. I sat there drinking bad whisky and reading *Great Expectations*, and a drunk man with a cleft palate came in to complain of injustice. He was almost incomprehensible, but the cause of his ill-humour may have been that a girl to whom he had entrusted his laundry had stolen all his shirts. He was listened to with gentle patience, and when he went away the flirting began again behind the desk, as loud as cockatoos. Someone told me about gambling in Kalgoorlie, where a game called Two Up had been in progress for several years, and at Mount Isa it was much the same, if not worse; thousands of pounds were won and lost in endless repetition. I put aside *Great Expectations* and listened to rousing anecdotes of sudden wealth and the abysses of instant poverty. Wealth was undoubtedly the better part, but no one, it appeared, regarded poverty as catastrophic. A fine, fat, friendly woman told a neighbour that her husband was on the beer again, and it was just too bad; and I thought of the lean, brown, half-naked men we had passed on the road from Bloomsbury, men in khaki shorts with infinitely shabby, large brown hats, and a feminine company that

we had perceived on the outskirts of a village.  There was
a flash of white, a dazzle of immaculate linen under the
glaring sun, and on a square of green turf one recognised
women in shining raiment.  Some strict and penitential
order of nuns, I wondered?  But no.  They were bowlers.
They were the opposing teams of two female bowling
clubs.—The drunk man with the cleft palate came in again,
but now his talk was quietly confidential.  He had retrieved his shirts, and I went back to my book.  Dickens,
I thought, was the kind of author that Australia needed.
With what a muscular virtuosity he combined, in the first
few chapters of *Great Expectations*, a supreme talent for story-
telling, the lurid compulsion of melodrama, and music-hall
wit!  A Dickens with a glittering eye for detail, for enormous reality and grotesque adornment—and, in his very
essence, a capacity for blandly accepting all and discerning
through a vision diamonded with perfunctory tears the foot
of a rainbow—is the proper author for Australia.

I went on a bus-trip to a district called Eungella.  We
drove through a great plain walled by hills that finally closed
in upon it and rose abruptly to 3000 feet, to a vast table-land
where dairy-pasture grew fresh and green and fine timber
rose to prodigious heights.   It was in a bus for tourists that I
rode, and a clever agreeable girl who was called a 'hostess'
drew our attention to objects of interest on the journey.
Some of them, such as the house of a prosperous physician,
seemed to be of no large or general interest, but she knew the
history of the sugar plantations that gave much of its wealth
to the district, and so complete was her knowledge that one
saw, as if through a screen of gallant make-believe, the
appalling lack of history, the emptiness of the land upon

which endeavour crudely lay. Here was the labour of pioneers, the first-fruits of enterprise won from a territory that had mere vacancy for its past : an endless past, or no past at all. Riches lay in it, still to be found and used, and its frail domestication touched emotion, touched nerves as well; but the lusty camaraderie of the settlers was delightful. Everyone whom we passed on the road waved and cried a greeting to our 'hostess' and our driver, for everyone knew everybody else, and though life had no depth in history it had breadth in friendship. A friendship stiffened by the hazards of life?—On our way back the bush-fires that were burning intermittently over all the east coast burst into new flames within a few yards of the road. Cattle grazed inno-cently under a pall of smoke, still turned to nuzzle grass that lay no more than the breadth of a football field from smouldering tree-trunks puffing steam, from a carpet of little pointed flames that overleapt the yellow soil. It was not a wholly placid existence that fostered geniality in the settlers.

In the highlands was a prospect of that sort of country which a romantic tale offers for their reward to daring, often desperate pioneers; a promised land gracious to the eye, rich in milk and sweetened by honey. A rain-forest guarded it, a damp green shade under Gothic pinnacles, a Gothic tracery of leaves, through which meandered a river in whose brown pools the shy duck-mole lived. The rich pasture of the highlands was the pioneers' reward, but the road through the valley was their monument, and the valley was still evidence of their tribulation. The settlers were still too few, their hold upon the land was light.

Midway on our journey was a village called Finch Hatton. In a droughty year it lay, under iron roofs, with a parched and desolate air, but at a cross-roads grew a tree of the utmost splendour. It may have been some sort of chestnut. It carried like Spanish ensigns, or lanterns for a festival, great flowers of scarlet and yellow, and among its branches, shrieking and clapping their bright wings, scampered a flock of green and ruby-throated parrots. A luxuriant vegetation was native to the land, birds were clad in brilliance, and its rivers, until lately, had harboured crocodiles. It lay, by a degree or two, within the tropic of Capricorn, and there is a harshness in tropical luxuriance.—There was a dark and woebegone tavern in Finch Hatton to which a plump red man, enjoying a lonely holiday, insisted on my going, and for some minutes we stood at a deserted bar and no one answered our call. Then a bare-footed woman with untidy hair came in. She was pale of face, lack-lustre, tired. She had to look after everything, she said, because her husband was ill. 'It's influenza, he's had it eight times. Yes, one after the other, he don't seem able to get rid of it. No, we haven't any beer, only English ale, and that's three-and-six a bottle.' Then a youngish man shambled in who looked, though it was late in the afternoon, as if he had newly and hurriedly got out of bed, and asked the bare-footed woman if he had paid his overdue account last night. 'Oh, I can't remember,' she said. 'Were you in?' 'Well, my wife says I came here to pay the account, but I can't remember either, so she told me to come and see.' The woman took from a drawer beneath the bar a tattered exercise-book, its pages blotched and blurred, and laboriously read some forty names and the sums they owed. 'I can't find your name anywhere,' she said. 'Are you sure you had an account?' 'I had an account all right, and I meant to

pay it.' 'Well, perhaps you did.  Better have a beer, now
you've come, though there's nothing left but English ale.'

In the sun-smitten street were gaudy advertisements for
a cinema, breezy invitations to a subscription dance.  An
excessively fat boy with bare legs and filthy feet sat on a fat
bay pony sucking an ice-cream cone, and a thin woman
peered anxiously into a shop-window that held a sombre
display of patent medicines.  My plump red friend said dis-
approvingly that the spirit of the pioneers was dead.  'We
don't seem to breed 'em nowadays.  We haven't got anyone
left of their quality.'  Two or three hours before he had
stood unsteadily on a vertiginous rim of the great plateau,
and looking down at the broad expanse of the valley far
below—olive-green and tawny, with violet shadows—he
had exclaimed in a sudden access of emotion, 'This solves
everything!'  But now, with the flavour of sour ale in his
mouth, he was pessimistic.  'We've only got eighty years of
history in these parts, and we're decadent already,' he
declared.

There was, indeed, in the valley an occasional likeness to
those parts of America where 'poor whites' live in a backyard, as it were, of industry and wealth; but these drab
patches were not typical of the country, and the cure for
them was obvious.  More people were needed.  The valley
and the highlands above it required the stimulus of company,
of a population two or three times as numerous.

Night fell upon Mackay—it was a Friday night—and
young men walked the pavements singing raucously, *When
Irish eyes are smiling*.  Girls with their tresses shining and
newly pressed by the hairdresser looked smart in summer
frocks.  A rising tide of mild intoxication filled the little

town—not drunkenness, not rowdiness and ill-humour, but a vulgar, balmy geniality. Queensland has its own customs, which are stronger than its laws, and its licensing hours do not seem to be prohibitive.

In the morning, quite early, I was jostled as I left the bathroom by a wild-eyed man in a garish dressing-gown who shouted to me, 'Salaam, sahib!' and under the rush of water in his zinc-lined shower sang loud and tunelessly, *If you were the only girl in the world, and I were the only boy.* . . . I ate my breakfast, and in the lobby that looked like a stage set for comedy read *Great Expectations* and waited for a car to take me to the airfield. By half-past nine there were several people sitting at the small tables, drinking beer, and a young woman, but already stout, came in and greeted a neighbour with strident amiability.

'Morning, Mrs. Weissnicht. I've just heard as how your washing-machine's gone bung.'

'Too true it has!'

'Well, can you beat it! Mine went bung last week.'

'No!'

'Too right it did. And Mrs. Harris's went bung the week before. . . .'

But I had to leave them, and never learnt what measures they took against affliction. The prosperous, tree-lined streets of the town were crowded with country people who had driven in to enjoy an idle Saturday. Smart shop-windows framed the abundant produce of the land, and expensive frocks for farmers' wives. Some of the buildings had verandas railed with intricately wrought iron in the colonial fashion that still survives in the poorest streets of Sydney, but the general aspect of the town was brightly, plainly modern. Decoration is old-fashioned. Tools, weapons, ships—all were decorated when tools and weapons and ships were made for enjoyment as well as use; but efficiency and the need of profit leave no room for enjoyment of that sort.

I flew to Cairns, which is a thousand miles north of Brisbane, and the view beneath was river-deltas, brown lands grotesquely carved by winding streams, headlands standing in brilliant relief against the onyx sea, sand-banks as pink as salmon. On the one side were the green pallors and white crusts of the Barrier Reef, on the other dry river-beds like dusty roads between the colour and shade of marching trees, and enamelled fields of sugar-cane. The airport at Cairns, swept by a hot wind, lay between abrupt and bushy hills. The sky threw down a tropical heat, but the water-front had a gaiety of appearance and something of the smartness of a town on the Riviera. Gardens lay behind an esplanade, broad streets were cleanly kept and shaded by lavish trees. The hinterland was immensely rich. Sugar grew in forests of thick stems, meticulously gardened by Italian immigrants who were said to be exclusive, stand-offish, who preferred to be Italian rather than become Australian; but whose industry was laudable indeed. Timber grew on the rolling heights of the Atherton Table-land—walnut, maple, tulip-oak, and black bean—and where the forest had been cleared the red soil bore abundant crops of maize. Tobacco grew, rice had begun to show another shade of green, dairy cattle flourished. Anything grew that was planted—and under the surface lay antimony, wolfram, tin.

I met an orchid-grower who had found a little plateau, some twelve hundred feet above sea-level, that was guarded by thickly forested mountains on either side and looked down a valley where a river glinted among the trees. He had cleared several acres of bush, he had built a house, and dug a garden. In less than twelve months his flower-beds were as full of colour as a florist's illustrated catalogue. The homely snapdragon, in large variety, and other modest natives of an English village flourished among the gaudy splendours of poinsettias, poincianas, hibiscus, and a deep crimson bougainvillea. His new orchard was an *omnium gatherum* where passion-fruit and papaws looked down at precocious raspberries which, planted in July, carried fruit in November. And in a long dark orchid-house hung hundreds of small brown bundles from which, quite soon, would sprout the mottled, striated, improbably shaped and fantastically coloured flowers that suggest, so often, the intrusion into botany of Hieronymus Bosch. 'But your customers?' I asked. 'Who will buy your orchids?' 'We'll have a restaurant and serve teas,' he said. 'In Australia people will go anywhere to look at things, if they can get a cup of tea as well. And when they've had a look at the view, they'll buy fruit and orchids.' 'But how will they get here? There's no proper road.' 'I'll have to make a road,' he answered thoughtfully.

Between Cairns and the almost deserted hamlet of Port Douglas—where the imaginative Louis de Rougemont once worked as a photographer—there was a restaurant that used crocodiles to attract customers. Three of them lay somnolent in home-made cages, and when the proprietor took a pole and went in to stir up the largest there were exclamations of lively anticipation from the tourists, and a concerted scream of alarm when the beast, with surprising speed, swung its ponderous head and opened a long, gaping, white mouth to snap.

'Where do they come from?' asked a simple-looking girl.

'Under a bush at the bottom of the garden, just where you did,' answered the nonchalant proprietor, and prodded the ten-foot crocodile in a tender place to make him show more interest.

'Well,' said the girl, 'that's not a nice answer.'

'No indeed!' said her friend indignantly. 'That just shows what it does to you, living with crocodiles.'

'How old is he?' asked an elderly woman.

'About seventy, I'd say. Just a teen-ager yet. They live to five or six hundred, if you let 'em.'

'And what do they eat?'

'Tourists, if they're lucky.'

A chorus of laughter applauded wit, and contentedly the travellers sat down to drink their tea and share their sandwiches with a tame kangaroo. We drove on, by a road that bordered a wind-pointed, brilliant sea, past cream-coloured beaches immensely long, and through tree-tunnels. We stopped for beer at a corrugated-iron and clapboard inn, and were served by a large man in a cotton vest who looked like an all-in wrestler. He was a Yugoslav who, before he took to innkeeping, had been a timber-jerker in Western Australia. His native place was Fiume. . . .

Once, long ago, I went to Fiume and in the ship met an Italian journalist who had marched with d'Annunzio's *Arditi*. On the wooded shore he pointed to places that were mapped for ever in his gallant memories.

'There, and there,' he announced in a voice that curdled thought, 'we left blood and hair!'

'Was there much opposition?' I asked.

Magnificently he smacked his chest, threw out his right arm in a splendid gesture. 'There was *no* opposition!'

The innkeeper had few regrets for the Dalmatian shore. 'So long as I have plenty cold beer, I should worry,' he said.

We dozed in the heat, we returned towards Cairns along the lovely sea-road, and beside a couple of mango-trees, laden with ripe fruit, the tourists demanded another halt. They got out and gathered mangoes, and in the bus they sucked the soft pulp, the juice ran down their chins, and fragments of the orange-coloured flesh besmeared their cheeks. Their brows were damp with sweat, the women's hair clung moistly to their necks. They were very happy, and began to sing. . . .

But in the evening I fell into conversation with two people who would not admit the soft and pleasant charm of northern Queensland, nor concede to Cairns the importance that the inhabitants claimed for it. They came from a sterner part of Australia, from a lonely sheep-station some eight hundred miles north-west of Brisbane. Longreach was their nearest town, and that a hundred and twenty miles away. Their mail came once a week, and then they had to drive seventeen miles to fetch it.

They were tall and good-looking; he with a bold masculine strength, she with fine features and easy charm. 'These places on the coast don't really count for much,' he said, 'and the big cities in the south do nothing for Australia. They don't give, they take. The real Australia and the real wealth of Australia's all in the interior. Wool and beef:

they're what matter, and chiefly wool.'   His far-off boundaries enclosed 190,000 acres, that carried a sheep to every
four, and impatiently he denounced the high prices of recent
years.   An inflated selling-price only meant inflated buying-
prices and a monstrously inflated tax.   Real values disappeared in a dust-storm of financial nonsense.   His father,
an Irish immigrant, had carved his first farm out of the bush,
but no one could do that nowadays.   No one could afford
to be a pioneer, and no one wanted to be one; because
there was no longer any profit in pioneering.   But pioneers
were still Australia's need.

His wife was not a woman who had been defeated by hard
work.   In her appearance, indeed, there was nothing to
show that she had ever been oppressed by it.   She might
have lived in happy ignorance of work.   'But I had to cook
for nine men,' she said, 'and that was when I'd two babies
to look after.   I'd one at the breast, and after dealing with
him for a bit I'd have to put him down and go back to the
stove.   They ate such a lot, I couldn't get used to it at first.
Two men would eat a leg of mutton between them.   But
he'd say, "They're good workers, give 'em plenty".   And
I had to.'

Ten years ago, she said, it had been impossible to get
cook, maid, or any sort of indoor worker.   And added,
with no thought of an appeal for sympathy, but with absolute
simplicity, 'No woman would ever live in a place like that,
unless she happened to have married someone she liked.'

I hired a boat to troll for mackerel on the Barrier Reef.
The skipper's grandfather, I quickly learnt, had come from
Glencoe.   He appeared to have been a warm-hearted and

impulsive Highlander, and had married an Irish girl who was a fellow-passenger in the emigrant ship. Their son became a farmer who went bankrupt in the 1920's, and of a considerable property retained nothing but two race-horses. For a little while he ran them on credit, but they never won a race and he had some difficulty in selling them. 'What were you doing at that time?' I asked the skipper. 'I was kangaroo-shooting,' he said casually, and told me, without affectation of singularity or any apprehension of unusual variety in his life, that he had been a carpenter, a mechanic, a builder's labourer, a building contractor, and a fisherman. Recently he had seen the possibility of making an easier living by taking out tourists, and he was about to furnish his boat with fishing-chairs and all that was needed for their comfort. It was a good boat, about forty feet in length, but his equipment as yet was a little crude. It consisted of two metal reels, about fifteen inches in diameter and fixed to the deck, on which were lines of twisted wire.

We left the creek and the buoyed channel, and a deck-hand began to prepare the bait. He had a bucket of small garfish, about ten or twelve inches long, and through one was passed the shank of a double hook, and a length of fine copper wire was threaded through its eyes and round its jaw to close its mouth. A piece of red rubber or a tuft of red cloth was fastened to the trace about a yard from its nose, to simulate the little fish that the gar was supposed to be pursuing, and the forty-foot trace of piano-wire was made fast to the line. The skipper handed me a pair of heavy gauntlets. 'When we start fishing,' he said solemnly, 'see that you keep 'em on!' And to impress his advice upon my mind told me a cautionary tale of an angler who, carelessly

NORTH TO THE SUN

holding a loop of the wire line round his bare wrist, had had his bait taken by a shark, and such was the strength of its sudden pull that his wrist was cut through, and his bloody hand fell overboard.

We headed out to sea, leaving Green Island on the starboard side—Green Island, where Captain Cook, Mr. Banks, and Dr. Solander went ashore to look for fresh water on the day before the *Endeavour* grounded, and nearly became a total loss, on a steep ledge of coral—and headed for Oyster Reef and Michaelmas Reef, some twenty miles off-shore. Our fishing-lines, extended on outriggers, trolled their bait about eighty yards astern, and presently I pulled in my first mackerel. It struck hard and plunged violently, but the strong tackle gave it no chance. Its colouring, of dark green markings on a pearly skin—a flash of silver as it sheered away—was very beautiful in the pellucid, jade-green sea, and after death it put on opal hues and a faint lavender. But I did not enjoy my fishing as much as I had expected to, because the tackle was too coarse to let one use skill, and oppose skill to strength with some degree of fairness. We caught nine mackerel, the smallest eight pounds, the largest twenty-five, and the skipper thought poorly of my character when I told him that I wanted to go ashore before nightfall; before the most profitable fishing hours, that is.—But I have no liking for mere slaughter.

The best part of the voyage was an hour when we lay at anchor beside a little sandy cay on which roosted a multitude of seabirds, while close above it hung like a canopy an equal multitude, shrilly calling. We had come slowly in, choosing our way between the purple shadows of coral-heads, and while the skipper cooked our lunch the deckhand and I launched the dinghy and rowed ashore. The whole population of birds rose in alarm, and in a reticulation of black and white their wings, for a moment or two, so covered the sky that the staring sunshine was broken into lozenges of light and shadow. They were sooty terns, and what appeared to be a black-and-white kittiwake. The cay was hardly more than an acre in size, and at one end of it lay chestnut-freckled eggs so closely dropped that again and again one had to step short or sideways to avoid them. The dropping-places—they were not nests—were in groups of four or five, each egg (they were still singletons) a couple of feet from its neighbour. The air smelt sour and acrid, and the angry birds came swooping at one's head, with fierce screaming, like waves of quite harmless little aeroplanes. But a short distance away the white sand beside the sea was covered with dark bodies as thickly as fly-paper in a Levantine butcher's shop in summer.

Australia was quite invisible, hidden by the smoke of bush fires. It was less than a cloud on the horizon, it was hardly a vapour in the distance. Round the scorching pallor of the little cay the blue Pacific seemed illimitable, and it was empty but for ourselves and the boat of an old man, who preferred to fish alone, that lay near by. The shoal-water was bright as young beech leaves, but farther out it was darker, then turned to blue; and in the intermediate distance it was mottled like tortoiseshell by underlying coral-heads and reefs. We rowed aboard and the skipper gave us a good meal of fried fish and salad.

We caught a few more mackerel, and leisurely returned to Cairns. In the mangrove-bordered creek where the skipper docked there lay old, sun-faded, patched and battered boats tied to stumps or piers in the mud, and little schooners that fished for trochus-shell from Thursday Island. Through a port-hole stared a black and bony face, motionless and without expression, but with gleaming eyes like fragments of trochus-shell stuck beneath its protruding brows. The skipper had an aged, rattling car, and drove me back to my hotel. It was nearly dark, and through the dusky air, close above us, flew with a slurring noise a covey of things with heavy, swollen bodies. 'Flying foxes,' said the skipper.

For my next journey—for prompting me to make it—I was indebted to Nevil Shute. 'See something of the out-back country if you get a chance,' he said. 'If you go to Cairns you can fly from there to Normanton and the Gulf. They're worth looking at.' And someone else had said, 'Too right! See the out-back, and tell yourself that's where the butchers' fortunes come from—and have a laugh.'

The journey began early in the day, and before the sun rose the airport was cool as a summer waterfall. But as soon as the sun showed above the hill-tops the coolness faded and shrivelled, and by half-past six the air was as warm as an August noon in England. Among the passengers in the waiting-room were three blackfellows, two of mixed blood; an elderly woman of determined aspect who owned an hotel in the out-back; a large and dignified man in a two-gallon hat, tight black trousers, and elastic-sided boots, who owned a cattle station; a lesser man, an engineer, who was going with him to repair a broken bulldozer; a pale, thin, still smaller man who was about to become a book-keeper on a remoter station; a white stockman; and a talkative, lively citizen of Cairns who was taking a short holiday and

for company had brought his saxophone.   There were also
two stewardesses, one who had had experience of 'the milk-
run'—so they called the service to the Gulf—and one who
was a novice.

The Dakota took off and climbed steeply over bright
fields of sugar-cane to clear the abruptly rising edge of the
table-land, and Cairns from the nearer sky looked very
comfortably neat and prosperous.   We still climbed, to cross
a great expanse of shaggy, broken highlands, where a less
kindly sky was full of tattered cloud.   The trees grew
sparser, the land more brown and bare, more deeply
wrinkled, and valleys had harsh patterns under stone cliffs.
The clouds dispersed, and a sullen haze covered a reddish
wilderness in which one could see neither house nor road.
I looked at the time-table and read the stations on the
route: Cairns, Abingdon, Croydon, Normanton, Miranda,
Vanrook, Dunbar, Koolatah, Rutland Plains, Mitchell River,
Galbraith, Delta Downs, and Normanton again.   Most of
them were cattle stations; two were ghost towns.

At a quarter to eight we landed at Abingdon on what,
to inexperienced eyes, appeared little better than desert
country; but trees grew fairly thickly out of the parched
soil, and their leaves were incomprehensibly green.   Sandy
shoals glared from a dry river-bed, and as we flew lower
red cattle were visible beneath the trees.   There was no
proper landing-strip, but we touched down, easily enough,
in a clear lane through the trees.   Black stockmen on rough
horses rode towards us, the station-owner and the engineer
got out, and with them were landed two or three sacks of
vegetables and a lot of newspapers.

Croydon, a ghostly remnant of prosperity in gold-mining days, was a tiny hamlet of corrugated-iron cottages, a corrugated-iron hotel, in an enormous featureless plain that thinly grew a multitude of slender trees. Here the woman of determined aspect left us, with the three black-fellows she had hired—they all carried musical instruments—and it was here, I think, that a fat and genial parson joined us: a man both simple and lordly, his circumference tightly confined in khaki shorts, a quick smile on his jolly red face, the spiritual comforter of 40,000 square miles with the generous title of Bush Brother.

We flew on to Normanton, another ghost town, where we discharged a cargo of bread, beer, ice-cream, and mail, and remained for an hour or so. The hotel at Normanton was unexpectedly pleasing. It was largely built of corrugated iron, of course, and numerous ants crawled on the dilapidated boards of the veranda. There were swing-doors leading to bar and billiard-room—or rather, swing shutters, for they reached neither to the ceiling nor the floor—and in the bar were two or three very big men, of formidable appearance, and two or three wizened, fever-stricken men who looked so frail that a strong breeze might have carried them away. The barman, scantily clad, was a perpetual fountain of sweat, and hens scrabbled in a backyard of splendid disorder. It looked wonderfully like the picturesque saloon that film directors used to build for a romantic 'western' picture; but there was no gun-play. The air was quiet, uncomfortably hot, and almost sticky with the scent of beer. A young man, cleanly shaved and more smartly dressed than the majority, came briskly up and strangely saluted me: 'Juan in China, isn't it? How are you?' And briskly walked away again.

We flew on, low above the ground and bumping violently in the hot air, to Miranda, Vanrook, and Dunbar, to Koolatah and Rutland Plains. From the height of a few hundred feet the country appeared to have no distinguishing features; all was reddish earth out of which the spindly trees miraculously fetched moisture enough to keep their leaves green, while dry water-courses left irrelevant beds across the plain. But the pilot flew surely, confident of his direction—'You get to the corner of this fence, and then you turn west a bit' —and with the most admirable dexterity landed his Dakota on the jolting, craggy surface of hardly visible clearings. Grey and scarlet cockatoos accompanied our landings and our takings-off. Sometimes a herd of wild horses galloped across the primitive runway, sometimes a panic-stricken family of kangaroos or wallabies flickered through the bush. But cattle in the meagre shadow of the trees stood motionless, invisible until we were close above them; many would die unless the rain came soon.

At one station an open truck full of black stockmen came slam-banging over the rough ground to meet us; at another we taxied to the very door of the homestead and got out to drink tea and lemonade under a giant mango-tree, to be offered sandwiches and little scones by a pale and pretty, sun-drained girl and her hearty, sun-reddened husband. The pilot wrote a memorandum to place certain bets for the man, the senior stewardess promised to buy films and stockings for the girl. The stewardess did a lot of shopping for women in the out-back stations, and she and the pilot were gatherers of news and transmitters of news to families in isolation. Somewhere we landed two blackfellows—lean of frame, quiet and well-behaved—

who were greeted with loud cries, clapping and hugging, by a welcoming party of their aboriginal friends; and somewhere as the plane lurched and swung, dropped in a pocket and jumped like a kangaroo on the hot air, I turned and saw the fat Bush Brother staggering up the central aisle, in one hand a quart bottle of beer, in the other a couple of glasses, and as he sat down beside me, his rosy face creased with pleasure, he exclaimed, '*Isn't* this the jolliest way of visiting your parishioners?'

A little while after noon we landed at the Mitchell River Settlement on the eastern shore of the Gulf of Carpentaria. We sat down to a lunch of strong tea and leathery steak under a canvas shelter. It was now so hot that the blazing sun seemed to pour down its rays with a ponderous and hostile force. There was a nursing sister from the Mission, a sun-bleached young woman with a tropical sore on her cheek and a foundling piccaninny clutching her knee, of whom I asked, 'Do you know what the temperature is?' And faintly she replied, 'I don't want to know, not now, but at six o'clock this morning it was 103°.' Round about us, passive but curious, stood aborigines in coloured shirts, and farther off, among the wispy trees, a more numerous company of women and children. Our holiday-making passenger from Cairns, who had brought his saxophone for company, said he could stir up all those gins and piccaninnies in no time, and playing a preliminary spring upon his instrument, set off like a wandering minstrel to woo their interest.

But they would not respond. They shrank behind the thin tree-trunks as he approached, and children took shelter in their mothers' shade. His confidence grew fainter as the gins retreated before him, and disappeared in the bush.    But he made a final effort, and approaching a sturdy woman who had stood her ground—a very black woman of hideous appearance—he played a syncopated version of *Annie Laurie*.   Her frowning features, of a truly remarkable ugliness, seemed to gather and concentrate into a scowl of diabolical malice, and as her bloodshot eyes shone ever more fiercely with the fires of hatred, his tongue faltered and *Annie Laurie* died as if she had choked upon a fish-bone. He returned disconsolate.  'They've got no ear,' he said.

A pair of dust-devils rose, swirling like genies in a tale of Arabian discomfort, at the end of the runway, and cockatoos chattered in the trees.   We took off, rising like a steeplechaser to a wall, and flew to Galbraith, and Delta Downs, and Normanton again.   We were to spend the night at Normanton, in the pub that looked like a saloon of the Wild West but was more genial in its temper.—The bar was now thickly occupied, and between the tall and burly men and the frail fever-stricken men a bridge had been created by a little domestic group.   A young couple had arrived from some far-out station, to fly to Cairns in the morning, and because there was no one to look after their baby while they drank, they brought it with them and set it on the bar.   The bar was awash with beer, the baby wore nothing but a napkin.   The baby crowed happily amid all the noise, and presently beer seemed to flow like a tide across the polished boards.

The largest of the burly men was tall as the doorway and almost as broad, his shoulders were prodigious, and in a large face that was all pugnacious ridges, under a forward-thrusting crop of hair, his protuberant eyes were bright, unblinking, and reddish brown in colour. His appearance seemed to threaten violence, but he used no violence because nothing disturbed his temper except a refusal to drink with him. And no one refused. Nor did anyone protest when sometimes, in pure absent-mindedness, he let his enormous hand come down on a cluster of change upon the bar, and extended his generosity right and left.—He was suffering from anxiety, I was told. He had recently got himself engaged to be married, and the parents of his fiancée had invited him to visit them in their home in Victoria or New South Wales. That it was incumbent on him to accept the invitation, he was well aware; but social occasions had always made him nervous.

I shared a bedroom with the saxophone-player, or nominally with him, for the partition walls were so scant and permeable that all a numerous company really shared a common dormitory, and in the morning, when we made an early start, we had to pass with averted eyes connubial beds in odd corners on our way to a tin shanty, in a yard among hens and goats, where a tepid shower-bath could be released behind a door that would not stay shut. Then a friendly young woman in the breakfast-room said, 'Steak and eggs?'

'Have you anything else?' I asked.

'If you don't want steak you can have eggs, and if you don't want eggs you can have steak. But most take both.'

'I'll take both,' I said.

In the bar, before seven o'clock, I paid my bill and exchanged greetings with four steady customers already drinking beer. One of them was the door-high, brown-eyed, formidable man newly engaged to marry; his

I

manner, in the early morning, was very gentle, and I suppose his nerves were still on edge.

We flew in air that was still calm, before the heat of the day had tumbled it, and with the homing skill of a godwit or a salmon the pilot found his way over the bleak, unmarked, unrecognisable red lands of the north. Australian National Airways maintains the service to the Gulf, which cannot be profitable. But the air-line is a life-line for the enduring people who live in the out-back and feed the cities with their labour : the independent, self-reliant men, and the patient women. A visitor may see a little rough comedy in the ghost towns of the country, but comedy is only surf on a strong and purposeful tide. For the men of the out-back life is hard, and if they were not sturdy they would not face it and could not endure it; but for women it is a penance that they suffer—as the woman from the station beyond Longreach had explained—because 'they happen to have married a man they were fond of'. And for them the air-line and its skilful pilots make life tolerable.

# XIX

## A CURE OF SAVAGES

In Korea I had read *Pride and Prejudice*, and enjoyed more than ever before its gaiety and round notes of laughter. In New Zealand I read a very good history of some parts of the last war, called *Infantry Brigadier*,[1] by General Kippenberger: a stern but lively book, written with authority and a cold, discerning eye. In Australia I read *Great Expectations*, and on my way to Port Moresby I began a biography,[2] remarkable for the tale it told, of Sir Hubert Murray of Papua. Gilbert Murray was a familiar name ('Euripides', one said; 'and Liberalism', one added), but of his brother Sir Hubert I had not known, and with increasing pleasure, with a growing respect, I discovered a man of singular character and that sort of moral greatness which is developed by stubborn pursuance of an ideal of some magnitude against the opposition of plain and simple danger, political hindrance, and the hardships of environment.

He was born in Sydney, but finished his education in England; after being expelled from school for punching the science master on the jaw, he went to Oxford and took a double first in classics. He supported a pugnacious temper with exceptional physique, and under Queensberry rules won the heavyweight championship of England before returning to New South Wales to be admitted to the bar. His habit of life contributed nothing to material success, for his

[1] Oxford University Press.　　　　[2] By Lewis Lett. Collins.

interests were scholarly, his liking and capacity for strong drink were alarming, and he was impatient of ordinary society. He did well in the South African War, and returned to Sydney with something of a reputation. At the age of forty-three he went to New Guinea as Chief Justice of a primitive country in the first, inchoate phase of colonisation, and for thirty-five years laboured to build an administration of dogmatic enlightenment. The welfare of the natives was his first charge. Clemency towards the savage but fear-stricken tribes, and stubborn resistance to the rapacity of white traders characterised his rule; and surviving the hatred of his numerous enemies he died, almost in harness, possessed of the natives' love, the white men's respect, and left a growing colony that had been moulded by his teaching and was still inspired by his example.

An heroic life in a country that seemed to require stability of mind as well as constitutional vigour. Precipitous high mountains, the lowlands covered by tropical rain-forest, impenetrable swamps. In a territory larger than Britain a native population dominated by mutual fear, at the mercy of sorcery, given to cannibalism, and quite unusually bloodthirsty. Quoting from Murray's unpublished memoirs, Lett told a story of the murder of an old man whom his murderers had found sleeping on a hill. Murray, naturally indignant, spoke hotly against such wanton crime, but his cook—who had brought him news of it—was of the same mind as the assassins. 'Do you think,' he said, 'that if I found an old man or a baby asleep, I would not kill him? My word, I would kill him all right.'

Murray reported this conversation to some people in his house, and a young man who could not believe that the nature of the Papuan was really so terrible, went off to question a native on whose fidelity he thought he could rely.

'If all the white men went away and left me behind, and you found me asleep under a bush, what would you do?' he asked.

The native considered the question, and then replied, 'Well, if I were sure that you were asleep, I would kill you myself; but if I thought you might wake up, I would get my brother to help me.'

An invitation to assist in murder was, apparently, never refused. There was a social obligation to accept. . . .

I put down the book and looked through the window. But there was nothing to see. We were flying through murky, viewless cloud. I thought of my old friend, the romantic doctor in Orkney, and wondered if he had been justified in regretting, for so long, his choice of marriage in preference to New Guinea.

The cloud scattered, and a broken, tawny shore appeared. We landed on sun-scorched ground, and were driven to Port Moresby. It was not immediately attractive to the eye, for the war had left some untidy wreckage behind it, and the architecture, for the most part, was of the modest, utilitarian sort that comes off the drawing-board of a government engineer. The land in the immediate vicinity of the town was parched and cracked by drought, and that seemed strange in an atmosphere excessively moist as well as extremely hot. I continued to feel oppressed by the humid air, but in a little while I discovered much for the eye's enjoyment in the mortal scene. For the casual travel-ler, who has no time to acquire an anthropologist's under-standing, it is a place to exercise a camera rather than the mind. The uninstructed European mind has no data on which to build the sort of comprehension that recognises kinship, with itself and each other, in, let us say, a Neapolitan dock labourer, a Swiss farmer, a Glasgow policeman, and a fisherman in Thorshavn. The Papuan native seems remote from these, of different origin, and, in a way, of different function in the world. But a camera, untroubled by speculation, would find enchanting views.

There was, near the town, a little palm-fringed bay in which a fleet of canoes harboured an amphibious population. With what appeared to be engaging simplicity—but doubtless it was governed by innumerable rules, taboos, and superstitions—men, women, and children lived almost their whole life in public, and the tumult of humanity, seen against a fleet of slender vessels on a glinting sea, made a hundred pictures to detain the eye. To detain the eye, and tease the brain.—Two or three miles away a fishing village sprawled upon the beach and lived in stilted houses built into the sea. Some of the houses were new, built at the expense of government, and they looked as good as the ready-made dwellings that shelter so many of our fellow-voters in Britain. But though I can, in part at least, understand and sympathise with the hungers and satisfactions of an ex-soldier in Wolverhampton, and a bus-driver's wife in Perth, I could feel no sensation of familiarity with the crumpled old women, the brown and isolated men, the lovely children of that wave-borne community.

In the streets of Port Moresby the most conspicuous features of the passers-by—opportunity again for the camera—were their hair and bosoms. The men, clothed simply in a wrap-around garment, a cinctured sheet, grew

their hair for adornment, and by virtue of a singular
fertility of the scalp could produce vast spheres of closely
curling wool—black pumpkins into which a face was
grafted—or towering busbies that they decorated with a
scarlet flower. Some clipped the ebullient crop to make an
aggressive ridge, a sort of helmet; these, I believe, were
what, a little rudely, were called Bouga boys: natives of
Bougainville.

Most of the women wore short grass skirts, as many of
these as a Victorian lady's petticoats, but nothing else; and
after a little while I began to see—or so I thought—a
relationship between the aspect of the face and the contours
of the bosom below it. If the one were pert or boisterous,
so in all probability were the others; if the superior features
were lack-lustre and a little sad, the inferior were often
similar. In our colder climate the art or practice of physiognomy is restricted to a study of the face; but for confirmation it should, perhaps, be extended to the waist.

I came a little closer to the reality of the country when I
met some of the men who governed it, and heard them
talk. They were all very willing to talk, for their primary
interest was Papua and its people. They would not live
there with less than a compulsive interest. They were
dedicated men—dedicated to the ideals of government that
Hubert Murray had inspired—but there was no pomposity
in their dedication. They were all Australian, and in the
Australian climate pomposity does not flourish. But, on
the evidence I heard, enthusiasm and a sense of purpose may
survive the heat.

Fear, they said, had been the governing condition of

Papuan life, and still was in the unadministered parts of the country. There had been no polity in the land, no society, almost no communication between the hundreds of little tribes that peopled it; the only bonds between a village in this valley and a village in the next had been their mutual fear and distrust. If a stranger appeared, people would hide. Then, if he was alone and did not appear too dangerous to assault, they would probably murder him.—That had been the traditional way of life, and it was one of the triumphs of administration, modest though it might appear, that a native could now travel far from his own village with no appreciable risk of assassination. Over much of the country the people had been given freedom of movement. But many fears remained. The power of the sorcerer had not been extirpated, and it was difficult to destroy the belief that death was unnatural. To the Papuan mind death always appeared to have been contrived, to be the consequence of someone's malignity, and from this belief sprang naturally the vendetta, or 'pay-back'. Death called for revenge.

But in recent years tribal raids, undertaken for revenge, had become rare events, and throughout the more settled parts of the country murder was of no more frequent occurrence than in many a city that called itself civilised. Murder had been discouraged by sedulous punishment: not heavy punishment, for execution was clearly too harsh a penalty for people who saw no crime in killing, but inevitable though lenient retribution. Two or three years in prison, for a first offence.—But a successful policy, and the partial grant of freedom from fear, had created new problems; for in a way the people had enjoyed their fear, and the plotting and planning of revenge had given them an absorbing interest in life—month after month of mounting excitement —and then at last the emotional satisfaction of slaughter, the physical satisfaction of a cannibal feast. Law and order had given them longer lives, but left a vacancy in life. And how could that vacancy be filled?

There were Christian missionaries at work, and from men who were not themselves overtly religious I was a little surprised to hear such high opinions, so widely prevalent, of the missionaries. Their courage was universally acknowledged. They lived far afield, in the wildest parts of the country. I heard—and the assertion was not contradicted —'We couldn't do without them'. But whether Christian doctrine could immediately compensate for the loss of terror's excitement and orgiastic satisfactions was gravely doubted; and there was no general confidence in the theory that regular work could wholly take the place of occasional cannibalism as an emotional fulfilment. There remained the long, patient, and uncertain process of education: not primarily a literary education, but instruction in the technique of an orderly life, induction into the responsibilities of social existence. When the village elders had been persuaded to accept authority, they no longer required the stimulation of a cannibal feast. . . . That, I think, was the conclusion; and it may lead one to look with a new eye at town councils, and even greater organs of authority.

I heard tales of the intricate and pathless swamps in the huge delta of the Fly, that look from the air like a lace shawl, and the flat, enormous, almost unpopulated plains beyond; of the limestone country, where the rocks are sharp as broken bottles; and the cold highlands that rise, almost on the Equator, to perpetual snow. I met a young officer with sun-dazed eyes who had just returned from four months of exploration in the highlands. He had had with him one other white man, eight policemen of the Papuan Constabulary, and a score or two of carriers. They had walked for eight hours a day and travelled an average distance of ten miles a day. They had nowhere been compelled to fight for their passage, but they had walked through villages where the natives clearly meditated an attack, and refrained only from doubt of its success. His purpose had been to find a stretch of country flat enough to make an air-strip. The clearing of an air-strip was the first step towards the establishment of order and the extension of law.

A day or two later I saw for myself the focal importance of a landing-ground when I flew from Port Moresby to a place called Tapini. It is eight days' march from the coast—there is no road—but in the air the journey lasted barely an hour. The aeroplane was a powerful, single-engined machine, the pilot a debonair young Dutchman. My fellow-passengers were a senior officer of the administration, a sergeant of the Papuan Constabulary and his wife, and one or two other natives; we carried also a mixed cargo of farm tools, tinned meats, and groceries. We rose into a sultry sky, and flying towards the central cordillera, that rises to some twelve or thirteen thousand feet, were soon blinded by a grey mist. We came out of darkness to see the mountain slopes ahead, like a rocky coast on which an ocean of cloud broke in gigantic, sullen waves. The pilot climbed a little higher, turned this way and that, and contemplated the scene. Aerial navigation over the mountain ranges of New Guinea is an art rather than a science, and he had to find, not only a particular valley in a countryside that entirely consisted of deep and shadow-laden valleys between truculent, high-rearing, narrow-crested ridges—but how to get into it, and if, on closer inspection, the approach should prove inopportune, how to get out again. He reconnoitred cloud masses, he explored the land, and set his course.

The valley was steep and narrow between mountains that rose on either side to six or seven thousand feet. We went down on a long slant, and the walls rose high above us. A third wall rose in front, for the valley curved abruptly to the right. But when it seemed that we were about to charge and splinter ourselves against the slope immediately ahead, a green shelf became apparent to the left. It was half-way down the valley, some three thousand feet above the stream at the foot of it, that ran like a twinkling gutter between descending roofs, and opposite the shelf—on which were a few brown-thatched houses—the pilot, banking steeply, turned hard aport, skimmed low across the precipitous edge of the shelf, and landed immediately on a strip of cleared ground which, rising appreciably, was broken-backed about the middle and thereafter ran level. We came to a jarring halt, and a little crowd of natives quickly gathered round.

The permanent population consisted of an assistant district officer, a cadet officer, and a doctor, all of whom were young; a handful of constables, a few of whom had wives, and some servants; and perhaps thirty short-term prisoners who lived in a gaol that could hardly be distinguished from the police barracks. But that day there were a good many visitors. There was another assistant district officer who, with a police escort, was on tour and had broken his journey at Tapini; and from the surrounding country had come a fairly large number of natives to be paid for public work they had lately done.—Keeping the foot-paths open, I think.—The men wore little red pouches between their legs, the women a piece of string; and many of them had the dazed and sullen look of slum children in Victorian photographs of mean streets and industrial squalor. They were very light and lively on their feet, small of stature but fairly well built, and some were remarkably ugly. If one lived among them, and worked for them, one would no doubt grow accustomed to their appearance, and discover in them the redeeming qualities of personality; but at first sight they were merely slum children living on nature's meanness in the squalor of the tropics. My visit has not been idle, I thought, for now, after some years of uncertainty, I know the political party to which I belong: I am for civilisation.

The pilot was anxious to leave as soon as possible, for cloud was gathering over the mountain-tops, and when the senior official who had come with me had made his inspection they went aboard again, charged down the air-strip, and leaping from the edge, swung right-handed in a steep turn down the valley. A little while later the visiting A.D.O., who was on tour, set off with his policemen and his carriers, and after a couple of hours we saw them, minute and scarcely moving figures, climbing slowly up a trail on the opposite mountain-side. The young men of the political service in Papua learn to walk. They walk up-hill and down for days on end, and for weeks on end; but they never walk on flat land, for there is none, except in the impassable swamps, where they can only travel by boat and keep to the rivers.

The A.D.O. who was my host took me to the new house he was building. Although it was far from finished it would, he said, be more comfortable than his old one, where the roof was beginning to fall. He was a young man of easy and pleasant manner, with six or seven years' service, who seemed to accept his lonely responsibility with quiet confidence. He had, I discovered, a pupil or apprentice on the station : a recruit to the service who had been sent into the wilds to show him the reality of Papuan government and see if he was suitable for a place in it. The average age of the three—of the A.D.O., the cadet officer, and the recruit—was something under twenty-four, but the doctor was a little older. He was a Lithuanian, and having some-how escaped the turmoil of Europe, appeared to find, in what seemed to me the rigours of colonial life, an abode of utter peace. He had decorated his small house with native ornaments and trophies of weapons, and snugly furnished it, as though he meant to settle down and spend his life in Tapini.

A native, who had just been brought in, lay in his hospital with a rough bandage round his head. When it was removed we saw that a piece of his skull, about the size of the palm of my hand, had been sliced off. An axe wound, a quarrel about a woman—or perhaps he had stolen a pig. To steal a pig, I gathered, was rather more serious than alienating a wife's affection. 'But he will live, he will be all right,' said the doctor. 'It is not easy to kill them.'

Someone showed me a bow and a sheaf of arrows that had been confiscated from a dissident, ill-tempered fellow. The pull of the bow must have been double the weight that is normal where archery is only politely practised—I could not bend it—and the arrows were five feet long, pointed with hideous barbs or steel blades filed sharp on both sides. I heard, not unnaturally, a good many stories of violence and sudden death, but when I spoke of the book I had been reading I found that Hubert Murray was still the dominating life of the place. The senior officials I had met in Port Moresby had all known him, and some had grown up under his eye; and in Tapini, among the young men, there was a common apprehension that government was somehow based upon philanthropy. The broken-backed air-strip was an outpost of government, an epicentre of philanthropy from which order had spread a little farther and law put out a protective hand.

It rained in the afternoon, and before darkness fell we were wrapped in cloud. There was cloud above and cloud below and cloud on every hand. We were suspended, invisible, in a region of woolly mist that thickened when the night came down. But in the morning the valley was clear, the air bright, and the mountains rose in sheer-sided splendour to majestic heights. And now, in that clarity, one could see that we were not quite alone. Far away, on the opposing hill, was a little patch of cultivation, and beside it two or three houses. They stood on a fearful slope, they seemed to be quite inaccessible from anywhere. And that was why they had been built there; for when everybody was an enemy, or would be if chance allowed, it was comforting to be inaccessible.

The day grew hot, it became—in that little scooped-out corner of the great valley—as hot as a ship's engine-room in the Red Sea; and I made a fool of myself. Two of the young men were going to walk up-hill to see the prisoners who, under guard, were cutting timber; and I said I would go with them. They set off at a great pace, up the precipitous path, and I kept level with them—or not far behind. Some exercise and a good sweat are probably just what I need, I told myself, to get rid of the abominable lethargy I've been feeling for the last week. And how profusely I sweated! My skin was awash in no time, and then, as still we climbed and my heart laboured and my lungs roared like a blacksmith's forge, I could feel my veins dry up as the ichor ebbed away, and presently it seemed as if moisture was being squeezed from the very marrow of my bones.— We had not far to go, it was only two or three miles; but the path was very steep, the sun was a furnace, the young men went like hill sheep, and in my folly I tried to keep pace with them. I used to walk well, and a few additional years of age should make no difference to that sort of aptitude.

We reached the timber where the prisoners were working, and using my hands like a squeegee on the boat-deck of a ship, I slightly dried myself. The prisoners were a malignant lot, I thought, and the most sinister-seeming and easily the most ill-favoured of them all was notorious for his success in stealing other men's wives. No man, even a Papuan, would have trusted him for a moment, but women —well, they had their reasons, presumably; and the aesthetic eye, after all, is a masculine organ, or of masculine origin. Morals, too, like machine-guns, were a male invention. Everything that has made life interesting, beyond the primal interest, and dangerous in excess of the earliest peril, has been man's addition to life. Women are innocent of all but the simplest and most abiding faults. . . .

We turned down-hill again, and a new sort of exertion started fresh fountains in my diminished body.  An hour or two later I felt curiously exhausted, and my heart was beating too fast and too perceptibly.  I concealed my slight *malaise*—I think I did—and again we had an evening of agreeable conversation.

Someone had shot a bird with brightly coloured, glittering plumage.  The A.D.O. had a houseboy, a merry little androgynous-looking fellow whose mop of hair was tinted with an orange dye about its outer parts.  He dressed the bird for our dinner, but kept the wings for his own adornment, and presently, clad in a new lap-lap and with the gay feathers pinned to his hair, set off with a tittering laugh and an umbrella in his hand to visit the police lines.  It began to rain again, and because there was no glass in the windows of the A.D.O.'s new house the lamps were presently surrounded by such coveys and buzzing hordes of moths and flying beetles as almost put out their light.  We sat late, talking of murder and enlightenment.

The aeroplane from Port Moresby was expected on the following morning, but morning found the valley full to the brim and topped like an exuberant soufflé with dense white cloud.  I shall have another day in Tapini, I thought, and settled down with a detective story.  I was still feeling unwell.  But about ten o'clock we heard the noise of an engine in the sky, and the valley-cloud was rising and breaking as it rose.  Through a rift that was more clearly visible from above, the flying Dutchman came slanting down.  He had failed, at his first attempt, to find Tapini, and gone back to Port Moresby.  This was his second trial, and because the whole flocculence of the sky was lifting now, he decided to wait for an hour or so before returning. When the majesty of the great view was unveiled, we went aboard. Seven or eight natives who were bound for a term of labour on plantations got into the body of the plane, and having said good-bye to my hosts I climbed into the cockpit beside the pilot.

We roared at full speed down the landing-ground, and having passed its broken back, bounced once, and were truly airborne. We crossed the edge, the cliff that fell into the valley below, and heeling violently, turned to starboard. Now it is not often, in the air, that one is disconcerted by a sense of height, but looking down through my window at the perpendicular cliff I became acutely aware of the underlying depths, and my discomfort was aggravated by the fact that the latch of the door was loose, and the door was rattling. If it falls open, I thought—and looked for something to which I could hold. But there was nothing except the pilot. I closed my eyes, and when I opened them again the view had become a handsome repetition of tall green ridges and valleys profoundly filled with shadow.

The next day, or the day after, I went to see a teachers' training college, some forty miles from Port Moresby, that lay in country like a spacious park of greensward broken by spinneys of tall trees. The road to it was rough and wild, beside a brawling stream that ran through a valley boldly picturesque; and the heat was still oppressive. The college had gathered its pupils from several parts of the country, from half-savage districts and more enlightened coastal areas and the outer islands; and though their features were widely different, the expression on their faces —

in contrast to the fear and sullenness of the untaught high-
landers—was amiable and alert. They were smart and
lively, self-respectful, and their quarters were clean and tidy.
I talked to them, and read the examination papers they
were writing. In its early phases, it appeared, their education was a pioneer's labour and had a pioneer's reward. It
cleared away the detritus of old tribal fears and customs—
it burnt the bush—and revealed a soil fit for cultivation.
These fresh and new-won minds were virgin soil. The
labour must have been hard, but the result was gratifying.
In our century, however, no one can see progress without a
shiver, without anxiety about its further course. A virgin
mind—the created virginity within a savage mind—too
often seeks a more positive impression than a liberal education cares to give. Our traditional education enlarges the
mind and makes it an open mind; on which, from other
sources, may fall the most undesirable seeds. And in new
soil they sprout quickly, they grow rank. Education is a
benign and necessary process, and to withhold it is iniqui-
tous; but from time to time one sees how dangerous it is—
and there is no protection against its dangers except more
education. Perhaps a mind that has once been opened
should be kept open—not wide open, but with a window
down—till the grave-digger closes it.

In a mild and unimportant way I still felt ill, but I flew
to Lae, across the central cordillera, and the pilot told me that
aerial navigation of the conventional sort was not always
sufficient in New Guinea. Neither compass nor altimeter
was wholly dependable, and before a pilot crossed the
cordillera, through one of the passes of ten thousand feet or
so, he would not only look ahead to see that his way was

clear, but turn a little and look behind to make sure that no cloud threatened to occlude retreat. Because cloud in front could rise with astonishing speed, and if there was also cloud astern, his position would be difficult and might be dangerous. But we had no opposition from the sky, and leapt the mountain barrier with a reward of views too vast and grandly desolate for description to encompass. With a reward, also, of cold air for a little while; but too soon we went down to lush greenery, a pretty coast, and the penitential heat of the old capital of German New Guinea.

A newly built settlement of bungalows, with restaurants and reading-room and canteen, housed the air-port staff and passengers on their way to the Admiralty Islands, New Britain and the Solomons. Lae is a junction, an aerial Crewe, in the island traffic, and the customers who go through are seldom intent on pleasure. Aeroplanes over New Guinea carry heavy freight because there are no roads to carry it, and across the archipelagoes they are workmen's trains that have taken to the air. A plane came in from Manus, in the Bismarck archipelago, and half a dozen men got out who had been labouring for a year on one of the rubble-heaps of war. Or so they described it. The Americans had made Manus a vast repository of weapons, military stores, equipment of all kinds; and when the war came to an end the stuff was all unwanted. Some was sold, at bargain prices, to the Chinese. More was destroyed. Aeroplanes were bulldozed into the bush. Labourers were still being hired to tidy up.—Or were they already beginning to rebuild its defences? I cannot be sure.—But whatever their purpose, the labourers drew handsome wages because Manus was far from their homes and its amenities were inconsiderable; and without too much effort, I was told, a man could make £22 or £24 a week.

There were three young Australians in the party, two of whom were depressed by their experience, but the other was cheerful enough in a defiant, rather brazen way. He had saved nearly £600—well, there was a lot of gambling on the island, and he'd been lucky too—and for the next six months he wasn't even going to think of work. A man who had already described to me how he had made, and lost, £17,000 in two years—I heard a lot about money in Australia and New Guinea—rebuked the young fellow for his improvidence, and told him that with £600 he could make a fine start in life. He needn't always be a labourer, he could set up in business. He ought to think how to better himself.—But why bother? asked the younger man. He was well enough off as he stood, he didn't want to be any better. Down in New South Wales he had a shack on the coast, and all he wanted to do was to lie on his back. There were plenty of rabbits about, it was easy to catch fish, and groceries would cost him £2 a week. Even allowing for a booze-up on Saturdays, he could live for a long time on £600.

It had been my intention to visit the highlands west of Lae, where many little tribes of the most backward sort had only recently been pacified and brought within the shelter of law; and where, it was said, there was land as rich and apt for development as the uplands of Kenya fifty years before. Land for cattle and land for crops, and though development was bound to be slow, because of the native policy—and also because there was no road into the highlands—development was certain: or so I was assured. And down towards the delta country there were the oilfields, of course. They knew the oil was there, they had been prospecting for years and struck oil again and again; what they were looking for was the big lake, and when they had found that they would start production. And the goldfields weren't exhausted, though the day was finished when a man could set off on his own, and wash enough to keep him happy. To get gold nowadays you needed the resources of a big company, and heavy machinery—and all the machinery had to be flown up because there weren't any roads. But the gold was there, and so was the oil, and up in the highlands there was land for crops and cattle.

Lae would become the centre of trade and virtual capital, not only of New Guinea, but of the archipelagoes to the north and east. There was a big future for the country, though there were plenty of difficulties to be overcome before it was realised. . . . I listened, and marvelled that anyone could retain such energy and enthusiasm in so depressing a climate. But whereas in Port Moresby I had heard only talk of the job to be done—of administration, and Hubert Murray, and a little anthropology—in Lae I listened to fine, confident anticipations of the profits to be made. I met a woman, a prospector's widow, who for a good many years had owned and managed an hotel famous for spacious hospitality and the lush irregularity of her customers' behaviour; and now she was building a new one, of considerable size and excellent design, that would be a credit to Lae if Lae should achieve the dignity of a capital city. She was so confident of its future that she foresaw a demand for luxury.

And if she were right, and optimism justified, would not Lae acquire the unique distinction of a capital city in a country whose prosperity was quite independent of roads? To build sufficient roads over the mountains, against the grain or with the grain of those abrupt and awful heights, was an unthinkable task.    Neither economist nor engineer would contemplate it.    But wealth lay waiting for use, and communication had been established with its sources : now sources and communications waited for development. Since roads were impossible, the traffic of the country must be airborne.    And perhaps roads, like railways, were obsolescent?    Perhaps New Guinea, emerging so lately from primeval sleep, from sorcery and cannibalism, would design a new landscape for the world's commerce, in which a pattern of dropping-zones and landing-grounds took the place of linear design, of highway and railroad track.    It had, indeed, begun to do so; the air-strip in the lonely hills was the modern substitute for a strategic road.

I was disappointed of my hope to see the new territories beyond Mount Hagen.    My untimely *malaise* found a new symptom, my weakness became intestinal.    The aeroplane that flew to the highlands was a little Dragon, well packed with cargo.    The flight would last nearly three hours; and that, in my incontinent weakness, was too long.    I did not care even to walk very far, but pottered about like a semi-invalid, and still could not think what had upset me.    Though it was a simple deficiency, and I should have known it.

Beside the cottages where passengers of the air-line lodged there grew a garden hedged with green and scarlet crotons : great scarlet leaves, and green leaves mottled with red and grey.    A trellised walk was hung with grenadillas, bright with purple flowers and heavy with pale-green fruit. Poinciana and frangipani grew between screens of multi-coloured, giant coleus of innumerable patterns. There were bananas in the background, hibiscus here and there, and tall red cannas. There was a tree with a foam of blossom that the gardener called a coral-tree, another with intricate and fanciful flowers that he called a bird-of-paradise.—The gardener was brown and thin, a great talker, of inoffensive complacency. 'I'm a man of many callings,' he said; 'I can turn my hand to anything.' He was a wheat expert, he had been a carpenter, and a metal-worker. He had been in business on his own, he had made £2000 a year, he had lost £4000 in the depression, he had played some part in municipal politics, and every Saturday afternoon he spent picking winners and listening to a broadcast of the race they ran. He'd made £15 last Saturday, but many a time he'd done better than that. And also, of course, he was a gardener. He had only been in Lae for nine months, and when he arrived there wasn't a flower of any sort to be seen. Well, look at it now. . . . Nevil Shute, I remembered, had told me that the typical Australian story was a good-luck story; but it seemed to me that there was more than a factual difference between the gentle melancholy of the English anecdote—as he remembered it—and the robust optimism of the Australian. Whatever the vicissitudes of fortune, the Australian appeared to have enjoyed them, and when he spoke of his adventures, of his ups and downs, he made them *sound* like a good-luck story. Was it the sun that coloured his memory? The sun that pulled passion-fruit and tall red cannas out of the soil as if it were a lucky dip?

I decided that *tourisme* in poor health was mere frustration, and changing my plans, booked an early passage back to Sydney. I went to call on the District Commissioner to apologise for my failure to visit his highland territories, and heard from him a tale of anger and revenge in the neighbouring hills. He had just sent instructions to three of his patrol officers to move into the troubled area, each with a party of ten or fifteen constables, and he seemed confident that they could deal with the situation.—The killing of a pig was the immediate cause of the raid, but that was only an incident in an old feud. The offended tribe had mustered an uncommonly large war-party: there were said to be three hundred men in it, under fifteen fight-leaders. They had sacked a deserted village whose inhabitants, being warned in time, had taken to the bush; and surprising another, had killed five men, one of whom they had eaten. Such were the details he had so far received. And now the raiders, returning to their own village, would find a police patrol in front of them, and the other two would join hands to round them up. An aeroplane was observing movement, and on the following day another would drop a load of handcuffs to facilitate the control of prisoners.—It was, said the D.C. calmly, a very easy country to administer, for there was no cohesion between tribes and no village was ever much inclined to help another. He was surprised to hear that I found the climate disagreeable. He had been brought up in the intense dry heat of the inner parts of Australia, and in contrast to that burning air he enjoyed the humid atmosphere of Lae. It was calm and restful, he said.

The day before I left I realised, quite suddenly, that in all probability what I had been suffering from was a deficiency of salt. In Korea I had daily swallowed a couple of salt tablets; nearly everyone did, in the heat of summer. But in New Guinea, where the climate was worse, I had done nothing to repair what sweat unloosed, and after I had drenched the hillside at Tapini there was probably no more brine in my blood than in well-water. My body had become tasteless, mawkish, and insipid. I lacked savour: no wonder I felt weak. A cannibal would have rejected me.

I needed salt. . . . But I shall not make an allegory of distress. I shall not insist on symbolism.

# XX

## RETURN TO HISTORY

FLYING southward over the Barrier Reef, the captain of the aircraft chose to speak of the autumnal colouring of Burnham Beeches. He had just come back from England, and the dying leaves, glowing like embers against the frosted blue of a fine November sky, had seemed to him even more beautiful than autumn shades in the Inland Sea of Japan. He had been in Japan a couple of weeks before, but Burnham Beeches held the better place in his memory. There was a richness in those old trees. . . .

That was a modern observation. No one, until very recently, could admire the same autumn in England and Japan and compare what he had seen, before the month was out, over the Great Barrier Reef of Australia. The aeroplane has done as much to alter our state of life as did the invention of the wheel; and with rather less time for consideration of what has occurred. But it is a vulgar fallacy to believe the world, in consequence, has been reduced in size. The aeroplane has revealed the world's immensity, and disclosed the complexities that a few hours may embrace. I had gone a long way since leaving home—it would be a ridiculous affectation to pretend otherwise—and now, when I had turned again towards home, I wanted to travel farther, but much more slowly. Movement was an excellent sensation, but I wanted to loiter. I felt, after flying so far and so fast, an atavistic desire to amble. I recalled an old intention, never realised, to walk from one end of Britain to the other : from the English Channel to the Pictland Firth. Not ambitiously, to see how quickly I could do it, but leisurely, to see everything else. I might still essay it—but not immediately. There was work to be done first, a paper mountain to be climbed, and the prospect of going home was a little dulled by remembering that home was also a prison in which, of my own volition, I would commit myself to another term of hard labour.

In Sydney I went aboard the P. & O. liner *Stratheden*, and within a day or two, in a colder air that smelt of salt, I was regaining vigour and a normal pulse. We called at Melbourne, Adelaide, and Fremantle, but I saw little more of Australia because no sooner had a view opened than hospitality reduced it to a dinner-table. I have no complaint, I enjoy a good table. But I cannot think that all Melbourne is so handsomely furnished as the house I saw, nor all its inhabitants so amiable as the few I met; and in Adelaide I spent an afternoon tasting wine at a nearby vineyard with—four, five, or six?—justices of the Supreme Court of South Australia, and this, though undeniably agreeable, and a remarkable exhibition of the judicious temper of the South Australian bench, cannot be regarded as typical of life in the state. I regret exceedingly the shortness of our stay in Fremantle, that allowed us only a few hours in Perth; for Perth, it was evident, had not only a very handsome situation on the Swan River, but a character of its own—a burly, expansive, independent character with a high regard for the look of things. There are goldfields in the hinterland to supply wealth, but what people boast about is the rich variety of their wildflowers.

We left Australia under a frieze of lightning, a running band of palpitating incandescence that lighted mile after mile of its black shore as we edged away and headed north for the tropics and the Indian Ocean. I felt, in that hour, no great attraction to the north. I had seen so much, but seen so little that my appetite for Australia was unappeased, and I wished the years would fall from me and I could stay and take a job in Perth or Sydney, in Adelaide or Melbourne, and then go walkabout and look for another. I knew the sort of novel that might be written about Australia; but one should be young to do it, and one would be the better of a good constitution.

There was consolation, however, in the calm and easy, the large and dignified comfort of the *Stratheden*. As soon as we had left coastal waters and were fairly on the open sea we settled down to a routine, a rhythm of life, that I remembered with affection and yielded to, once again, with gratitude. The aeroplane for duty, the aeroplane for commerce, but ships for pleasure. . . . The changing sea, the extravagance of sunset, the outrageous violence of a Line squall. Idle gossip, and little experiments in friendship. Very good food, and a steward at one's elbow. The clean-washed, empty deck at dawn, and sleep medicined by salt winds. A pretty girl—two pretty girls—at the next table, and a deck steward who had scandalous and charming tales about an English cricket team. Conversation of a different sort with a classical scholar, of more than college fame, who said after church on Sunday morning, 'What a delightful character St. Paul had! That speech of his in Athens: so witty, so apt, so precisely what the occasion demanded and his audience required. It was a piece of great good fortune that St. Paul had so much to do with the development and presentation of Christian doctrine. He was a clever, intelligent man; he had advantages that some of the disciples lacked.'

I was going home—home to history and conversation that could gossip of great occasions—and though I was sorry to turn my back on the newer lands, I was devoutly glad that I lived in a world of history. It made life more interesting, and to have beneath one layer upon layer of history was to be cushioned against the shocks of future time.—History rose also upon the sky-line, and a Sinhalese gentleman of lordly stature and benignly plump looked through my window one morning and proudly exclaimed, 'We are now in sight of home! There is Adam's Peak, where Buddha left his footprint.'

Ceylon stood in profile on a pale-blue sea, and Adam's Peak rose tall against a pellucid sky, taller because Buddha had trod its heights. Buddha and St. Paul were peaks in the landscape now. . . . I felt, or my mind experienced, the greater ease of an older life when I went ashore; and in Ceylon my spirit enjoyed ten days of comfort, my corporal parts relished the luxury of a temperate heat. Ceylon is a gentle, domesticated fraction of 'the East'. The sun is ardent, but the air is kind; the rain-forest grows in superb abandon, but a good road divides it, villages have pacified it. Here is 'the East' for unadventurous travellers. Here, immediately visible, is natural beauty in great abundance, and of the very sort that one expects. It is a Royal Academy view of 'the East'. The highlands above Kandy are of noble pattern, spacious in extent; they are all that highlands should be, and many of the tea-garden coolies who work there have delicate and charming features : they are labourers who look like the creatures of an idyll. At Galle, and at Jaffna in the north, there are noble fortifications that recall the splendour of colonial empires that crossed the sea before our larger navies had been launched; there is the piety of Dutch churches beside the piety of Hindu temples.

If I were a wealthy man and had, shall we say, a favourite niece, a romantic girl who had dreamed of temples, palm-trees, and elephants in ritual procession, but had never been out of Britain, I would take her to Ceylon and say, 'This is Taprobane of the Greeks, Serendib of the Arabs, rich in sapphires and garnets, in topaz and moonstone; luxuriant with satinwood, tamarinds, ebony, and quite enormous rhododendrons; procreant of sun-birds, ibises, and little elephants; dowered with a history that goes back to a tooth which Buddha shed, and whose slightly later chapters you can read in the *Rāmāyaṇa*—and everything it possesses can be seen without peril, undue effort, or discomfort. Come and enjoy it.' And she would not be disappointed.

Neither was I. It was now late in December, and mindful of the climate to which I was returning I swam wherever I could, at Galle in the south and in the very early morning with friendly Tamils in a green pool near Jaffna, after walking bare-footed through a melancholy temple; in a sun-reflecting dam in the bare highlands above Kandy, and in the surf at Mount Lavinia. Such kindly water was a luxury beyond all hope or purchase in my own country.—I had, indeed, to lecture a few times, to pay for pleasure, but after practising my repertory for eight weeks in New Zealand I could do that without much effort; and here and there it brought unexpected rewards.

In Kandy I saw some part of a dancing, elephant-proud pilgrimage to the Temple of the Tooth, and in Jaffna, where all the countryside is a testimonial to the Tamils' industry, I saw a new exercise in iconography in a municipal building where I was paying my respects to an official of the town. Behind his desk hung a coloured portrait of Gandhi—but gone was that engaging, gap-toothed grin, so knowingly derisive of all who opposed him, that enlivens the more characteristic photographs of the Mahatma, and in its place was a gentle mouth whose lips, it seemed, had just closed upon 'Suffer little children . . .' Above his gleaming head, that in life reflected the blaze of the Indian sun with a peasant's hardihood, rose a sentimental, golden light that was not quite a halo, but looked like a tentative first sketch of a halo. Already, without much hesitation, it said 'Believe in me'.

I went to swim again at Mount Lavinia, and got up early in the morning to fly to a country where there might well be ice on every puddle.—We stood at the air-port, my host and I, and a Sinhalese photographer demanded that we pose with another passenger, a learned critic, not of literature, but of golf: Mr. Henry Longhurst. 'At this hour of the morning?' I said. 'Not likely!' But my host spoke of courtesy and so forth, and grumbling still, we moved into a group. The photographer was exigent. 'You must come closer,' he said. 'You must look intimate, and also, please, be animated.'—Now I am neither a race-horse nor an actress, creatures whose ability may in some degree be judged by appearance, and I became, I admit, increasingly ill-disposed towards the photographer as he persisted in his demands that we stand ever closer and look yet more amiable. But to conclude the tiresome business as quickly as possible I addressed Mr. Longhurst and my host, neither of whom showed the smallest sign of animation, in a voice that harshly imitated a gramophone record which had been played too often : *Now tell me, Mr. Linklater, what you think of Ceylon. Tell you what I think of Ceylon? Sure I'll tell you. I think it's lousy, I've hated every minute I've been here, and my only glint of hope is to see it vanishing astern. If you want to know what I think of it in one vital pregnant word, it stinks.*

The photographer took his picture—perfunctory animation on the torpor of early morning—and we boarded the aeroplane that flew to Karachi, that flew across Arabia, that landed at Cairo and Rome, and suddenly discovered below its windows such a wealth and expanse of beauty as I had not seen in all my voyages in the farthest Orient and the deep Antipodes. For the Alps had been pelted by a snow-storm from the north, and their northern sides were white, but their southern slopes were dark and bare. We flew between the Matterhorn and Mont Blanc, and away to the south stood the *corps de ballet*, poised by Degas, of mountains in starched muslin that might at any moment point their toes and dance. Half a continent, orchestrated by winter, intoned the praise of elegance. . . .

A moment or two later I got out in London, and some forty-eight hours after swimming at Mount Lavinia I drank a cup of tea in my club and looked at the evening papers. To my horror they had a paragraph about Ceylon, entitled : LINKLATER SAYS IT STINKS.—I remembered my early-morning joke, and sadly I thought : If I had said 'Ceylon smells sweet, Ceylon is the abiding scent of Taprobane, a memory like frangipani of the Arabs' Serendib', why, not a newspaper in the world would have paid attention.   But I had been overheard in a parody of the air-port interview, and instantly my fictitious denigration had become 'news'. One touch of malice makes the whole world kin, for half the world takes pleasure in a slight to the other half, and the other half is delighted by the opportunity to feel aggrieved.

I had managed my long journey without mishap until the very end; and then someone poked a stick between my legs.

# XXI

## A MEMORY OF HILLS

PERHAPS it was in 1921, and certainly it was in August, that I met Stewart and Cheyne—medical students with whom I was friendly—and found we were in the same plight of poverty. That was in Aberdeen, where in the society I kept, at that time, such embarrassment was fairly common. We went to a pub, and debated what to do. Another friend appeared, who had just returned from Deeside, and told us that if we were looking for healthy employment and an interesting experience, together with a small stipend, we could get what we wanted on a grouse moor of which he knew. We had another drink, and discovered that our problem had been solved. We gathered a simple equipment of old clothes, a pot or two and a frying-pan—shaving material, a few enamel plates, and some groceries—and borrowed a tent. And two days later we took train to Ballater.

Our destination was a glen that divides the hills to make a ragged corridor from the broad valley of the Dee to the rougher country about the source of the Don. General Wade had built a road through it in 1720 or thereabout, and close to one of his hump-backed bridges, that now seem so truly Scottish in design, we made friends with a shepherd and his wife who agreed, for some small payment, to rent us an unused loft in their cottage and let us pitch our tent beside a fast-running stream close beside it. Then, assuming a decent and respectful mien, we called on the head keeper of the estate and were hired as beaters for a season of grouse-shooting. The tenants would be shooting driven birds for four weeks, on five days a week, and our pay would be eight shillings a day. We were well pleased with our bargain, and set up our bell-tent in a lively satisfaction that the shepherd did not seriously impair when he told us that on the longest day, when the beaters drove the farthest and steepest marches, we would have to walk some twenty-five miles of high-pitched heather.

On the morning of The Twelfth we assembled with our fellow-beaters near the shooting-lodge, and the head keeper, a stern and grizzled man, regarded us, and addressed us, very much in the manner of a company commander to whom had been committed a forlorn hope and whose troops were only such as Falstaff led. We presented, indeed, a somewhat uneven appearance. There were three or four crofters of middle age and middle size, with drooping moustaches, who could be depended on to keep walking and do what was required, and one heroic figure, the very picture of a Highland champion, sublimely strong and innocently handsome, who, it was said, would gladly stay for ever on the hill because he had a shrewish wife who gave him no peace at home. There were a few younger men, amiable and stout enough of limb, but dubiously convinced of the seriousness of the occasion. There were two little boys, foundlings from a Glasgow orphanage in boots too big for them, whose foster-mother had sent them out to earn wages that would supplement the allowance she was paid for them; and there were the three of us, unhappily conspicuous. In order to be inconspicuous we had put on our oldest and most ragged clothes, but the other beaters, to meet the gentry face to face, had dressed themselves very respectably : not as if for church, indeed, but well enough for a cattle market. Even the little Glasgow foundlings had polished their enormous boots till they shone like top-hats in the heather. But we drew attention to ourselves because we were so ill-attired.

An under keeper led us at a great pace over a little neighbouring hill, and a mile or two farther on stationed us at wide intervals round half the base of a much larger hill. When all were in position a whistle blew, and we advanced. We all carried long sticks, of birch or hazel, and now and then someone thwacked the heather and uttered a disturbing cry. But in the early stages of a drive that was excess of zeal, and all we really had to do was walk steadily forward, up the hill, keeping our distance and guided by experienced beaters on the flanks and in the centre. When a covey rose before us we would shout and wave our sticks to send it in the proper direction, and because it was a good year for grouse there was movement in plenty and the harsh whirr of wings on either side. The grouse is an excellent bird, but created for sport and the table, and so one had no compunction in guiding it to its appointed death.

As we approached the top of the hill, and prepared to go down on the other side towards the butts, the beaters on the left drew a little closer together, to prevent birds flying back across them, and those on the right swung round and marched the quicker to maintain the rhythm of the drive, and covey after covey, with the slope of the hill to help them, went swiftly and with wildly beating wings across the guns, and from the fringes of the flocks dead birds fell with a thump in the heather, birds fluttered and fell in a long slant, birds staggered and declined upon the other side, and bold birds with an extra dash of speed went safely through.

We who were novices had been told by the old hands, 'Now take care of yourselves when you come in sight of the guns, for we don't know what they're like yet—we don't know if they can shoot or not—and if they can't shoot grouse they'll maybe shoot a beater. So go slow when you get near them, and keep your head down.'—We went slowly indeed when we came within sight of the butts, but the excitement of seeing birds falling like a plummet, or descending in a furious tangent to their curving line of flight, was too great to let us use much caution; and none of us, on that first drive, was peppered. All of us, before the month was out, came sometime under the hail of spent pellets, but our guns were good—though one or two were a little reckless—and no one suffered from wild shooting.

There were two more drives before lunch, and two after lunch; and on that first day we walked home, a little wearily, to our tent, having covered nearly twenty miles of rough heather. But we were not unduly tired, and thoughtfully we boiled potatoes and ate a large, dull supper. We woke stiffly in the morning, and the second day seemed harder than the first. The third day was the longest, and we walked over steep country; but we took home with us a brace of grouse that had fallen, not to the guns, but to our sticks. Before we set out on the fourth day's marching we ripped open the linings of our coat-pockets and turned them into poacher's pockets. Our supper, presently, was no longer bully beef, but something much more appetising.

Though our guns were good—two or three were first class—they wounded many birds, and after the first few days the beaters began to put up a few grouse that could fly only a little distance, and then fell fluttering down. The drives were long, the beaters for most of the time were invisible to anyone in authority. A quick run through the heather, an agile pursuit, a deft blow with a long stick of hazel—and there was a dead grouse for a poacher's pocket. By the second week we were coming home every night with something in our jackets, and our tent-pole became a game-larder of growing richness.

We borrowed a big iron pot from the shepherd's wife, and lived on stewed grouse. We let them hang for three or four days, then plucked and cleaned them, filled them again with a stuffing made of oatmeal, onions, and chopped innards, sewed them up, and stewed them with more potatoes and onions in a pot that was never emptied. It presently acquired a rich, brown, permanent gravy, and every grouse was dowered with the inherited flavour of its predecessors. Never, since then, have I eaten game so good.

We had to borrow another pot when a foolish salmon became imprisoned, in a falling stream, in a bright green pool below our tent. A ledge of shining granite overhung the pool, and sometimes the salmon lay within its shade. One evening it left the pool—splintering the green water to a thousand emeralds—on the point of a short gaff. Another salmon came into our larder when we surprised a troop of disgusting little boys stoning a poor fish that had been trapped in a shrinking basin of the main stream. The little boys, stricken by consciousness of their guilt, ran away when they saw us, and promptly we saved the half-dead fish from disrespect, and had it for our Sunday dinner.

We lived very well indeed—the shepherd's wife baked

floury bannocks for us—and every day we strode, with increasing confidence and ease, across the splendid hills, and breathed the Highland winds, and exchanged jocular and simple talk with our fellow-beaters. I heard one day—a Sunday, when I had gone with the shepherd to look for some ewes that had taken their lambs too far afield—a piece of good advice. 'You'll never be able to walk,' he said, 'till you learn where to put your feet. Watch your feet, man, watch your feet!' And I learnt that if you never put your feet on failing ground, on bog or a shifting stone, but always choose a firm hold, you save yourself fatigue, and with a little practice you can watch your feet with no more effort than keeping balance on a bicycle. And another day, on the topmost hills, I saw marksmen more fierce and frightening than our employers with their expensive guns.

I was walking with the head keeper, who was angry and perturbed. For the first day since the season began there were no birds to drive, no birds to shoot. And then, on the top of the hills, we saw the reason. 'There they go!' he said, and following the direction of his hand I saw two long and shallow, wavering dark clouds moving from our open heights down to the wooded slopes of Strathdon. 'And that's what's done it!' he added, pointing to the sky. And there, above the fleeing packs of grouse, were two eagles descending in wide circles from the pallid light of a clouded sun.

For several days we walked in vain, and few birds were shot; and perhaps because sport grew dull we were given a holiday, and the holiday let loose ambition. We heard that on the day of our vacation the King would be shooting on the other side of the glen, and now that we knew the whole craft of beating, and could walk with anyone, we would beat for the King, we decided. King George V was said to be the best shot in Britain.

We shaved more closely than was usual, we dressed more carefully, and set off early to speak to his head keeper. He was a burly man, with authority below a look of joviality. He listened patiently and told us that every youngster in the place had been clamouring for a job that day, 'And I must give the local lads the first chance. But if I can find a place for you, I'll take you. I'll let you know.'—I cannot remember his name, but it may have been Macbeth. That seems unlikely, but no other name will come to my mind.

We waited, and saw the King arrive, and with him the Duke of York. We watched him talking to Macbeth, and with dismay we saw Macbeth give his directions to an under keeper, and the troop of beaters set off into the hills. We had been left out, we were not wanted, and like a rain-cloud disappointment fell upon us. We stood ill-at-ease, shuffling our feet, and said half-heartedly, 'Well, we may as well go'. But then, still reluctant to leave, we were held fast: the King and the Duke of York were coming to speak to us. When they were twenty yards away we clapped to attention like the Brigade of Guards—boot-heels resounding, chests like pouter-pigeons, head up and chin in—and to our astonishment the King said he was sorry.

Macbeth had told him of our appeal, he said, but Macbeth had the ruling over matters of that sort, and if he could not employ us, there was nothing to be done about it. But he was sorry we had been disappointed. We stood, a little breathless, and muttered 'Yes, Sir'. The King, in his voice that was rough about the edges and genial in essence, asked who we were and what we did. Shyly, in overlapping words, we told him, and with a flicker of amusement in his beard—looking at our posture—he asked, 'Have you been in the Army?' We told him the names of our regiments, and he talked to us a little longer; and at his right shoulder the Duke of York looked at us all the while with steady and percipient eyes. He was of our generation, he knew us better than the King. The old King was quite simply the Chief of the Clan, the Captain of the Ship; but the Duke had trodden the years that we had trodden, and he did not smile when the King smiled.

Then, marvellously, the King said, 'If you'd like to stay and see me shoot, you can go down there, but you'll have to keep still. They always give me the lowest butt, and the birds will come over it, I expect, with this wind. So if you'd like to do that, I'll make it all right with Macbeth.'

We uttered, inarticulately, a chorus of thanks, and tried, as the King and the Duke turned and left us, to exalt the stiffness of our position to a yet taller rigidity, a loftier respect; and then hid ourselves in a hollow below the King's butt and waited for the grouse.

They came in great numbers and at prodigious speed, for the wind was with them and the slope of the hill determined their course, and from the edge of the coveys the King took them down with inerrable aim. We knew, by that time, something about good shooting, and every bird that fell to the King's gun was dead in the air before it dropped. When a large covey came, and another closely followed, there were two, three, four dead birds in the air before the first had fallen. It was shooting as the ordinary first-class shot may dream of shooting. It was the very summit of marksmanship, the nonpareil of shooting, and while we watched—and we knew what to look for—not a bird came fluttering down, but every one was a meteor falling or a plummet dropping straight. Two or three of our own guns, across the valley, were good; but the King who had treated us so gently was supernacular.

That, of course, was the apogee of our month, but its remainder was not immemorable. The labour of walking became a pleasure as our muscles grew more apt and our lungs elastic. The mornings grew colder, the frost came, and the grass was spread with a pale and sparkling coverlet. We still fed uncommonly well, and our employers, who had learnt that we were only amateur grouse-beaters, invited us to tea one Sunday in their shooting-lodge. We put on our better clothes, and went.

Our hosts were very kind and quite simple in their manner towards us. They talked seriously about the art and difficulties of shooting, they wanted to hear what we had learnt; and what we said of the King's marksmanship impressed them deeply. It was Stewart or Cheyne—both were much bolder than I—who fluttered the calmness of such talk, above the tea-cups, by saying that there was competition among the beaters for certain places in the line. For places that would bring them, in the concluding stage of the drive, opposite to Mr. So-and-so and Mr. Such-and-such. But why? they asked. 'Well, they're the best shots, and there's no chance of us getting peppered,' said Stewart or Cheyne. A certain embarrassment was evident, for a moment or two, and our masters appeared thoughtful. But the tenant, who was a good shot, dispelled the little sense of strain by asking us if we would like to see their larder; and led us to a lower floor where on racks in a cold room hung hundreds of grouse, which on the following morning would be sent to London to be sold. 'It seems a pity,' said he, or perhaps his wife, 'that you, who have done so much to give us these birds, can't enjoy eating them. I wonder, if we gave you a brace, if you could manage to cook them in your tent?'

We looked at each other, with an affectation of doubt, and thoughtfully said that we could, at least, try. Our host considered the birds upon the nearest rack, but before he had decided upon the brace to give us, Cheyne, or perhaps Stewart, said, 'Here's a couple of nice ones, we could manage these.' And with warm expressions of gratitude we went home and added a brace of fine young birds to our larder on the tent-pole.

Cheyne, to take some appointment in a hospital, had to leave us a few days before the end of the season, but Stewart and I completed the four weeks of our engagement, and said one evening, 'Let us walk back to Aberdeen. By Strathdon and Alford it's fifty-six miles. Surely we can do that?'

So on the last Friday, after only a morning's work, we set off at six o'clock in the evening, and walked into Aberdeen with no more pain than the blistering of our toes. We had trained our legs to carry us, but all our walking had been on heather, and our feet were not armoured against hard roads. We reached Queen's Cross, in the western part of the city, exactly at noon on Saturday—fifty-six miles in eighteen hours—but we were limping badly, and we said good-bye with a falsely lugubrious prognosis of the week-end's exhaustion. Bed for us, we declared. Bed until Monday morning at the earliest. But neither of us meant what he said, and we met again that evening—at a dance.

What prompted this recollection, in the early weeks of 1952, must be fairly obvious. The King had died, and John Donne was disingenuous when he said, 'If a Clod bee washed away by the Sea, Europe is the lesse, as well as if a Promontorie were'. That was spoken for the crowd, that was pietistic demagogy. The loss of even the dearest Clod is invisible beyond his parish boundary, but the death of a King, like a plough in old pasture, stirs up a myriad minds and over a continent will cast memories to the top. It was something to have seen two Kings together—him who was, and him who was to be—against the plain and empty background of a highland moor; and no great profundity or scope of imagination is needed to guess that in the eye of history, three or five hundred years from now, they will stand as clearly and as simply outlined. To have had two good Kings, of their absolute and native virtue, in the catastrophic season of our two great wars will be recognised as one of the marvels of good fortune in our annals; perhaps a myth-making sequence of good fortune, the centre of an epic theme if our successors, five hundred years from now, have the appetite and mind for epic.—But when memory suffers a large upheaval, there are little private stirrings (mole-hill or worm-cast) that reach the surface too; and after I had thought of the Kings, there remained a *sensation* of those days in the hills, of the wind breaking over the tops and the frost in the morning, and in the parcel of regrets that I had accumulated through the years I found a bitter complaint that I had not, since my grouse-driving summer, used my legs enough. I had not walked far enough, or often enough. I had not seen enough of what can only be seen by going to it afoot.

Indolence, of course, was the major reason, but a subsidiary was that in my trade of letters—or in my experience of it—a surplus of health, an extreme of vigour such as mountain-walking bestows, does not help one to sit patiently at a table, take ideas to pieces, and break them into little words which, set down in the proper order, will rebuild the picture for a reader's understanding. An author, to do his proper work, should be somewhat below the peak of perfect health. Give him, by long days afoot, a feeling of splendid robustness, and he will be too proud—too assured of sufficiency—to bend himself to a laborious and essentially a humble task : a breaking-down and the building-up again. Most certainly he must deny himself the higher pleasures of the field, the sporting pleasures, whose reward is not only health but a satisfaction, spurious perhaps, but so successfully delusive that more serious labours appear quite irrelevant. Even fishing is dangerous.

In the spring of 1952—in a cold, belated spring—I was invited to catch a salmon, if I could, in the river Carron. My host was a retired Admiral of an XVIIIth-century nobility of figure, and with the candour of his sort he said : 'Conditions are about as bad as they can be, but there's no sign of them getting better. The river's low, and it doesn't look as if it's going to rise. There are some fish in the pools, but they've been there too long, and I've caught nothing for a week. But if you want to come, come now, because it may be quite hopeless later on.' So naturally I went, and took a trout-rod with me—a nine-and-a-half-foot dry-fly rod—because experiment could be excused by the improbability of success. It was a day of horrible north-easterly weather, a day of biting cold; and when, after lunch, the wind grew less, it began to rain. The rain blew inland to the hills, and a hail shower followed. But the fascination of the running stream, though it ran so low, still held, and about five o'clock I was fishing a good pool that had deep water at the one end, under some leaning trees, and at the other twinkled over a shallower bed of pebble-stones. I drew my fly to the edge of the faster current, and felt a little drag upon it, then a slow, untroubled, powerful movement. I checked my line, and tentatively raised the top of my little rod. And then the salmon spoke. It ran up the faster water at enormous speed, and my line went out, crying with a voice of wild astonishment. My heart beat loudly, my cold fingers put a gentle brake upon the line, my rod was bent to a half-circle, and the salmon paused. He tugged and jerked, and for half a minute his strength seemed uncontrollable. Then he slid backward in the stream, and I began to feel, not mastery, but some equality with him. I could not bully him—my rod had not strength enough—but whenever he stopped pulling I drew him towards me, and as soon as he ran again I let him take line. I could feel at once when he slackened speed. With so light a rod I was in close and delicate contact with him, and when he turned sideways to the stream the weight of the current fell on my wrist almost as closely as on his flank. He ran down-stream, he leapt once, and plunged in deep water as though to burrow in the river-bed. He sulked and hung heavy for a while, and I shouted to my fellow-fisherman—the Admiral's other guest, a Captain in the Navy—who came hurrying to my help. My fish leapt again, a surly splash. I brought him close to shore, and the Captain, making ready his gaff, said, 'Do you want me to take a chance? I think I can reach him.' 'Not yet,' I said. 'He isn't ready, and if you don't mind waiting——' 'I'll wait for ever,' he said. 'I'm enjoying this as much as you are. Take your time, and don't hurry.'

The fish went off again, at full speed, to the top of the pool, and now I played him with infinite caution; for my hope of landing him was growing steadily, and patience would improve it. Slowly and reluctantly he came down-stream again, and twice ran to the far side; but he was growing weaker, I could manage him now, and when at last I drew him in he lay upon his side, defeated, and very beautiful. 'He's too lovely to spoil,' said the Captain; 'I'm not going to put the gaff in him.' And stepping into the cold water he laid cunning hands under my fish and firmly tailed him. I tapped him on the head and he lay on the bank, a perfect salmon of twelve pounds' weight.

Our XVIIIth-century host saluted the capture with XVIIIth-century generosity, and after an hour or two I drove home, slowly and cautiously. I was working hard on a book—that is, I had been working, till the day before, but all the next day I lived happily in a memory, exact from minute to minute, of my fishing, and had no thought for anything else. The taking of a salmon, when all the conditions were against it and my weapon was a trout-rod, looked so like a real achievement that for twenty-four hours I felt no other need to justify my life. It was, I suppose, an atavistic sentiment, the lively ghost of some long-buried ancestral satisfaction. Before the Norsemen came to Orkney it was Pictish land; and my pleasure was so deep that its origin, I dare say, lay in the heart of a Pict who had gone fishing.

Salmon are dangerous, but there are worse perils to an author who likes a country life. I have only once shot a red deer, and I am fortunate indeed that it did not happen till I was fifty: too late, that is, to form a habit. That excitement was deeper, as the labour to attain it was more strenuous. There was hard walking, for several hours, over a great treeless forest, there was a long stalk that brought no result, for the day was almost breathless but little draughts of air circled about the flanks of the hills, and the deer winded us, and galloped off with that easy, leaping tread that swallows a valley and devours a mountain with no effort. Again we approached them, and an aeroplane, an Anson trainer, flew low and frightened them. There was one last chance, said the stalker, and that was to reach the far side of a hill, round whose circumference they seemed to be moving, in time to meet them. And now we really walked. We had not been loitering before, but now we covered the heather in long strides like men who had some purpose of high honour to compel a punctual arrival; and after walking till my heart seemed swollen to the size of a rugby football, I had to crawl, up-hill, in soft black peat and keep my head and backside low to the ground and still obey the stalker's injunction to make haste. And when I saw the stag I admitted I could not hit him.

He was couched in the heather, and all that showed was his branching head and the back of his neck. He was facing

the other way, but a little youngling stag was moving about
and sometimes looking towards us. The stalker said there
was a hind as well, and the hind would surely wind us, or
see us, and give the alarm. But I thought I could not hit
the back of a stag's neck, the breadth of a girl's thin hand, at
rather more than a hundred yards, and I must wait, I said,
till he rose. 'Then for God's sake keep still,' muttered the
stalker fiercely. 'There's the hind now,' I whispered, when
suddenly she appeared and stood staring straight at me, her
long ears a menace of intelligence, her round black eyes a
stare of imminent detection. 'Keep still, keep still,' murmured the stalker, a little behind and below me; not
fiercely now, but in the voice of a man praying in secret.
And for a long minute, with my chin on the peat and a fly
tormenting my neck, I endured the accusing gaze of the
hind—and then she stamped her foot, and on the instant
the stag was up, and for a moment stood superb, his
great head high and turned a little towards me, his off
fore-leg crooked at the knee for action. I put up my
rifle, and fired. I saw the up-flung tail of the hind, and
as she disappeared the stag fell sideways in a ponderous,
absolute descent.

We ran towards him—'Re-load,' said the stalker—and
there he lay on grey moss and a grey boulder, quite still.
We watched him for a few seconds, and he made no movement. He was dead, and I loved him dearly. For a moment,
I suppose, I loved myself, and him I loved because he contributed to me. But whatever the niceties and shadows of
the sensation, it was both a profound and exalted feeling—
profound because its origin lay in the heart of an ancestral
Pict, perhaps, and exalted because I had driven my body

to an exertion far beyond its custom and killed my stag—
my only stag—with the cleanness of instant death. And
we stood two thousand feet above the sea, with the bare,
enormous forest all about us, and the wide, unsullied sky
above. . . .

There are great dangers and great temptations in a
country life, and a writer who lives in the country, and
stays indoors, must have a passion for his work, whether
it is good or ill. Indolence, it may be, is an acquired characteristic—acquired for his protection and the prosecution of
his task.

# XXII

## MAN AT WORK

For a couple of years I had been carrying in my mind—in a small mixed cargo of ideas, images, and situations that might some day build a story or two—the picture of a man, not of English blood, who had inherited from English teaching and example of an older day the individual confidence of our Victorian age, and because he had been born and nurtured somewhere in the outer parts of the Empire, had been unaffected by the changing spirit of the centre and retained a strong Victorian equanimity long after that temper had expired in the country of its origin. I had added something to the picture from tales I had heard of this or that potentate in the East; and in his company I saw a woman, an English woman of respectable birth who had been driven from home, not in revolt against the tyranny of Victorian parents, but by the tyrannous exaction of modern government. How these figures first entered my mind I cannot precisely remember; but I had known something of them for an appreciable time, and very dimly, as if through morning fog, I saw dispute between them and the shadow of an action in which both were involved. But before I could see it clearly I must wait, I knew, till I had found a background against which the mist would dissolve: a background, that is, which would suggest an appropriate action. I wanted a secluded scene—a cut-off, remote, enislanded situation— and a few days after I had left the almost inaccessible outpost at Tapini it occurred to me that topographically it was very suitable, and from different acquaintances in New Guinea I heard some details of native thought and practice that promised, or seemed to promise, interest to the story that was gradually taking shape in my mind. To be brief about it, I had left New Guinea with what appeared to be a match between a couple of characters I had taken with me, and a background I had found there; and on the voyage to Colombo I wrote a rough draft of the first scene of a play. My imagined characters began to put on life, and the action I was inventing for them seemed appropriate.

Before Christmas had faded and the New Year had risen I set to work in earnest, and within a month I had written something which, on paper, looked like a play; but was not. It is one of the hazards of the trade, and one of the writer's penalties, that hard work can be put into failure as inconspicuously as into success. A good novel or a good play conceals the labour of its making; and the labour of writing a play that is no play, or a novel that will not be finished, is hidden away in a drawer of the writer's table. My play had a broken back: it had two themes, that is, which were not dramatically riveted together. It contained a character, a principal character, whose antecedence had not been sufficiently established.—These faults were shown to me, and I admitted them. I put the play aside, not for burial, but to await re-writing. I could mend its faults, I thought, but not yet. Now I had to attend rehearsals of another play, whose history had been full of incident and imposed variety.

It began a long time ago, when I conceived an exuberant admiration for Ben Jonson, and wrote a book about him that I now consider extravagant in some ways, but whose extravagance I cannot deplore because it matches the circumstances of his life and reflects the warmth of my feeling for him. He had, among his other gifts, an effrontery like genius in appropriating the work of older authors whom time, but not he, had forgotten; and presently it occurred to me that my homage might justify a little borrowing from him. His play called *The Alchemist* was built upon a situation, familiar to Elizabethan audiences, that again became common in our own times. Plague in the XVIth century drove the well-to-do from London as bombs did in the XXth; and in both ages knavery found sustenance in folly. I wrote a light-hearted play of which the scene was a mansion in Belgravia, whose owner had fled from the menace of the Luftwaffe and whose empty rooms were exploited by a batch of contemporary coney-catchers; and when James Bridie asked if I had anything that the Glasgow Citizens' Theatre could use, I sent it to him.

James Bridie was an old friend. I had known him for twenty-five years or more, and the longer I knew him the more I loved him. He was a greater man and a much better dramatist than critics or the commonalty have yet recognised, but that is a failure which time will repair, and for the moment I am not concerned with his genius. It was in his character as a man, not in his quality as a writer, that he commanded the next move; and perhaps I should explain that in conversation—or in argument, to which conversation so quickly inclines in Scotland—he had two advantages: he could be absolutely contrarious and contradictory without intending unkindness or causing offence, and to unreasonable question or unsubstantiated assertion he opposed a rock-like patience masked in gentleness, and often countered with Socratic innocence. In a motor-car he sometimes preferred to sing, and as his repertory was enormous and included the Metrical Psalms and the songs of Marie Lloyd, the operas of Verdi and the curious ballads of the first great war, his companions—his late opponents, perhaps—had no choice but to capitulate and join the chorus.

He was at his best, I think, in a party where he was host. He was very generous, he had a long experience of playing the host, and he played with enjoyment. He liked to encourage and extract the drama of casual encounter. He was a tolerant and sympathetic listener, and he could be a magnetic listener: he could pull words out of reticence. Sometimes, too, he could be mischievous.—There is a story of a party at which James Agate was unwilling to be witty because he wanted to talk about his ill-health: Bridie had been a distinguished consultant, and Agate, like so many laymen who find themselves in colloquy with a doctor, thought the occasion convenient to tap his host's professional knowledge.

'Bridie,' he said, 'I'm not well. I haven't been feeling well for some weeks, but I'm not going to bore you with physical symptoms. It's the state of mind I'm in that's worrying me. The fact of the matter is that I'm drinking myself to death.'

'Yes?' said Bridie.

'I want you to be serious about this. I'm in a bad state, physically, and I suppose that's why I'm drinking so heavily. But if I go on like this, I'll kill myself.'

'If that's what you want to do,' said Bridie, 'I've always

heard that drink is one of the pleasanter ways to go about
it. It gives you time to reconsider your decision——'
  'I have asked you to be serious, Bridie.'
  'I'm being perfectly serious.'
  'Can't you see that something should be done about it?
Can't you suggest anything?  Here am I, drinking myself
to death——'
  'On what?'
  'You may not believe it, but I'm drinking half a bottle
of whisky a night!'
  'Well?'
  'Half a bottle of whisky a night, I tell you!'
  'But what else?'

  The telephone rang, and I heard his voice.  'I've read
this play of yours,' he said.
  'Well?'
  'It's no good.'
  'Oh.'
  'It's very bad indeed.'
  'I'm sorry to hear that.'
  'But the idea's good, and if you'll re-write it——'
  'I'm certainly not going to do that.'
  'Yes, you've got to.  We're going to produce three plays
at the Edinburgh Festival next year, and yours will be one
of them if you'll do it again and make a proper job of
it.'
  'But I don't want to——'
  'I think you should.  It's no good as it stands, you see,
because you're writing about the war years, and everybody's
sick to death of the war, and you've set your scene in

London, and you don't know anything about London. But bring it up to date, and change your scene to Edinburgh——'

'You're asking me to write a new play!'

'Yes.'

'And invent a new set of characters!'

'That's what you should do.'

'I'm damned if I will!'

'Well, think it over. And remember you've got to do it quickly. . . .'

I went back to my room, seething with anger, and an hour later I admitted that Bridie's criticism was just and realised that I could not, in any case, say *no* to him. I saw that a new construction could indeed be raised on the old plot, and within a few weeks I had written a Scottish play. The telephone summoned me again.

'It's a lot better,' he said, 'and I think it will do if you'll make some alterations here and there.'

'Where?'

'Tony Guthrie will tell you. He's read it too, and he wants to talk to you about it. If he and John Casson come to see you next Saturday, can you put them up for the week-end?'

'We'll be delighted. . . .'

Tyrone Guthrie and John Casson arrived, and we dined together. Guthrie, with his commanding height whose authority an imperial profile reinforced, towered above the company, and close behind him loomed his triumphant production of *The Three Estates*. With masterly imagination, with a capacious grasp of its unwieldy burden and a sparkling eye for detail, he had made the ancient, obscure, and forgotten satire an admired and conspicuous success,

and when I thought of that large hand falling, that percipient vision intent, on my scenes and dialogue, I felt a
little constrained and nervous. I was more at home with
John Casson, who before his engagement with the Citizens'
Theatre had taken the hardihood and energy he derived
from his father Sir Lewis and Dame Sybil his mother into
the Fleet Air Arm, and flown—till he was shot down—
against the German forces in Norway: he had been
stationed in Orkney, and when I grew alarmed by too
close and critical talk of the theatre, I could gossip with
him of foul weather and notorious characters we had
known.

We dined, and dismissed my wife, and went to work.
It was about midnight, I suppose, when she reappeared,
in a dressing-gown, and with apprehension on her face
enquired, 'What's the matter?' 'Matter?' we said. 'You
woke me up, you were making so much noise.' 'We've
been discussing the play, that's all.' 'You were shouting. . . .'

My constraint had been banished by the enthusiasm with
which Guthrie trounced my construction—my nervousness
had evaporated in the warmth of his disdain—and we had
indeed been arguing with some vigour. But when we met
again on Sunday morning we were suddenly on easy terms
and friendly terms. I readily agreed to make five or six
of the alterations that he declared were necessary, and he
calmly accepted my refusal to change one or two passages
that I considered essential. The play was much improved
by his advice, and the gaiety and vivacity with which he
directed it made it a popular success, though all the critics
but one or two denounced its frivolity and said it was quite

unsuitable for such an important occasion as the Edinburgh Festival.

Nor was it allowed to remain in the shape in which it was acted; for among the visitors to the Festival was Frank O'Connor, and one evening I listened, mutely, to his criticism of a middle act that lasted too long and a first act that did not begin soon enough. He has a persuasive voice, strong in tone and profoundly deep. About his words hung the booming echoes, as it seemed, of an imagination that had caverned deep into earthly knowledge. His voice was imperative, and thrilling, as the ghost of Hamlet's father in the cellarage. It shook my pretty satisfaction as a seismic murmur shakes the orange-groves of California, and sadly crashing, dully thudding down, fell branches of my dialogue and the fruits of fancy. I promised him that I would make the changes he advised, and when I had done so the play was manifestly trimmer and tidier than it had been. I felt very grateful to him.

About eighteen months later it went into rehearsal again —now entitled *The Mortimer Touch*—with a new cast and a new producer. It was an excellent cast, led by Pamela Brown, Roger Livesey, and George Relph; and the producer, George Devine, made no demand for rearrangement of the scenes or re-writing of the principal parts. In a false confidence I waited for the opening night, at Brighton, and I thought the performance went very well. But a few weeks later, at the Duke of York's theatre, a chilly air descended on the third act, in which I thought was the prettiest comedy, and I shivered slightly in the falling temperature. The play lingered for a little while, and gently expired.

I had, however, no time to nurse and cosset disappointment, for I had undertaken to write some account of my walkabout year, and I had already begun the prelude (in a wrong key) that began it. Now with a quire of paper before me and a new book to fashion, the old problems reappeared —the problem of selection, the problem of the proper tone— and to deal with them I must turn my back on summer. How wonderful is man's faculty for work, and what an estrangement from the natural world!

Somewhere I have confessed the uneconomic habit of my work—the laborious waste of time, the patient fishing of a sluggish loch till the fish begin to rise—and because the rise often comes late in the day I seldom go to bed before the next morning, and to keep the balance I do not get up very early. I breakfast alone, and for company I take, almost at random, a book from the shelves. Not a new book, but an old one of which I can read a couple of chapters without the compulsion to devour it all. And one morning, after some dispiriting days when I could not make my story seem fresh and sound true, and as many pages were thrown away as were written, I came down and took by chance the picaresque *Adventures of a Bookseller* by Pino Orioli.

Orioli was a friend of Norman Douglas, and occasionally his publisher. I had known both of them, but not intimately except in their books, when, newly married, I lived for some time in Fiesole. Orioli was the easier to know: a kindly and exuberant man who offered, as freely as windfalls from an abundant orchard, anecdotes and tales of his unusual life for the entertainment of all his companions. Many of the anecdotes were scandalous, but as gay and lively as a horde of little boys in a swimming-pool, and in his voice, as he told them, was a recurrent splash of laughter. He had begun his career at the age of twelve, as apprentice to a barber in Alfonsine. A passion for learning had educated him. He became a bookseller whose primary interest was incunabula, and a publisher of limited editions. He was a gourmet, and on his travels filled his diary with local recipes.

Of Norman Douglas I felt a little shy. I had read most of his books, and I knew the Scottish countryside in which he had been born. His red face beneath a silver coverlet of hair was inscrutable yet seemed benign; but I was overawed by his breadth of scholarship and greater breadth of experience. I had met, at that time, few authors, and I was properly respectful of the author of *South Wind* and *Old Calabria* and *Siren Land*. I was, I think, too respectful for his liking, who preferred enjoyment to honour. But I cannot have made my reverence offensive, because after lunching one day with him and Orioli, at Betti's in the Via dei Tosinghi in Florence, they took me—in the late afternoon, when our luncheon concluded—to Orioli's bookshop on the Lungarno delle Grazie, and with another bottle of wine on the table they began to make presents to me of books that Orioli had published, that Norman Douglas and Richard Aldington and D. H. Lawrence had written. I left, I think, several of them behind me, but I carried off a toppling pile in my two arms, and called a cab, and drove up the hill to Fiesole.—And now, after reading a chapter of Pino's *Adventures* at the breakfast table, I gave no thought to my work for several hours, but searched for all the volumes I had been given beside the Arno nearly twenty years before.

Pino's *Adventures* was one of them. Another was Richard Aldington's *Stepping Heavenward*. There was D. H. Lawrence's *Last Poems*, and large and square, in thick, pale-blue boards, Norman Douglas's *Capri*. I found Richard MacGillivray's essay on Douglas, and then, rich in patterned gold, a little book whose pages measured seven by four and a half inches, on the title-leaf of which was printed:

PANEROS

SOME WORDS ON APHRODISIACS
AND THE LIKE

and on the following leaf, printed and written:

This Edition is issued to
Subscribers only and limited to
two hundred and fifty copies,
numbered and signed by the
Author. The price will be doubled
after first of March, 1931.

This is No. *83 and it is for*

 *Eric Linklater*
  *from Norman Douglas*
  *and from the publisher*
  *Pino Orioli*

  *and from*
  *Norman Douglas*

At first sight, I admit, it looks as if the duplication of the signature were a vinous oversight, an ebullient carelessness after a luncheon party that had lasted too long; but I thought I saw in it something more than that. Norman Douglas was dead—he had died a day or two after the King's death—and from that distance his doubled name was like a symbol of generosity. As though he had said, 'When you give, give with both hands'. I read the book again: it was mannered, stylised, compact of remote and curious learning, flavoured drily with a fescennine humour. It might almost have been written by my ghostly neighbour Sir Thomas Urquhart of Cromarty. And towards the end of it I read: 'Seek masterpieces not in merchants' houses, but on the roadways'. It was a justification of what I had done.

I considered my books from the Lungarno delle Grazie and thought: Of all the minor gifts, books are the most agreeable, and in the fashion and restriction of our times only minor gifts can be made. There is no one left who will present a parting guest with a cheque for £1000, an elephant, an ocean-going yacht, or a pair of dancing girls; and in the habit and narrower circumstances of this age, such gifts (or most of them) would be embarrassing. But how welcome is a book, for given books read doubly well.

I saw, then, at least a partial solution of my current problems—the problems of selection and tone for the book I was writing—and I made a list of thirty people to whom, for one reason or another, I felt inclined to give a present. They were of different shapes and sorts, of different age and condition, but with all of them I had some connexion of mutual kindness, and to these thirty, I resolved, I would address myself. I chose an audience, that is, and thereby clarified my task. I had to tell a true story—true in temper and in such detail as I cared to use—and the tone of it must be agreeable to my audience. Not all of it, I realised, could give equal pleasure to all of them, but for everyone there would be something of particular interest, and the remainder would not feel burdened, if I could help it, by the rest of the tale.

I went back to my table. I tore up a few more pages, re-wrote what I had written, and started another chapter. Beyond my window the summer painted new colours on the hills and like a *pointilliste* enlivened the dancing sea; but I stayed indoors. I turned my back upon the growing summer—oh, the perversions of humankind!—and sat at work. That was the end of my walkabout year.

THE END